Business Communication

Business Communication

Sean Keegan

CLANRYE INTERNATIONAL
www.clanryeinternational.com

Clanrye International,
750 Third Avenue, 9th Floor,
New York, NY 10017, USA

ISBN: 978-1-64726-074-3

Cataloging-in-Publication Data

Business communication / Sean Keegan.
p. cm.
Includes bibliographical references and index.
ISBN: 978-1-64726-074-3
1. Business communication. 2. Business writing. I. Keegan, Sean.
HF5718 .B87 2021
658.45--dc23

For information on all Clanrye International publications visit our website at www.clanryeinternational.com

CLANRYE INTERNATIONAL

Table of Contents

Preface

This book is a culmination of my many years of practice in this field. I attribute the success of this book to my support group. I would like to thank my parents who have showered me with unconditional love and support and my peers and professors for their constant guidance.

The exchange of information for promoting the goals of an organization is known as business communication. It also seeks to increase profits within the company. It is a broad field, which encompasses various topics such as marketing, customer relations, consumer behavior, brand management, employee management, event management and interpersonal communication. Business communication utilizes various media channels such as the Internet, radio, television, ambient media and word of mouth. Some of the applications of business communication are presenting business ideas, making plans, executing decisions and reaching agreements. This book provides comprehensive insights into the field of business communications. Such selected concepts that redefine this field have been presented in this book. It aims to serve as a resource guide for students and experts alike and contribute to the growth of the discipline.

The details of chapters are provided below for a progressive learning:

Chapter - Introduction

Business communication refers to the process of interaction between employees and management in order to achieve business goals. It includes business report, business presentation, business memo, business letter, employee suggestion systems, etc. This chapter has been carefully written to provide an easy understanding of business communication.

Chapter - Types of Business Communication

There are different types of business communication which can be classified as interpersonal communication, corporate communication, written communication, and oral communication. The topics elaborated in this chapter will help in gaining a better perspective about these types of business communication.

Chapter - Levels in Business Communication

Business communication has been divided into different levels for effective communication. It involves organizational communication, internal communication, external communication, upward communication, lateral communication, etc. This chapter discusses these different levels of business communication in detail.

Chapter - Technology in Business Communication

Business communication relies on several technologies for the development of business. A few of such technologies are email, Skype, messaging, business phones, video conferencing technology, etc. All these various technologies used in business communication have been carefully analyzed in this chapter.

Chapter - Marketing Communication

Marketing communication consists of advertising, societal marketing, direct marketing, events and experiences, public relations and publicity, brand management, interactive marketing, personal selling, etc. This chapter closely examines the concepts under marketing communication to provide an extensive understanding of the subject.

Chapter - Public Relations

A strategic communication procedure that forms favorable relationships between firms and their public is called public relations. Some of the models that fall under its domain are press agentry model, public information model and two-way asymmetric and symmetric model. This chapter delves into the subject of public relations to provide an in-depth understanding of it.

Sean Keegan

1

Introduction

Business communication refers to the process of interaction between employees and management in order to achieve business goals. It includes business report, business presentation, business memo, business letter, employee suggestion systems, etc. This chapter has been carefully written to provide an easy understanding of business communication.

The word "Communication" has come from the word "communis", which means common. Thus, communication signifies sharing of ideas in common. The dictionary meaning of communication is to convey or exchange information and share ideas.

It is a process through which two or more persons transmit or exchange thoughts and ideas among themselves. "Communication is an exchange of facts, ideas, opinions or emotions by two or more persons."

Communication is the process of transmitting information and understanding from one person to another or from one unit to other unit with a view to getting the desired response from the receiver. Through this process two or more persons exchange ideas and understanding among themselves to achieve the desired effect in the behaviour of another person.

It is a two-way channel for transmitting ideas, feelings, plans, commands, instructions, reports and suggestions that influence the attitude towards an organisation's objectives. The communicator's goal is to convey the meanings or ideas without distortion. Success of the leader and the enterprise depends upon adequacy of communication.

It is the responsibility of the managers to establish and maintain the channels whereby they can convey their own thinking and policies to the subordinates, and can receive their reactions and an account of their problems.

"Communication is the sum total of all the things one person does when he wants to create understanding in the mind of another. It is a bridge of meaning. It involves a systematic and continuous process of telling, listening and understanding."

The definition involves two aspects in communication:

First, there is something which is transmitted, such as facts, feelings, ideas, etc. It implies that there must be a receiver if communication is to occur.

Second, the definition emphasises the understanding element in the communication process.

Sharing of understanding would be possible only when the person to whom the message is sent, understands in the same sense in which the sender of message wants him to understand.

So, communication involves something more than mere transmission of the message or transmission and physical receipt thereof. The correct interpretation and understanding of the message is important from the point of view of organisational efficiency. Effective communication, as such, might be the accurate transmission and receipt thereof, and its correct understanding.

"Communication is the process of sending and receiving messages. However, communication is effective only when the message is understood and when it stimulates action or encourages the receiver to think in new ways."

Communication made among persons to convey their personal information, message or thought are personal communication; but exchange of information, facts and ideas relating to business may be termed as "Business Communication". Business Communication refers to the communication relating to business activity which means providing goods and services to the consumers with a view to earning profit.

It is a process through which information, facts, ideas, orders, advices, decisions, etc. are conveyed, sent or exchanged between/among the persons associated with business. Thus, Communication relating to trade, law, Finance, administration, management, etc. of a business enterprise may be termed as 'Business Communication'.

The success of a business enterprise depends largely upon good communication. Effective communication wipes out the hindrances in achieving the target of a business enterprise. Ineffective communication or communication failure may cause loss of money, time, energy, opportunity and even goodwill of a business.

In this age of globalisation every business enterprise, big or small, requires proper communication for its existence. The success of any business concern largely depends upon successful communication.

In this age of speed, complexity and competition, sending of information regarding the product to the ultimate consumer is very important. Unless they know about the product of the business enterprise, it is not possible for them to make contact and buy the product. Communication plays a vital role in this sphere.

Elements of Business Communication

Business communication involves six basic elements. They are as follows:

Message

This is the subject-matter which is transmitted or passed by the sender to the other party or group of persons. This might be opinion, order, suggestion, attitude, feeling, view, etc.

Sender

He/she is the person who intends to make contact for passing information and understanding to other person.

Receiver

The person to whom the message is meant for is known as receiver or communicate.

Channels

Information is transmitted through certain channels (e.g., radio, television, telephone, letter, e-mail, etc.). The media is selected by the sender considering various factors.

Symbols

These are the words, actions and signs which are passed on by the sender while communicating with the receiver.

Feedback

When the receiver acknowledges the message of the sender and responds back to him/her, feedback takes place. Without feedback communication is incomplete.

Features of Business Communication

Business Communication has certain features or characteristics which enable us to distinguish it from other communication.

A Communication to be Business Communication must be:

- Practical,
- Factual,
- Clear and brief,
- Target-oriented,
- Persuasive.

Practical

Effective business communication deals with the practical aspect of the information explaining why, how, when and the like queries. It avoids impractical, imaginary, unnecessary or repetitive information to eliminate waste of time. It conveys important information to the receiver.

Factual

In general a business message contains facts and figures in place of overall idea. Important date, place, time, etc. should be clearly mentioned in a business communication.

Clear and Brief

The language used in business communication should be simple, clear, brief and without ambiguity. Sometimes charts, photographs, diagrams, etc. are used to condense or clarify the information.

Target-oriented

A business communication must have a specific objective and must be planned properly so that the objective can be achieved.

Persuasive

Business communication often plays a persuasive role. It persuades an employee to perform his/her duties, a customer to buy a product or service etc. The basic characteristics mentioned above are related to the message or information of the communication.

The Process of Business Communication has Certain other Characteristics. They are:

Integral Part of Management Process

Communication encompasses those activities by which the ideas, opinions and decisions of the managers are conveyed to the subordinates of different ranks. It also involves the exchange of facts, feelings, suggestions and responses between the superiors and subordinates.

Communication, in this way, puts the people into action, guides and directs their activities, regulates and co-ordinates them for proper work performance. A manager, thus, performs the management functions through communication and managerial positions become the communication centres to receive information from various sources for its transmission to relevant points.

So, communication is a part and parcel of management function, and is, thus, an integral part of management process. That is why, "the first executive function is to develop and maintain a system of communication".

Two-way Traffic

Communication does not only mean its downward movement from superior to the subordinates it implies both the transmission and reception. So, when conveying any information, a manager should know its reactions and responses. Otherwise, managerial task of guiding and directing will be ineffective.

A man should, thus, not only speak, inform and order, but should also be able to listen, answer and interpret. Communication, therefore, involves two-way traffic from the managers to the employees and from the employees to the managers. It is not complete unless the message has been correctly understood by the receiver and its response becomes known to the sender.

Mutual Understanding

The basic purpose of business communication is to bring about understanding between individuals in the organisation. It is an important element for establishing human relationships. A leader can lead and a manager can direct effectively by establishing perfect understanding with the subordinates, peers and superiors in the organisation.

The greater the degree of understanding presents in the communication the more possibility that human action will proceed in the direction of accomplishing the goals.

Pervasive

The subject-matter of business communication covers a wide range and extends to all functions—purchases, production, sales, finance, recruitment, wages, dividends, market standing, innovation, productivity, etc. It also moves through all levels of management— upward, downward and sideways. Business communication is, thus, said to be a pervasive function.

Continuity

Communication is an ever-present activity and without it an organisation cannot exist. Communication is as necessary to an organisation as blood circulation in a living body. Therefore, the managers should ensure that adequate and smooth communication flows in all directions.

Breakdown of communication results in misunderstanding, creation of unfavorable attitudes, hostility and conflict. So, communication must be a continuous process and move up, down and sideways for active participation of all concerned.

Specific

A business communication is generally specific in nature. It means that a particular communication should deal with a single subject at a time. This is necessary for the effectiveness of communication. Multiplicity of subject in a communication has the possibility of creating confusion which is dangerous to sound management. It must be specific with regard to the information intended to be conveyed or received.

Result and not Cause

Sound communication is the result of competent management, not the cause of it. Business communication is a means to an end and acts as a tool in the hands of the managers. Successful handling of this tool depends upon the competence of the managers. It is not an independent activity, rather an essential ingredient of managerial function.

So, good communication does not produce good manager. But good manager is nearly always a good communicator. Misconception of management process often leads to poor communication.

Internal and External

Business communication is primarily internal. It is, thus, a part of administrative function and intended to apply to the members belonging to an organisation. Orders, instructions, suggestions and even public notice announcing the annual general meeting of a company are some of the examples of internal communication.

But nowadays, many communications move beyond the organisational horizons and touch the outside population exceeding the organisation's own (e.g., advertisement). Business communication may thus be internal and external.

Different Types

Business communication may be of different types—formal, informal, upward, downward, sidewise, written, oral, etc.

Feedback

A communication cannot be complete unless and until feedback or response of the recipient is made. Feedback may be written, oral or gestural. Sometimes mere silence may also constitute a feedback.

Objectives of Business Communication

The main objective of communication is to give information and to persuade different persons. Other objectives include conveying suggestion, opinion, idea, advice, request, etc.; imparting instructions, guidance and counseling; providing training; giving warning; appreciating good work; boosting of morale; etc. In the case of a business enterprise the main objective of communication is the improvement of its activities, all-round development of the organisation, and ultimate success in its operation.

Giving Information

The primary object of communication is to make the members of an organisation aware of its goal and acquaint them with all the relevant information. This helps the business enterprise to achieve success through concerted efforts of all the people concerned. It is a fact that well-informed people can achieve better.

The managers should know in details the social, political, economic and other conditions of the place where the business is situated. Information regarding the employees, consumers and competitors should be at their fingertips. Employees, likewise, should be well-informed about their positions, powers and responsibilities in particular, and the aims and objectives of the organisation in general.

Information regarding demand for a particular product, the taste, liking, etc. of the consumers; availability of raw materials, credit facility, advertising media; latest government rules and regulations, etc. are required for the production and selling of the product.

Information can be obtained from past records, books, journals, newspapers, government publications, seminars, conferences, exhibitions, trade fares, etc. The other sources of information are the chambers of commerce, structured questionnaires, radio, television, internet, etc. Whatever might be the sources, the information must be reliable, accurate, complete and latest.

Persuasion

To persuade means to make other people decide to do something, especially by repeatedly asking them or telling them the reasons why they should do it; in other words, influencing other people to believe or to do what one wants. This is one of the important objectives of communication.

The seller often influences the buyer through persuasion to buy his/her products rejecting earlier decision to buy other products. This persuasion should be so planned that the buyer becomes least conscious of being persuaded and even if he/she becomes conscious, he/she should be made to understand that it is for his/her own interest. Actually persuasion is an art which should be suggestive in nature rather than coercive.

Conveying Suggestion

Communication helps in conveying suggestions, opinions and ideas. The workers who are actually engaged in the work know better the loopholes in it and can suggest to the managers the ways to plug the loopholes. This is an example of upward communication. In big offices, suggestion boxes are provided and suggestions are received throughout the year. Sometimes further communication is made with the suggestions for clarification. Interaction of suggestions and ideas help the progress of an organisation.

Suggestions are not in the nature of order or advice and are, therefore, never obligatory to follow them. Either acceptance or rejection is possible in the case of a suggestion. Some executives, supervisors or managers who have a false notion of self-dignity, self-respect, higher position, etc. may not accept a suggestion, even though it is good one because it comes from lower level. But dynamic executives welcome constructive suggestions in the interest of the organisation.

Advice

One of the objectives of business communication is to advise an individual or a group of people. The manager advises the subordinates about the ways and means of better performance. Advice involves personal opinion and it influences the opinion and action of the other persons to whom advice is being given.

Today's business world is very complex and no one can be an expert in all the spheres of business. So, a businessman has to take advice from experts regarding the matters in which he is not well-informed. For example, he may need advice regarding banking, insurance, stock exchange, tax rules, legal procedures, etc. Within the business the managers, supervisors and executives may advise each other (a case of horizontal communication) and the subordinates (downward communication).

Motivation

Communication is made to inspire, to motivate, and to create a sense of loyalty among the employees. Through communication their morale is boosted up and it leads to better performance. Regular communication is necessary for motivating the employees and infusing in them a positive attitude towards work and a healthy relationship with the managers. This, ultimately, increases managerial efficiency.

Motivating someone means inspiring but not forcing him/her to do something. A motivated worker is an asset of any organisation. The greater the motivation, the lesser is the cost of supervision, because a motivated worker never neglects his duties.

Motivating factors include monetary incentives, security of job, job satisfaction, good working environment, participation in decision-making, fixation of target, etc. Money works as a good motivator. A worker works overtime when he/she is allowed extra wages. Security of job motivates an employee to devote himself/herself wholeheartedly to the job.

If an employee is satisfied with the job, he/she gets pleasure in doing it. Good working environment attracts him/her to work in co-operation with other members. Workers' participation in decision-making gives them a sense of being part and parcel of the organisation. Fixation of production target, sales target, etc. of an organisation helps the workers to work together to achieve the target. Thus, different factors of motivation contribute to achieve performance excellence of an organisation.

Training

To meet the need of an organisation, senior employees may need to be trained to update them about the new technological developments so as to adjust themselves to changing work environment or job demands. The new employees may also require training at the initial stage to cope up with the methods, techniques and systems of work in the organisation.

Communication is the key to all these kinds of training. Such communication can be made through classroom teaching, lectures, seminars, short courses, conferences, educational tours, film shows, etc. Not only the ordinary employees, but the managerial staffs also need to be trained in the process stated above.

Instruction, Guidance and Counselling

One of the objectives of business communication is to manage the employees by means of imparting instruction, providing guidance and arranging for counseling. Legal, vocational and medical guidance and counseling are provided free of cost for the employees in a good business organisation. Doctors, lawyers, coaches, etc. are employed for the purpose. The underlying objective of such assistance is to keep the employees physically fit and mentally alert so that they can work whole-heartedly for the well-being of the organisation.

Giving Warning and Appreciating Good Work

It is very much necessary to appreciate a good worker. It will encourage him/her to strive for better performance and greater involvement. It makes the employee conscious about his/her responsibilities. On the other hand, it is also necessary to give warning to the employees who tend to be in disciplined, non-accountable and unproductive or create disturbance. The objective of both appreciation and warnings may be accomplished through oral or written communication.

Resource Utilisation

Communication checks wastage of the resources of the organisation and helps their better utilisation. Lack of knowledge or lack of proper direction in time may cause the waste or misuse. Communication helps to bridge the gap of knowledge through instruction, advice, etc. and waste or misuse of resource is minimised. Not only material resources, but also the financial resources, human resources and other resources are utilised properly through communication.

Management Efficiency

One of the objectives of business communication is to increase efficiency of the management. If there is a good network of communication (formal and informal), the organisation can be managed efficiently and effectively.

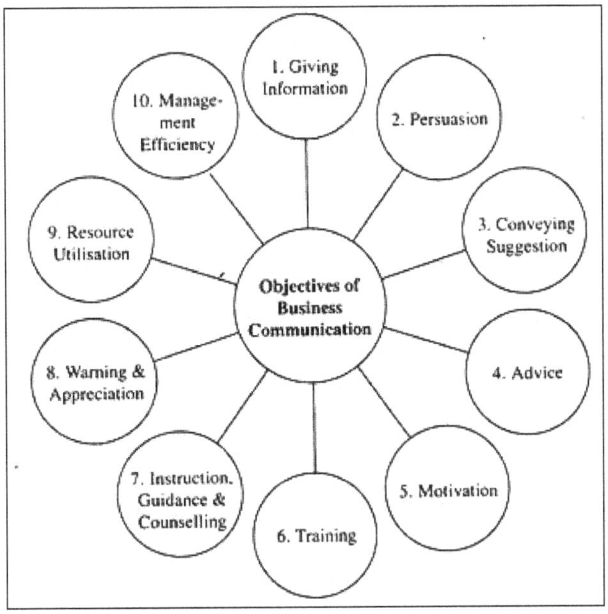

Objective of Business Communication.

Steps of Business Communication

The process or steps of communication involves a series of actions and operations undertaken for the fulfillment of a certain end or objective.

The Basic Communication Process Involves the Following Steps

- Clarifying the idea or problem,
- Getting participation in developing a solution to the problem,
- Transmitting the idea or decision,
- Motivating others to take action agreed upon,
- Measuring the effectiveness of communication.

The Following Elements are Involved in the Process of Communication

- A communicator (a speaker, sender, issuer).
- Transmits (says, sends, issues).
- Stimulus (message, orders, reports).
- Communicate (addressee, respondent, audience) to influence his behaviour as seen in his response (reply, reaction).

The process of communication can best be expressed by Laswell's popular five 'Whs': "'who' says 'What' in 'Which Channel' to 'Whom' with 'What effect'?"

In the light of the above, the process or steps of business communication can be described as follows:

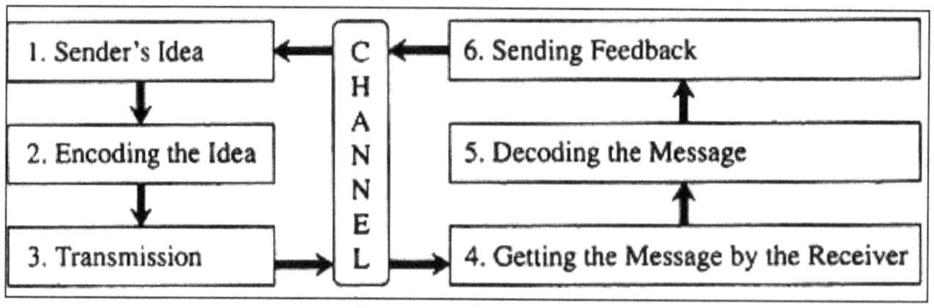

Process of Business Communication.

Sender's Idea

The first thing in communication process is to be familiar with the idea or problem to be communicated. If the communicator has no clear view of this idea or problem, its reception on the other end may give similar obscure idea and may thus be misunderstood. So, the process of communication demands full and clear view of the idea or problem to be communicated.

Encoding the Idea

When the idea is converted into a symbolic form in terms of some kind of language, it may be termed as the encoding of the idea. The language may consist of words, symbols, charts, diagrams, gestures, etc. This encoding depends upon the personal characteristics of the sender as well as the receiver. The style, length, form, clarity, etc. of the message varies from person to person.

Transmission

In transmitting the ideas or decisions, certain matters are to be taken into consideration. The first consideration should be to select an appropriate channel (i.e., verbal, non-verbal, written, etc.) and a medium (telephone, e-mail, letter, face to face conversation, etc.).

This selection depends upon urgency, distance, availability of means, cost and time factor, etc. Next thing is to determine the person or persons to whom such ideas or decisions are to be communicated. So, the selection of right course and right person for communication is essential for its effectiveness.

Getting the Message by the Receiver

The receiver must get the message to make the communication fruitful. Suppose a letter or e-mail is sent to a person. It is not possible for him/her to go through it and understand its meaning unless it is received by him/her.

Decoding the Message

Decoding means understanding or bringing out the meaning of the message. It is very vital. If the receiver understands the message in the same sense as the sender intends, the objective of communication is presumed to be fulfilled.

Sending Feedback

Feedback is the receiver's response to the message. Having understood the message the receiver reacts to it and responds accordingly. The feedback evaluates the effectiveness of the message. If the sense of the message is realist properly, the feedback or the response will be desirable and, if it is not, one has to understand that there are some barriers in the process. Steps are required to be taken for the removal of such barriers.

Channel

Channels are the routes or paths of the communication. The sender's idea is transmitted to the receiver through this path. Again, the receiver sends feedback to the sender through the channel. Thus, channel is used at least twice in the process of communication. Oral or telephonic message, letter, different audio and video media, computer, e-mail, fax, etc. are the popular channels of communication. Selection of channel depends upon the nature of the message, necessity, urgency and situational conditions.

Noise

It is not a separate step in the process. It may be present at every step and make the communication less effective or ineffective. Noise distorts the message and conveys ideas not intended by the sender resulting in chaos, confusion and complexity.

Channels of Business Communication

Channels are the routes or paths through which messages are sent or received.

Examples of Channels

1. Here ABC are the three persons and there are three channels of communication between AB, BC and CA.

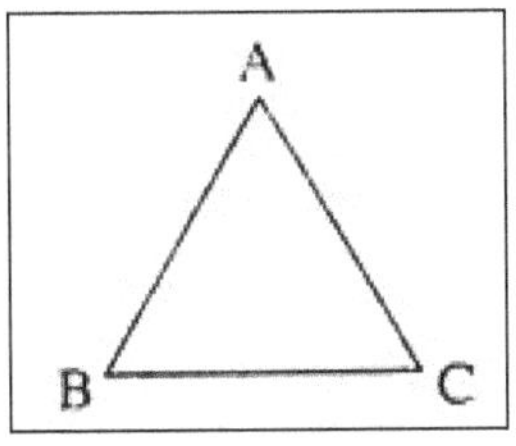

Channels of Communication.

2. Here, ABCD are the four persons and there are six channels of communication between AB, BD. DC, CA, AD and BC.

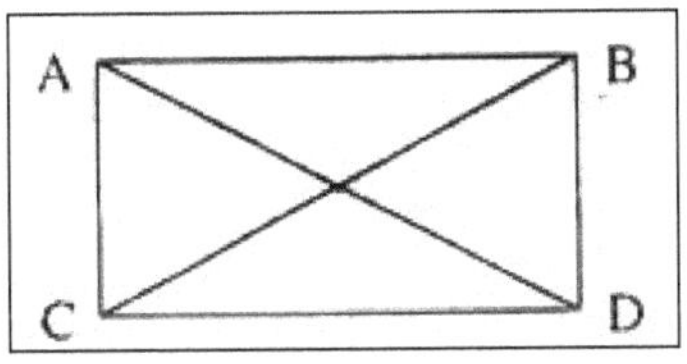

Channels of Communication.

3. Here the number of persons are five— ABCDE—and ten channels of communication between AB, BC, CD, DE, EA, AC, AD, BD, BE and CE.

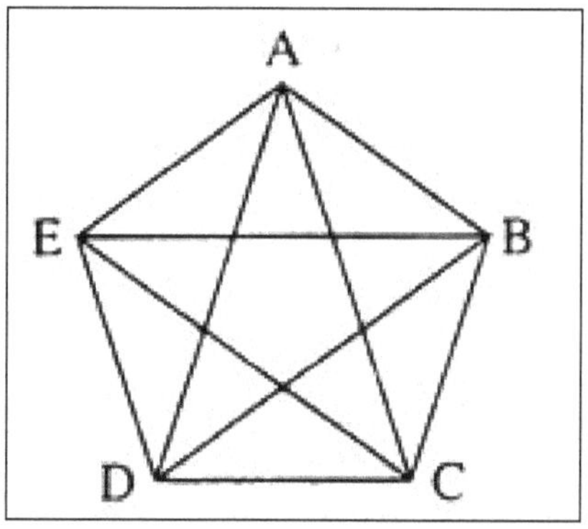

Channels of Communication.

If channels are used for the purpose of communication relating to any business activity, such channels may be called 'the channels of business communication'. A departmental manager issuing orders to the supervisors in writing is an example of business communication.

Its direction is downwards as it is made by a superior to his subordinate. Here a downward channel is used. Again, the communication is expressed in writing. Therefore, a written channel of business communication is in operation. Once again, as the communication is carried on through an official route, it is a formal communication channel also.

Classification of Channels of Business Communication

Channels of business communication may be classified from different viewpoints as follows:

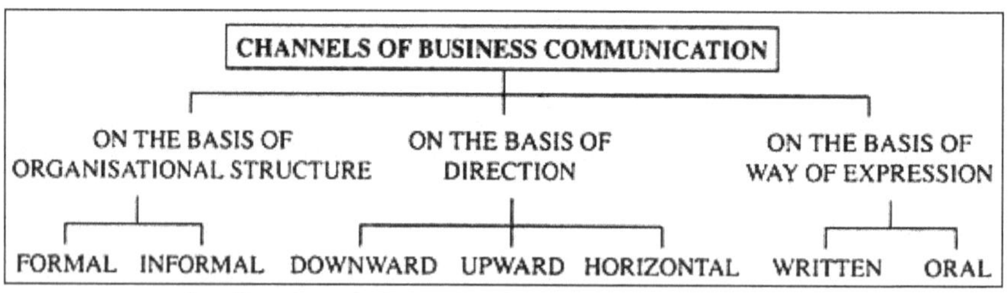

Classification of Channels of Business Communication.

On the basis of Organisational Structure

On the basis of organisational structure, the channels of business communication may be divided into:

- Formal,
- Informal.

Formal Channel

When communication is carried on through structured, organised or official route, the channel is called 'Formal Channel'.

Informal Channel

Non-structured, unofficial and unorganised route of communication is 'Informal Channel'.

On the Basis of Direction

The Direction of Business Communication Channels may be:

Downward Channel

Channels used for flowing information from top towards bottom are called 'Downward Channel'.

Upward Channel

Communication of information from lower level to upper level is possible through 'Upward Channel'.

Horizontal or Lateral Channel

When communication takes place between the persons of same rank a 'Horizontal Channel' is said to be formed.

On the Basis of Way of Expression

On the basis of the ways or means of expression business communication channels are of two types:

Written Channel

When communication takes place in writing through letters, memos, reports, proposals, e-mail, faxes, etc. 'Written Channel' is said to be in use.

A Written Channel is Often Selected in the Following Cases:

- Immediate feedback is not required;
- The receiver stays in a far off place and cannot be brought to contact easily;
- Distortion of message is not desirable;
- Detailed, complex and planned messages are required to be sent; and
- Permanent record is necessary for future reference.

Oral Channel

'Oral Channel' includes different media e.g., face-to-face conversations, speeches, meetings, telephone, voice mails, audio and video tape, teleconference or video conference, etc.

An Oral Channel is to be Selected if:

- Feedback is required immediately.

- The receiver of message or audience can be brought to contact easily.
- Interaction is necessary.
- Simple messages are communicated.
- No permanent record is to be kept.

Levels of Business Communication

Levels of business communication may be determined on the basis of direction of communication and the ranks or positions of the persons with whom communication is being made.

It may be Classified as:

Lower Level Communication

When information flows from the persons occupying higher positions to those at lower levels, it is called 'Lower Level Communication'. The flow of communication being downward it is also called 'Downward Communication'. It is usually conveyed through oral or written orders, reports, manuals, etc. and is the most common practice in all business organisations.

In an organisation, people at lower levels have a high degree of loyalty, faith, respect and sometimes a mixed feelings of fear and obedience towards the people of higher levels. This leads to high degree of acceptance of the communication.

In the lower level communication there is a possibility of distortion of information through gossip or 'grapevine' communication. In such a case the ultimate objective of communication is lost. So, care should be taken to send the information, message or order and receive feedback without any loss, alteration or distortion of information.

Upper Level Communication

When communication moves upward from the subordinates to the superiors, it is called 'Upper Level Communication'. The means of upper level communication includes the submission of reports and suggestion, opinions and attitudes, complaints and grievances, etc.

The upper level employees can understand the pulse of the lower level employees through such communication. But, it is less common because it is less favoured by the top managers due to its troublesome and perplexing nature.

The effectiveness of such communication depends upon good superior-subordinate relationship and intention of the superiors to remove the grievances and honour the emotions of the subordinates. The subordinates should also be co-operative and avoid unnecessary criticism, fault-finding attitude, complaining for fake or baseless grievances, etc.

Horizontal or Side-wise or Lateral Communication

'Horizontal or Sidewise or Lateral Communication' takes place between the people of same level in the positional hierarchy of the organisation through oral or written method. Communication between the employees or supervisors or managers of the same department or another department is examples of horizontal or lateral communication. It helps to promote understanding and coordination in the organisation. It is especially important in large or decentralised organisation.

Importance of Business Communication

The significance or importance of business communication is increasing very rapidly day-by-day. The business world of today cannot move smoothly without the help of communication. It makes a business enterprise dynamic and increases its efficiency. It is regarded as the motivating force that leads to industrial harmony.

It can be used as a device for controlling the business activities to ensure the achievement of organisational goals. The role of communication in business is as essential as the blood veins or arteries in human body. In its absence, a business organisation would cease to exist.

Business communication has a significant role to play in management whose objective is to direct the individual efforts for securing overall co-ordination of organisational activities. It performs the energizing function in the organisation by transmitting information, facts and ideas and thereby making co-ordinated efforts possible. Communication can, as such, be regarded as basic to the functioning of an organisation.

Theo Haimann has rightly said that the success of management activities, to a great extent, depends on good communication system. Communication creates favourable work environment, motivates the workers to work hard and, thus, management activities become easier. Through communication process it is possible to supply all necessary and important messages or information at all levels of the organisation.

Business communication promotes managerial efficiency and induces the human elements in an organisation to develop a spirit of co-operation which finally leads to peak performances. The process of leadership depends on effective communication. Sound communication system is an essential requirement of good labour-management relations.

With the help of communication there is better understanding of the objectives and policies which encourage co-ordination. Growing importance of human relations in every business with customers and workers has made communication the life-line of business. Producers are required to make sales appeal to their customers.

The subordinates are required to communicate their grievances and complaints to their superior, otherwise they may lead to conflicts. Proper communication helps in implementing the decisions effectively and leads to smooth running of the business. It creates mutual trust and confidence and builds up the morale of the employees and, thus, provides job satisfaction to them.

Business communication is all the more important in management because the success of an enterprise depends upon how effectively its employees understand one another. Most of the problems of business can be attributed to poor communication between the managers and workers.

So, lack of communication or poor communication will affect a business in different ways. It will greatly affect understanding of the employees, place them in utter confusion, create apathy to their work, hinder their willing co-operation, put co-ordination out of gear and invite dislocation, chaos and conflict in all business affairs and, ultimately, the very survival of the business will be at stake.

The importance of effective communication in management has been widely recognised in recent years. It has become one of the most vital factors in the efficient performance of management. It has an important bearing on management affairs from different points of view.

Above discussion of the significance of business communication may be stated point- wise as follows:

Movement of Information

Communication helps to move information from one place to another and from one person to another. It develops a chain of understanding among the workers of different levels in a business enterprise.

Efficient and Smooth Running of Enterprise

The smooth and efficient functioning of an enterprise entirely depends upon the effectiveness of the system of communication. It provides the basis of direction and actuates people to action in accordance with the desires of the management authority. "Communication serves as the lubricant fostering the smooth operation of the management process."

Promotion of Management Efficiency

Communication encircles all the functions of business management. So, without it, no function of business management can proceed towards its desired goal. It is the tool of managerial efficiency. The managerial efficiency depends upon getting things done through other people by making them know and understand what the manager wants them to do. It is the work of communication to keep the employees informed of everything necessary for smooth work performance.

Proper Planning

Communication is very helpful in planning the activities of business. It provides the managers information and ideas necessary for sound planning. "Only through good communication can company policies and practices be formulated and administered." Secrecy of information creates suspicion among the workers and separates them. Understanding of the common problems unites them for showing a better record of their performance.

Basis of Decision-making

Communication helps the managers to take essential decisions and conduct vital operations. The quality of decisions made in an organisation entirely depends on the volume and quality of information available to the management authority. In the absence of effective communication it may not be possible for top management personnel to come in closer contact with their subordinates.

Basis of Co-operation

By promoting mutual understanding and meeting of minds, communication paves the way for co-operation. Communication creates condition for mental acceptance of the work before its actual performance. This mental acceptance is the will- to-do before actually doing it. Communication involves understanding and willing acceptance of orders and instructions and acts as the basis for individual and co-operative efforts.

Means of Co-ordination

Co-ordination implies orderly group efforts to provide unity of action. This unity of action is the result of team work which, in turn, depends, to a great extent, upon clear understanding of the organisational goals, the mode of their achievement and situation of the work. The function of the business communication is to get the workers fully informed of everything relating to the work and bring a perfectly tuned harmony in their work.

Job Satisfaction

Proper communication system extends mutual trust and faith. It thus creates confidence in the ability of their manager, promotes their loyalty to the enterprise and stimulates their job interest. Proper communication system enables the subordinates to bring to the notice of the managers their viewpoints, grievances and troubles. This facility raises the morale of the workers and, ultimately, leads to job satisfaction for high performance.

Establishment of Public Relations

A business enterprise comes into contact with several social groups, e.g., customers, investors, trade unions, government and the local community. It must maintain cordial relations with each of these groups to develop a favourable image. It must continuously strive to convince the public in general that its actions are taken in the interest of the society. No public relation can be established without communication.

Establishment of Effective Leadership

Effective leadership is established through communication. The ideas, orders, instructions, direction, etc., of the leader or manager is transmitted to the subordinate employees through communication. The manager can influence them and create a healthy relation by wiping out misunderstanding and distrust between management authority and subordinates through communication.

Assisting Motivation

Communication creates motivation. Through it the managers and employees are well-acquainted with the latest information relating to the organisation. This leads to avoidance of hostility, acceptance of reality, change of attitude, consciousness of responsibility and—ultimately—motivation to work.

Loyalty

The confidence and loyalty of the lower employees on the management personnel increases as they become aware of the competence of efficiency of their boss through communication. It helps to strengthen mutual trust.

Accomplishment of Goals

Communication fulfills the organisational objectives through co-operation and co-ordination among the managerial and working staff. Interconnections between the managers and subordinate employees are established through effective communication system.

Industrial Peace

Workers' unrest is a problem today. It is communication which can establish peace in the industry. Two-way communication helps to develop mutual cooperation and understanding. Through downward communication the management personnel send their orders, instructions, directions, etc. to the subordinates.

On the other hand, the upward communication helps the subordinates to convey to their superiors their demands, grievances, complaints, suggestions, etc. Thus, through communication of facts and information between the superiors and subordinates, industrial peace can be established.

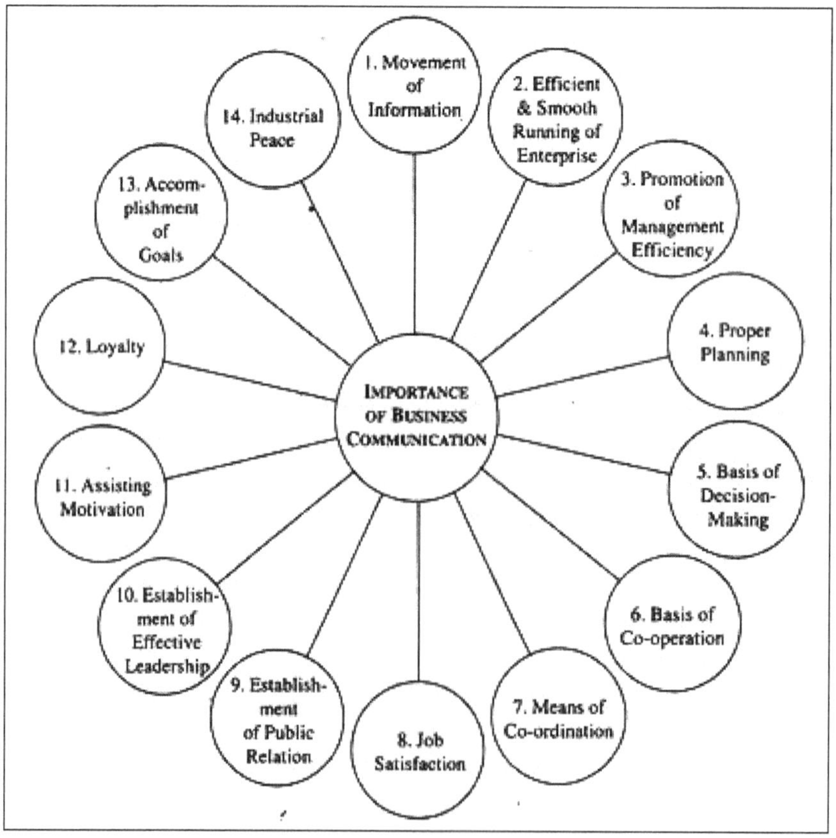

Importance of Business Communication.

Business Report

A report is an impersonal presentation of facts. Report is very much important in the field of business, trade and commerce. The main purpose of writing a report is to present some important information impersonally. A business report may be defined as an organized statement of facts or events or any situation relating to business or commercial interests prepared after an investigation and presented to the interested persons with or without recommendations. It facilitates the evaluation of progress and decision making process for business purpose. A business report is usually a type of upward communication in which communication process starts from lower level to upper level i.e., an employee makes a report and submits to related upper person to make usage of it. Such communication is basically authoritative and the level of authority depends on the subject and usage of a business report.

In other word, a report which contains business affairs is called business report. Generally a business report is an impersonal presentation of facts and information relating to business, trade and commerce. It is an orderly statement of information that assists in decision making and problem solving.

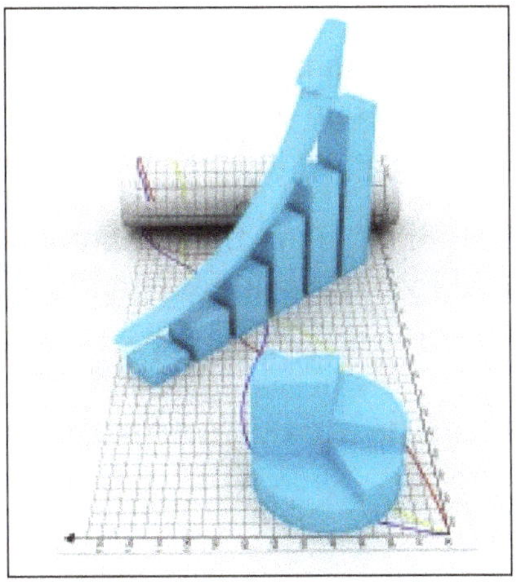

A business report may include graph presentation too.

Characteristics of Business Report

Business reports carry information on facts related to business activities. The very nature of business report differentiates it from other reports. The unique characteristics of business report are discussed below:

- Specific Issue: Every report, including business one, is written on specific subject. It is written to fulfill certain need.
- Pre-specified Audience: An important characteristic of report is that it has a pre-specified audience. Usually a report is written for a limited number of audiences and the need of the audience is always kept in mind.
- Specific Structure or Layout: In preparing report, certain structure or layout or format is followed. The layout or structure of report is almost same in every case.

- Written on Past Events: In most of the cases, the reports are written on past events. Most of the business reports carry the reasons of happing the incident, the ways of recovery etc. Reports are also written in past forms.
- Neutral in Nature: In drafting reports, impartiality it strictly maintained. No biased or non-objective material is included in it. Biased report may lead to disastrous decisions.
- Factual Information: Business report is always written based on factual information. The data collected on specific events is factual, not factious.
- Joint Effort: A report is an outcome of joint efforts of a group of people. No one can personally or solely prepare a report. Now-a-days, in most of the cases, committee is formed containing three to seven people for furnishing a report on certain incident.
- Orderly Presentation: The information of a report is presented orderly so that the audience can get his needed information from where it is located.
- Upward Flow: The direction of a report is always upward in the organizational structure. The higher authority normally assigns the duty of preparing reports to their immediate lower authority and after preparing the report, they submit it to their boss or higher authority.
- Some Additional Aids in Presentation: A report is always presented in an attractive way. In addition, analytical reports contain executive summary, contents and index, necessary charts, graphs and design and conclusion and recommendation etc.
- Signature and Date: It is customary to put the signature of the reporter with date at the end of the report. If it is prepared by a committee, signature must be given by each member of the committee.

Types of Business Reports in Business Communication

The business reports are classified on many basis:

Reports on the Basis of Importance or Frequency

The reports are classified into two types. They are ordinary or routine reports and special reports.

- Ordinary or Routine Report: Ordinary reports are prepared and presented before the managing director at specific intervals or to the next authorized person in the business routine. The reports shall be submitted either daily, weekly, fortnightly, monthly, quarterly, bi-annually or annually. This type of report contains mere statement of facts in detail without any opinion or recommendation of the reporter.

  Examples for routine reports are Report of Directors to the Annual General Meeting, Auditor's Report to the Annual General Meeting, Sales Report, Production Report and the like.

- Special Report: This type of report is prepared and presented before the top management on specific request. It usually contains the opinions or recommendations of the reporter with the help of facts and arguments. Examples for special report are opening of branch, introducing a new product, Improving the quality or changing the shape or size of the product and the like.

Reports on the Basis of Legal Formalities

The reports are classified into two types. They are formal report and informal report:

- Formal Report: Formal report is prepared in a prescribed format and presented before the competent authority in an established procedure. Reports submitted by officials or committees of constituted bodies (example: Companies, Cooperative Societies, Local Bodies etc.) are usually formal report.
- Informal Report: Informal report is prepared in a format of the convenience of the reporter and presented directly before the required person as and when demanded. An informal report is presented as in the form of letter or memorandum. Generally, it takes the form of a person to person communication.

The formal reports are classified into two types. They are statutory report and non-statutory report.

Reports on the Basis of Function

The reports are classified on the basis of function into two types. They are informative and interpretative.

- Informative Report: An informative report is prepared and presented with the help of available information at the maximum with regard to an issue or situation.
- Interpretative Report: An interpretative report is not only contains the facts, views and opinions of reporters and others but also includes the causes for an issue or an event and required remedial action with recommendations.

Reports on the Basis of Meetings

Whenever a meeting is organized in any business organization, a report is prepared by the secretary or any other individual about the proceedings of the meeting. Such reports are classified into two types. They are Verbation Report and Summarized Report.

- Verbation Reports: A verbation report is a complete word by word record of all discussions made at a meeting. For example, Appointment of an Auditor. A resolution is passed in the meeting. Likewise, Directors are appointed and the remuneration and perquisites of key personnel are fixed by passing a resolution. In this case, a report is prepared by including the verbation record of the resolutions passed with the names of the proposers and seconders, manner of voting and results.

  However, the verbation report should not be confused with the minutes of the meeting which is the official record of the proceedings and the decisions arrived at in the meeting.

- Summarised Report: A summarized report is prepared with the help of the essential details discussed in the meeting. This type of report is prepared for sending to the press or to shareholders of the company or members of the institution.

Reports on the Basis of Nature of the Subject Dealt with

The following reports are included in the report which are classified on the basis of the nature of the subject dealt with:

- Problem Solving Report: A problem may arise in any one of the department or in the whole organization. Hence, the top management may seek a report for solving the problem. When, the reporter collects various information to find the causes for such problem. Moreover, the report is concluded with the ways of solving the problem. Such type of report is called Problem Solving Report.
- Fact Finding Report: A machine may be breakdown in the factory premises. Sometimes, there may be a rivalry between the two group of workers. Now, the management wants to know the real reason for machine break down and group clash between the workers. In this case, the reporter analyze the incident through detailed investigation and find the truth. Finally, the reporter presents the facts in the report form before the top management.
- Performance Report: The business organization wants to know the performance of each department periodically or performance of a branch or performance of newly appointed employee or performance of existing employees for promotion, transfer and the like. The management is not in a position to take a decision without knowing the performance. Hence, a reporter is asked to prepare the performance report for anyone of the reasons mentioned above.
- Technical Report There is a lot of changes made in the technology. Whenever a company is going to introduce mechanical process instead of manual process, the level of technology required assessed. Sometimes a design may be changed in the existing product, if so, latest technology should be adopted. In this case, a detailed report is essential to top management for taking a decision. Such type of report is called Technical Report.

Reports of Committees or Subcommittees

Committees or Subcommittees are formed by the top management to prepare the report on any one of the issue. The followings are included in the reports of committee or subcommittee.

Standing Committee Report: Standing Committees are permanent in nature and are entrusted to deal with some continuing aspects of the business organization.

For example: Finance, Performance of Employees, Performance of Departments etc. These matters are continuously watched by the standing committee and submit the report at frequent intervals.

Special or Adhoc Committee Report: Special or adhoc Committees are appointed to deal with special investigation and are dissolved as soon as the presentation of report. Hence, the life of special committee is temporary.

For example: Fire occurrence or Accident incurred within the factory premises. The causes for fire or accident are find out by forming special committee.

Minority Report: Committees or subcommittees are appointed to submit the report based on the investigation of special subject. Generally, three members are selected to form a committee or sub-committee. One member being the chairman of such committee or subcommittee.

If the members have different opinion or views over the subject matter dealt with, the dissentient member may append the notes of dissent or may submit a report separately. Such report is termed as Minority Report. Even though, the dissent members must sign in the majority report with dissent note.

Majority Report: Generally, all the members of the committee or subcommittee including chairman have unanimous opinion among them. If so, only one report is prepared and presented before the responsible body. If not so, majority members of the committee or subcommittee have different opinion than minority members. In this case, majority members are going to submit a report before the responsible body. Such report is termed as majority report.

Reasons to use Business Reports

To prepare an excellent report, it helps to understand what the report will be used for:

- Summarize: Reports help to explain a complicated idea, process or the company's financial status in a clear, understandable way. Months of accumulated data, or years of research, might be summed up in a short report. Of course, it may not have every detail that was uncovered in the research, but the report will give those who read the report a concise summary of the research or data.
- Simplify: The people who will review your report may not have the time, desire or skill to evaluate all the data and research that's behind it. In any case, they have their own jobs to do. Your report gives them what they need to know.
- Clarify: If 10 people were to read and review all the data and research results you have gathered, they would come to a variety of different conclusions. Your report ensures that they're all operating from the same vantage point because you're giving them all the same data.
- Persuade: Say your company wants to persuade investors to put up capital to fund a new idea. Your report will be included in the business plan that will be shared with the investors. Other associates will compile the company's profit and loss statement and other financial status reports, but your report will be a sales projection outlining where the company believes the untapped markets are, and the sales they could yield. The financial statements are important, but your report is the one that could persuade on-the-fence investors to come aboard, or not.
- Prove a point: Business reports are often used when tough decisions have to be made, such as whether to downsize, which could involve layoffs. No one wants to go in that direction, but when the report is in front of them, showing the steady decrease in profits compared with expenses like salaries, it's clear what needs to be done. Or, on the positive side, reports can show whether the company is in the position to expand into exciting new directions.

- Solve a problem: You've been in meetings where discussions of a problem go around and around without arriving at a viable solution. But, if you share your reports on the big projection screen, everyone is looking at the same issue at the same time. Viewing a tangible document, with tables and graphs that show where the situation really stands, allows everyone to analyze the same material together and arrive at a solution together.

Example for Writing Common Reports

According to Purdue University's Online Writing Lab (OWL), most business reports don't have a universal format. Check to see if your company has a preferred format for the report you're writing. If not, you're free to compose it any way you see fit. However, OWL has suggestions that can help you make sure you're covering all the bases and writing the best report you can.

- Keep it brief.
- Know your audience and write to them.
- Use headings and highlight important points.
- Put your most important findings, arguments or points first.
- Decide whether to include your conclusions or leave that to the readers.

The content of your report will vary depending on its purpose and its audience. For an internal report, the audience already knows about the company, so you don't need to fill them in on those details. A public report, however, or one with multiple audiences, would benefit from some background information about the company.

Title/title page. Every report needs a clear title that explains what it will reveal. This isn't the place to be clever; transparency is key. For a short or informal report, a simple title at the top of the page, followed by the dates, if applicable, will do. For example:

Summary of Income and Expenses, First Quarter 2018

Formal reports need a title page that includes the title, date and author, for example:

Summary of Income and Expenses First Quarter 2018 Prepared by (your name) If the report is being prepared for a specific person or group, add that after your name, for example: For XYZ Company, Inc.

Introduction: Start with a short history or pertinent background information about the company, if you think it's needed. Then briefly explain why this report was prepared. If the report is presenting research findings, briefly explain the research methodology. For a short report, this should be a few sentences. A formal report might include an entire page. Some formal reports begin with an Executive Summary that gives an overview or synopsis of the report so that, if this is all someone reads, they'll still understand the report.

Table of contents: In a long report, list sections and visuals with page numbers.

Body of the report: Here's where you put your data, the crux or most crucial information of your report. Include visuals such as charts, diagrams, tables or graphs rather than text alone. Visuals show people what you want them to know and they are interactive, which keeps your readers' attention. Tables, graphs and other visual substantiative documents are the "proof" of what you're reporting. Always start with the most important data first.

Results: This section is optional and depends on your readers. Do you want to tell them how to interpret the results, or let the report speak for itself?

Conclusions: Formal reports need an ending summarizing the results, whether they were expected or came as a surprise, and how they will affect future decisions.

Exceptions: Annual and quarterly reports are examples that may be more creative. Particularly, if the business is reaching out to the general public, such as a hospital's annual or quarterly report, the updates may be best told through compelling stories of lives saved or employees performing state-of-the-art techniques. Businesses might relate their progress this way, too, by interviewing employees undertaking cutting-edge research or inventing new, exciting products.

Business Presentation

Business presentation can be defined as formal information about the business products or practices. It is typically carried out by using the audio and visual presentation material such as statistical documents, projectors, flip charts, whiteboards, and much more. The most common examples of the business presentations are intra-organization and sales presentations. Generally, the suppliers conduct the sales presentations in front of a potential customer with the aim of pitching their services, whereas the intra-organization presentations conducted by members of a company in front of their coworkers with the purpose to introduce new operations or policies.

Importance of Business Presentation

Business presentations are often utilized by the organizations and companies as a way to sell an idea or product for motivating the audience or training purposes. The presenter needs to prepare and rehearse before a business presentation for becoming confident. There are many factors that determined the effectiveness of a business presentation.

Connecting

A memorable bonding experience between the audience and the presenter is created by the interactive business presentations. This type of presentations involves the audience and helps in the driving home the overall message.

Informative

Every listener wants to know about the main nuggets of information such as learning tricks for improving the performance or how to overcome problems. A great presentation leaves the audience with a good piece of information that should be eye-opening and enlightening.

Inspiring

It is very important that a business presentation should be able to capture the attention of the audience. It should consist of the elements of a story, complete with anecdotes, lessons, conflicts, and resolutions. In addition to this, the presentation also required targeting on the important points from the start for capturing the attention of the audience.

Appealing

The impact of a business presentation on the audience is also affected by using visual or physical props. Some of the factors that mostly appeal the audience are screen projectors, handouts, slides and body language of the presenter. However, the exact impact of the props greatly depends on their relevance to the presented information.

Types of Business Presentations

There are basically four types of business presentations stated below:

Group Presentations

The findings of a team are communicated by the group presentations. Generally, these types of presentations remain informational in structure and seek to convince the people for accepting new programs and strategies.

Presentation Aids

Nowadays, the computer programs such as Flash and PowerPoint are used by the presenters for enhancing their presentation. Even the simple blackboard can augment the business presentations by capturing the feedback and questions of the audience.

Persuasive Presentations

The main motive of a persuasive presentation is to convenience the audience for supporting certain views. Generally, it outlines an organization goal or problem and then follows it by the statements for detailing the present state of affairs.

Informative Presentations

This type of presentation consists of educating the audience. It consists of status reports or summaries and starts with an overall goal that follows the action and specific plans. In simple words, a business presentation plays a vital role in the advancement of any organization.

Purpose of Business Presentations

Effective business presentations can help an organization to reduce internal conflict and increase external sales. Business presentations can be used to confirm a company's financial viability, to cast vision for a managerial staff and to honor the accomplishments of valued employees. Business presentations often take on distinctive characteristics depending on their overall purpose and the audience for which they are intended.

Information

Many business presentations, such as quarterly accounting reports and departmental project updates, serve the primary purpose of communicating information. These presentations provide ideas, opinions and data for a specific audience. In preparing an informative presentation, you seek primarily to teach your audience about your chosen subject. To do so, you need to learn about your audience and how much they already know about the subject, and you need to gather accurate, reliable and credible information. Referencing specific authority figures and providing significant data can also help your audience to better understand your subject.

Persuasion

Some business presentations have a primary purpose of persuading an audience to adopt a certain belief or to make a specific choice. Persuasive business presentations occur both internally, such as when a manager seeks to convince the staff to begin recycling, or externally, such as when members of one company makes a sales presentation to members of another organization. When you prepare a persuasive presentation, you seek to provide credible information in a compelling way, and you seek to craft an effective argument as well. Persuasive presentations often involve proposing a change in belief or action that may either reinforce or change the status quo.

Motivation

Business presentations may at times serve the purpose of not only persuading the audience to accept a certain perspective, but also motivating the audience toward a specific action. Motivational presentation use persuasive tactics. These presentations, though, focus more extensively on igniting the emotions and feelings of the audience. Sales managers, for example, may give a motivational speech during the annual sales meeting, just as a coach will make a motivational speech to a football team at halftime. Understanding your audience's priorities, concerns, and motivations will help you to spur your audience to action.

Celebration

Other business presentations serve the purpose of celebrating some aspect of business culture or some individual or group in a business community. Celebratory business presentations include toasts given at dinners and events, goodwill speeches made on historically significant dates, inspirational speeches given during a memorial or eulogy, and congratulatory messages recognizing achievements. These presentations help to demonstrate an individual's commitment to the company and his coworkers and to show the company's commitment to its employees and its ideals. Developing celebratory business presentations often involves researching your subject and practicing your delivery, as well as considering the needs and concerns of your audience.

Business Memo

A business memo is a short document used to transmit information within an organization. Memos are characterized by being brief, direct, and easy to navigate. They are less formal than letters but should maintain a professional, succinct style. Often, the purpose of a business memo is twofold: to identify a problem and propose a solution. Other times, memos may provide or request factual information.

Business memos are designed to accommodate busy readers who want to find the information they need from the memo quickly and easily. In writing a business memo, you should structure your memo to accommodate three kinds of readers:

- Those who read only the executive summary.
- Those who skim the entire memo for its key points and a few details they're interested in.
- Those who read the entire document for the details that support its major claims or recommendations.

Bear in mind that these readers may have different purposes in reading the memo. Often, readers need to make policy and action decisions based on the recommendations. Others may want to obtain specific information (evidence) needed to understand and justify policy and action decisions. Readers may also want to get a sense of your professional ability and judgment.

In determining the purpose and audience of your memo, ask yourself: Who is the intended recipient of this memo? What do I want the recipient to do after reading the memo? What information will the recipient be looking for in the memo? These kinds of questions will help guide your content, structure, and style choices.

Writing an Effective Business Memo

As stated above, an effective business memo is brief, direct, and easy to navigate. The following five writing strategies help readers to navigate business memos easily and quickly:

- Present the main point first: This may be the single most important guideline about the structure and content of memos. Readers should quickly grasp the content and significance of the memo. If readers have a question or problem, they want to know the answer or solution immediately—if readers want more information, they can continue reading. In other words, supporting details should follow the main point or conclusion, not precede it.

- Maintain a professional, succinct style: The style of your writing should be appropriate to your audience: In this case, your audience is your boss, your coworkers, or both. So, your style should be professional, straightforward, cordial, and easy to read. To achieve such a style, use short, active sentences. Avoid jargon and pretentious language. Maintain a positive or neutral tone; avoid negative language if possible. In addition to making memos easier to read, a professional writing style also improves the writer's credibility.
- Create a very specific subject line to give the reader an immediate idea of the memo's (or message's) subject and purpose. The subject line should orient the reader to the subject and purpose of the memo and provide a handy reference for filing and quick review. Suppose, for instance, that you were writing to request authorization and funding for a business trip. You'd avoid a general subject line like "Publisher's Convention" or "Trip to AWP Conference" in favor of something more specific like "Request for funds: AWP conference." The last example would tell the reader the subject and what she was being asked to do about it.
- Provide a summary or overview of the main points, especially if the memo is more than one page. Often referred to as an executive summary, the first paragraph of a long memo or message serves these functions:
    - Presents the main request, recommendation or conclusion.
    - Summarizes then previews the main facts, arguments and evidence.
    - Forecasts the structure and order of information presented in the remainder of the memo.
    - Like the subject line, the executive summary provides a quick overview of the purpose and content of the memo. The reader uses it to guide both a quick first reading and subsequent rapid reviews.
- Use format features, such as headings, to signal structure and guide readers to the information they're seeking. Headings provide an outline of the memo, enabling the reader to quickly see what the major topics or points are and where to find them in the memo. Make headings parallel with each other and as specific as possible. Other format features that signal structure and guide readers include short paragraphs and blocks of text, lists set off by indentations, numbers or bullets, or generous use of white space to guide the eye.

Standard Memo Heading

Though the format for a memo may vary from one organization to another, the standard heading consists of a series of clearly labeled lines that convey key information about the memo's contents and its distribution. The following are standard elements of a memo header:

Date:	The date on which the memo is distributed
To:	The person(s) to whom it is primarily
addressed	
(sometimes with job title)	
cc:	Name(s) of anyone else who receives a copy

(sometimes with job title)

From: Name of the writer, usually followed by

his/her

handwritten initials (sometimes with job title)

Subject: or Re: Concise statement of the memo's topic

Importance of Business Memo

Quick email messages about company happenings have become a common method of communication in offices, but this casual form of communication is not suitable for all occasions. While informal emails may have replaced the interoffice memo in some situations, business memos still have a place in the office. Business memos follow strict guidelines in terms of format, with a header, opening, summary and closing. The business memo should be formal, and managers may send the formal document to employees via email.

Company Policy Changes

When management changes a company policy that affects all employees in an organization, a business memo is an appropriate method to disseminate the information. The business memo provides the formality and authority a company-wide policy change requires. Managers and supervisors can post the business memo in an area visible to all employees.

Announcements

A business memo is an appropriate type of communication to use when making company announcements such as an employee promotion. Companies also use the business memo to welcome new employees who will fill a vital role in the organization. The business memo documents the important announcement. Email can serve as the delivery method for a memo, but the memo should be written in a formal business format. Business memos can also announce a new product line for the company. Management can also send out a business memo to announce that the business hit a target or goal. Other company announcements may include holiday parties, new benefit programs, stock information or the acquisition of a new client.

Action Request

Business memos are appropriate when management makes a request of all employees. For example, during an open enrollment period for health insurance, the human resource manager can use a business memo to inform and request that workers turn in policy changes by a specific date.

Reminders

Employees and management can also distribute a business memo to remind workers about a task that workers must complete. A reminder memo can relate to office behavior, such as cleaning up the company break room.

Business Letter

A business letter is usually a letter from one company to another, or between such organizations and their customers, clients, or other external parties. The overall style of letter depends on the relationship between the parties concerned. Business letters can have many types of content, for example to request direct information or action from another party, to order supplies from a supplier, to point out a mistake by the letter's recipient, to reply directly to a request, to apologize for a wrong, or to convey goodwill. A business letter is sometimes useful because it produces a permanent written record, and may be taken more seriously by the recipient than other forms of communication.

General Format

Margins

Side, top and bottom margins should be 1 to 1 1/4 inches (the general default settings in programs such as Microsoft Word). One-page letters and memos should be vertically centered.

Font Formatting

No special character or font formatting is used, except for the subject line, which is usually underlined.

Punctuation

The salutation or greeting is generally followed by a comma in British style, whereas in the United States a colon is used. The valediction or closing is followed by a comma.

Form

The following is the general format, excluding indentation used in various formats:

[SENDER'S COMPANY NAME]

[SENDER'S ADDRESS (optional if placed at bottom)]

[SENDER'S PHONE]

```
[SENDER'S E-MAIL (optional)]

[DATE]

[RECIPIENT W/O PREFIX]

[RECIPIENT'S COMPANY]

[RECIPIENT'S ADDRESS]

(Optional) Attention [DEPARTMENT/PERSON]

Dear [RECIPIENT W/ PREFIX]

[First Salutation then Subject in Business letters]

[CONTENT]

[CONTENT]

[COMPLIMENTARY CLOSING (Sincerely, Respectfully, Regards, etc.)]

[SENDER]

[SENDER'S TITLE (optional)]

[SENDER'S ADDRESS (optional if placed at top)]

Enclosures ([NUMBER OF ENCLOSURES])
```

Indentation Formats

Business letters conform to generally one of six indentation formats: standard, open, block, semi-block, modified block, and modified semi-block. Put simply, "semi-" means that the first lines of paragraphs are indented; "modified" means that the sender's address, date, and closing are significantly indented.

Standard

The standard-format letter uses a colon after the salutation and a comma after the complimentary closing.

Open

The open-format letter does not use punctuation after the salutation and no punctuation after the complimentary closing.

Block

In a block-format letter, all text is left aligned and paragraphs are not indented.

Modified Block

In a modified-block format letter, all text is left aligned (except the author's address, date, and closing), paragraphs are not indented, and the author's address, date, and closing begin at the center point.

```
company name and address
          date
           TO
```

Semi-block

Semi-block format is similar to the Modified block format, except that the first line of each paragraph is indented.

Modified Semi-block

In a modified semi-block format letter, all text is left aligned (except the author's address, date, and closing), paragraphs are indented, and the author's address, date, and closing are usually indented in same position.

Parts of a Business Letter

Like most of the letters a business letter also has a layout which includes various divided parts.

These parts are:

- Letterhead: A letterhead is topmost heading printed on letter paper. The heading consists of name, address generally accompanied by a logo of the organisation. Most professional firms have their own pre-designed letterhead. Pre-printed Letterheads showcase the repute of a company; in terms that that company can afford to have these and is not miser in using some extra ink. However smaller firms may not have it. They use their name, address where the letterhead would be placed.
- Date: The date has to written exactly below the letter head. The date is important part of a letter and is used for reference. The date is supposed to be written in full with day, month and year. Example – 31st May 2012 or May 31st, 2012
- Recipient: Recipient or Receiver's name and Address is next part of a business letter. This part included the Name of the Receiver, his Designation and Full address inclusive of phone and email.
- Salutation: Salutation is word of greeting used to begin a letter. It is courteous gesture and shows respect to the receiver. Dear Sir/Madam etc. are specifically known as Opening Salutation.
- Body: Body is the main part of the letter. The message of the letter is to be clearly mentioned in the first line, itself. The body has the relevant subject matter which is to be divided into a number of paragraphs, mostly 3-4 or more depending upon the matter. If there are instructions etc. these are to be in a bulleted or numerically listed in separate lines. The Last Paragraph should sum up the whole letter and offer any assistance or take a course of action as required or instructed.
- Closing (subscription): Closing refers to the end of the letter. It is courteous and shows a mark of respect towards the recipient. Yours Sincerely or Sincerely etc. are specifically known as Closing Salutations.

- Signature: Sign your name after a few spaces. If you have your Printed Name, then sign above the line containing your typed name. Signature is to written in Black or Blue Ink. If you have an electronic signature you can use that too. Scanned image of your signature can also be used, if it confers with rules of your organisation.
- Sender's Name, title and contact information: If not provided in the letterhead, one can include his Name, Title, Address, Phone, Email etc. in separate lines.
- Enclosure: If you have attached some documents, Type Enclosures few lines after the Signature of Senders Info. Provide the number and type of documents attached e.g. 'Enclosures (2): brochure, resume'.

Business Letter Styles

There are Four Styles, or Indentation Formats used for writing business letters:

Full Block Style: Block letter format is commonly used to correspond between businesses and between individuals and businesses. Its main purposes are to inform, request or register a complaint.

In full block format letter:

- All the text is aligned to the left margin.
- All lines are left justified.
- Paragraphs are not indented.
- Paragraphs are separated by double or triple spacing.
- Everything is followed by a single blank space in most case but there are exceptions: three or four spaces follow the date; two spaces follow the body; three or four spaces after the closing (enough room for a signature); and two blank lines after the sender's title.
- There is no punctuation in the addresses.
- There is a comma after the greeting, although some in the U.S. prefer a colon.
- The closing is also followed by a comma.

Semi-Block Style: Semi-Block letter format is as mentioned, has partial formatting of a full block style.

In Semi-Block Format Letter:

- All text is aligned to the left margin.
- Paragraphs are indented.

Modified Block Style: Modified block format is a conventional way of writing formal business letters. Its format is applicable to both print and email correspondence. Its main purposes include cover letters, thank you letters, letters of resignation and sales letters.

In Modified Block Format Letter:

- All text is aligned to the left margin, except for the author's address, date, and closing.
- Paragraphs are not indented.
- The author's address, date, and closing are usually indented three inches from the left margin, but can be set anywhere to the right of the middle of the page, as long as all three elements are indented to the same position.

Modified Semi-Block Style: In modified semi-block format there are partial elements of modified block style.

In Modified Semi-Block Format Letter:

- All text is aligned to the left margin, except for the author's address, date, and closing.
- Paragraphs are indented.
- The author's address, date, and closing are usually indented in same position.

Types of Business Letters

Sales Letters

Typical sales letters start off with a very strong statement to capture the interest of the reader. Since the purpose is to get the reader to do something, these letters include strong calls to action, detail the benefit to the reader of taking the action and include information to help the reader to act, such as including a telephone number or website link.

Order Letters

Order letters are sent by consumers or businesses to a manufacturer, retailer or wholesaler to order goods or services. These letters must contain specific information such as model number, name of the product, the quantity desired and expected price. Payment is sometimes included with the letter.

Complaint Letters

The words and tone you choose to use in a letter complaining to a business may be the deciding factor on whether your complaint is satisfied. Be direct but tactful and always use a professional tone if you want the company to listen to you.

Adjustment Letters

An adjustment letter is normally sent in response to a claim or complaint. If the adjustment is in the customer's favor, begin the letter with that news. If not, keep your tone factual and let the customer know that you understand the complaint.

Inquiry Letters

Inquiry letters ask a question or elicit information from the recipient. When composing this type of letter, keep it clear and succinct and list exactly what information you need. Be sure to include your contact information so that it is easy for the reader to respond.

Follow-up Letters

Follow-up letters are usually sent after some type of initial communication. This could be a sales department thanking a customer for an order, a businessman reviewing the outcome of a meeting or a job seeker inquiring about the status of his application. In many cases, these letters are a combination thank-you note and sales letter.

Letters of Recommendation

Prospective employers often ask job applicants for letters of recommendation before they hire them. This type of letter is usually from a previous employer or professor, and it describes the sender's relationship with and opinion of the job seeker.

Acknowledgment Letters

Acknowledgment letters act as simple receipts. Businesses send them to let others know that they have received a prior communication, but action may or may not have taken place.

Cover Letters

Cover letters usually accompany a package, report or other merchandise. They are used to describe what is enclosed, why it is being sent and what the recipient should do with it, if there is any action that needs to be taken. These types of letters are generally very short and succinct.

Letters of Resignation

When an employee plans to leave his job, a letter of resignation is usually sent to his immediate manager giving him notice and letting him know when the last day of employment will be. In many cases, the employee also will detail his reason for leaving the company.

Importance of Business Letter

Businessmen must establish contact with the people and then only they can develop their organisations. Importance of communication is very great in business life. There was a time when the size of business was normally small and varied means of communication were not available, direct meetings or face-to-face communication was practised by the businessmen. Later on, the policy of sending representatives for direct contacts was introduced. All these methods have their limitations.

The importance of business letters as the cheapest and most extensive form of communication was first realised in USA and UK and now this method has been accepted as the best method of communication all over the world. This has been possible with the introduction of ever growing postal services. In the meantime standardisation of the form and the style of business letters have made them more popular and acceptable by all.

The commercial correspondence has a language of its own which is markedly different from personal letters. Day by day improvements are being made in the form and the style of business letters making them more impressive, meaningful and compact.

A large number of books on the subject are available in the market in the aid of the business world. Invention of different machines for the purpose makes business letters fast in production and in distribution.

It does not mean, however, that other means of communication have been abandoned.

Advantages of Business Letter Communication through letters occupies the largest share in the total volume of communication because of the following advantages:

- Letters are less costly than other means of communication.
- Letters can be sent to long distant places by post within a short time. Of course, letters may be sent by messengers within neighbouring areas.
- Letters are drafted after proper thinking and planning and so the subject matter can be presented in a systematic and logical way.
- The ideas conveyed in letters are clear and free from ambiguity.
- The size of a letter may be big or small as required.
- Letters simultaneously provide evidence and exact copies can be retained.
- Same communication may-be made to a number of persons at a time, through duplicating or printing.
- Many unpleasant and delicate matters which cannot be spoken face to face or through mechanical devices can be written in letters in a discreet language.
- Letters are suitable for all types of communication.
- There is standardisation in form and style readily acceptable by the business world. Even internationally accepted code language is used.

Employee Suggestion Systems

A suggestion box is a device for obtaining additional comments, questions, and requests. In its most basic and traditional form, it is a receptacle with an opening, like a voting box.

The suggestion box is used for collecting slips of paper with input from customers and patrons of a particular organization. Suggestion boxes may also exist internally, within an organization, such as means for garnering employee opinion.

Variations on this method include paper feedback forms which can be sent via postal mail, such as the "We value your input" or "How was the service today?" cards found in some restaurants; solicitations to provide comments over the telephone, such as a voluntary survey at the end of a transaction with a call center, or even an invitation on a printed store receipt to call and complete a customer satisfaction survey (sometimes offered with a product discount); or the placement of feedback forms on an institution's website.

Including mechanisms for customer comments beyond an ordinary point of service has several benefits. Suggestion boxes provide some degree of detachment (or sometimes, especially with computer-mediated communication, complete anonymity) from the person or service that a customer may be critiquing, and may therefore yield more frank and open feedback, thereby providing greater opportunities for obtaining accurate market research data and improving customer relations.

"Drop Your Ideas in the Suggestion Box".

The internal routing of comments within an organization may also provide those without direct contact with customers a realistic appraisal of the quality of customer care being given. The external routing of responses to received suggestions, such as by posting responses to questions and requests on a physical or virtual bulletin board, may also help educate consumers and improve a company's image and customer loyalty.

Modern Versions

Internet suggestion box for employees in a factory.

The physical box, as a post box, was replaced by electronic places or addresses; like postal service systems replaced, in the 2000s, by email. But the traditional function, "*obtaining additional comments, questions, and requests*", still exist as demand, collecting information with input from customers and patrons of a particular organization, or means for garnering employee input.

In some contexts the modern suggestion box is a webpage with an anonymous form, or a simple email address, for example to an audit department. In other contexts, it turned into a complete issue tracking system, named issue tracking system, which allows the following main features (that was impossible with the old classic suggestion boxes):

- Store the entire history suggestions in a database: Each suggestion receives a "ticket number", and a detailed suggestion-form is stored;
- Allow the user and the company monitor the status on your routing: Each ticked receives an *status*, that changes with its progress in the audition feedback or the problem-resolution.

Employee Opinion Gathering

Gathering employee opinion with a suggestion box can also be fruitful, especially in groupthink-prone environments and within a corporate culture that adheres to a "shoot the messenger" mentality. However, as with the use of anonymous suggestion forms from the public, allowing unsigned comments may sacrifice accountability and make the feedback system prone to abuse.

Recording received suggestions in a database can help track any trends. While some systems keep suggestions private, some systems make suggestions public, allowing other people to endorse the suggestion rather than creating a similar one. This voting system allows organizers to quickly see what is most suggested.

The term "employee suggestion systems" refers to a variety of efforts businesses make to solicit and utilize input from their employees in hopes of achieving cost savings or improving product quality, workplace efficiency, customer service, or working conditions. These efforts range from simply placing suggestion boxes in common areas to implementing formal programs with committees to review ideas and rewards for those that are adopted. The ideas generated can range from simple quality of work life improvements, like putting a refrigerator in the coffee room, to larger streamlining issues that can save the company thousands of dollars per year, like switching all salespeople's cellular phones from individual contracts to a group contract with a discount vendor.

Some companies assume that since they cultivate an open relationship between employees and management, ideas for improvements will surface informally, without explicit prompting. But experts note that formal suggestion systems encourage employees to really think about their jobs and want to participate in the operation of the company. Formal suggestion systems let employees know that their ideas are valued. Such systems may even increase motivation and foster loyalty and teamwork among employees. And these benefits come in addition to the positive impact employee suggestion systems can have on a company's bottom line. "Millions of dollars are being saved by listening to the company's greatest asset—its human resource." Wells went on to discuss a study which uncovered savings of more than $624 million in 2003 in 47 companies in which 450,000 people participated in programs.

Elements of a Successful Suggestion System

"The goal of a successful suggestion system is to tap the reservoir of ideas and creative thinking of all employees for the improvement of the working process and products,". "To do so requires proper understanding by everyone of the process, management support of the system, encouragement and meaningful rewards, and a structure to make sure nothing falls through the cracks." The elements of a successful employee suggestion system can be divided into four main areas: management support, program structure, program visibility and promotion, and recognition and rewards.

Management Support

The first element of a successful employee suggestion system is to demonstrate buy-in from top management. Managers must show enthusiasm and commitment toward the program if it is to generate the desired results. A small business owner might begin by sharing his or her vision for the company with employees. Employees who understand the company's overall mission are more likely to submit valuable ideas that will help the company achieve its goals. The next step might be to make sure line managers support the suggestion system and do not feel threatened by it. It is also important for managers to raise the topic frequently in meetings and incorporate the positive results of employee suggestions into periodic progress reports. Managers should also be encouraged to submit suggestions themselves, although they should not generally be rewarded for ideas that fall under their normal strategic planning responsibilities.

Program Structure

The next element of a successful employee suggestion system is structure. Experts recommend placing responsibility for program development and implementation with a single administrator. This person should begin by selecting a committee of employees—from all parts of the organization and representing various demographic groups—to help administer various phases. The administrator and employee committee should then develop clear rules to guide employee efforts in providing suggestions. Suggestion programs tend to be more successful when employees are encouraged to make reasonable suggestions within the parameters of their own work experience. "The real goal is to generate as many ideas as possible, and, over time, to improve the quality of the suggestions through feedback and encouragement,". It is important to develop a clear policy statement that covers all aspects of the suggestion program and make sure that both managers and employees understand it. If employees view the process as open and above-board, it will help eliminate any suspicion about how ideas are reviewed and rewarded.

Program Visibility

Another important element of successful employee suggestion programs is visibility. After all, employees cannot be expected to participate in a program if they are not made aware of it. Experts recommend launching suggestion programs in a highly public manner, with announcements, newsletters, parties, etc. Employees should come away with the idea that management intends to give full consideration to all suggestions and plans to act on the best ones in a timely manner. The suggestion system itself should also be widely publicized and promoted. Examples of possible systems include the familiar suggestion box with written forms; the old-fashioned bulletin board for posting ideas and results; a special toll-free telephone line to allow employees to phone in suggestions; or more sophisticated systems based on e-mail or postings to a dedicated Web site. Once the system has been introduced, it is important to follow up with ongoing promotional activities in order to maintain employee interest.

Recognition and Rewards

Another vital element of successful employee suggestion systems is recognizing participants and providing rewards for good ideas. Employees are much more likely to participate in a suggestion program if the ideas they submit receive quick and thoughtful responses from management. Experts recommend setting a timetable in which receipt of an idea will be acknowledged (ranging from 24 hours with electronic systems to one week with more traditional systems). Then employees should be notified within 30 days whether or not their ideas will be adopted. Even in cases where an idea is not used, the employee who submitted it should be thanked for his or her participation in the program. It may be helpful to provide a small, tangible reward for employees who submit an idea to the suggestion system for the first time, such as a T-shirt, pen, or umbrella.

To ensure the success of a suggestion system, it is also important to publicize the suggestions used and their positive impact on the company. One way to do this might be to hold an annual dinner honoring the people who made suggestions over the course of the year. Many companies also establish reward systems for employee ideas that lead to cost savings or process improvements. For example, some companies distribute a fraction of all the savings provided by the employee suggestion system as part of their annual profit sharing programs. Experts acknowledge that it can be complicated to develop an appropriate reward system that recognizes valuable employee contributions without creating jealousy and resentment among fellow employees. Some suggest that this task might best be delegated to an employee advisory committee. The key is to evaluate ideas based on factors like innovation and ingenuity as well as monetary value when establishing rewards.

Advantages and Disadvantages of the Employee Suggestion Box

When employees are given opportunities to participate in decision making at work, they feel empowered and assume more ownership of their work. Allowing employees to make suggestions through vehicles such as the suggestion box is not enough, however. To be effective, you've got to take employee suggestions seriously and treat the comments respectfully.

Motivation

Employees gain a sense of pride about the organization when they're given opportunities to participate directly in decisions or make suggestions they know will be considered. They become motivated to work even harder for the company and develop a stronger desire to see the business succeed. When suggestions repeatedly go unnoticed or employees rarely receive feedback about the suggestions they enter into the box, they can become resentful and lose motivation. If you don't take the suggestion box seriously and occasionally incorporate useful suggestions, it's better not to have one at all.

Control

Managers who are expected to take employee suggestions seriously may believe the process undercuts their authority. When asked to review and consider employee suggestions, they are reluctant, feeling they will lose respect of their staff if they don't maintain complete control. In reality, managers who remain open to suggestions and welcome new ideas from their employees generate a higher level of respect from employees. Staff becomes more loyal to a manager who uses their constructive suggestions. Employees are more prone to honor the boss's authority when they receive praise and notice for timely and positive suggestions.

Criteria

Too often, employees receive no guidance from management about what kinds of suggestions you're looking for, how to approach various topics and the process by which changes are made in the company. Simply placing a suggestion box on the wall without any instructions encourages frivolity and unproductive suggestions. When you institute a suggestion box, advise employees of the types of contributions they can make. Give them details about the company goals and future plans so they can base suggestions on facts instead of guessing at your intent. Arm employees with all the information they need to make informed suggestions so they will reap the benefits of being involved.

Expectations

A suggestion box cannot cure what ails your company. Employees may become impatient when changes don't occur as quickly as they would like. You could actually undermine the process by giving employees the impression that positive suggestions can be incorporated at will. They need to understand the process of change in your company as well as your priorities. Employees and management must understand that a suggestion box and the resulting employee suggestions take time to initiate. Using the suggestion box must remain consistent for it to be effective. Make sure employees retain realistic expectations of how long it will take for some suggestions to be considered. At the same time, encourage them to continue participating so that employee participation becomes an integral part of your culture.

References

- Business-communication-meaning-elements-and-features-with-diagram, business-communication -70142: yourarticlelibrary.com, Retrieved 23 January, 2019
- Definition-of-business-report: bconsi.blogspot.com, Retrieved 16 June, 2019
- What-is-business-report-characteristics-of-business-report: bizcommunicationcoach.com, Retrieved 13 April, 2019
- Types-of-business-reports-in-business-communication: accountlearning.com, Retrieved 04 May, 2019
- Importance-types-and-what-is-business-presentation: studymafia.org, Retrieved 10 June, 2019
- Purpose-business-presentations- 7875472: bizfluent.com, Retrieved 16 January, 2019
- Writing-business-memos: writingcenter.gmu.edu, Retrieved 18 February, 2019
- Weighing-pros-cons-employee-suggestion-box-33254: smallbusiness.chron.com, Retrieved 18 March, 2019

2

Types of Business Communication

There are different types of business communication which can be classified as interpersonal communication, corporate communication, written communication, and oral communication. The topics elaborated in this chapter will help in gaining a better perspective about these types of business communication.

Communication Systems

Communication systems are the various processes, both formal and informal, by which information is passed between the managers and employees within a business, or between the business itself and outsiders. Communication—whether written, verbal, nonverbal, visual, or electronic—has a significant impact on the way business is conducted. The basic process of communication begins when a fact or idea is observed by one person. That person (the sender) may decide to translate the observation into a message, and then transmit the message through some communication medium to another person (the receiver). The receiver then must interpret the message and provide feedback to the sender indicating that the message has been understood and appropriate action taken.

The goal of any form of communication is to promote complete understanding of a message. But breakdowns in communication can occur at any step in the process. Business managers need to understand and eliminate the common obstacles that prevent effective communication. Some of the causes of communication problems in business settings include:

- A lack of basic language skills.
- Differing expectations and perceptions on the part of senders and receivers.
- Selectivity or the tendency for individuals to pick and choose what they retain when they receive a message from another person.
- Distractions such as ringing telephones, scheduled meetings, and unfinished reports.

Good communication should be complete, concise, clear, concrete, correct, considerate, and courteous. More specifically, this means that communication should answer basic questions like who, what, when, where; be relevant and not overly wordy; focus on the receiver and his or her interests; use specific facts and figures and active verbs; use a conversational tone for readability; include examples and visual aids when needed; be tactful and good-natured; and be accurate and nondiscriminatory.

Unclear, inaccurate, or inconsiderate business communication can waste valuable time, alienate employees or customers, and destroy goodwill toward management or the overall business. As we enter the information age, the importance of communicating clearly grows and the emphasis on written communication increases. "Companies once covered for poor writers by surrounding them with people who could translate their thoughts onto paper. But this strategy has proved less practical in the bottom-line-driven information age, which requires more high-quality writing from more categories of employees than ever before. Instead of covering for non-writers, companies are increasingly looking for ways to screen them out at the door."

In the early years of corporate America, business managers operated on a strict basis of top-down communications. Whatever the boss or owner of the company said was the law. In most cases, strategies for doing everything from selling product to dealing with employees would be discussed behind closed doors. Once those decisions were made by managers, lower-level employees were expected to put them into effect. Employees had little input; they did as they were told or found work elsewhere. Such management attitudes, particularly when they applied to worker safety issues in such places as coal and steel mines, led to the growth of labor unions. If nothing else, unions had the power in many cases to slow or shut down production until management listened to the demands of the workers.

In reaction to union demands, corporations eventually set up communication systems where rank-and-file members could speak their minds through union representatives. Although the unions provided the impetus for corporate managers to implement such systems, managers eventually realized that employees could have meaningful input into solving company problems. When presented with the opportunity to contribute, many employees jumped at the chance. This sort of feedback came to be called bottom-up communication.

In today's business environment, most corporations encourage employees to take an active role in the company. Employees who notice ways to improve production are encouraged, and usually rewarded, for passing those ideas on to managers. Employees who submit ideas that withstand intense study can be rewarded with a percentage of the savings to the company. Employees who are harassed on the job are strongly encouraged to report such harassment as far up the chain of management as necessary to stop it. Regular employee meetings are held where the lowest-level employee can stand up and ask the highest-level manager a direct question with the full expectation that a direct answer will be offered in return.

Business managers have also developed a method of monitoring how the company is running while meeting employees halfway. Sometimes called "management by walking around," this method of communication calls for top managers to get out of their offices and see what is happening at the level where the work is performed. Instead of simply reading reports from subordinates, business owners visit factories or service centers, observe employees on the job, and ask their opinions. Although the practice is both praised and denigrated regularly by business management experts, this form of communications does serve to keep the boss in touch.

Preparing Effective Messages

Perhaps the most important part of business communication is taking the time to prepare an effective and understandable message. According to Murphy and Hildebrandt, the first step is to know the main purpose of the message. For example, a message to a supplier might have the purpose of obtaining a replacement for a defective part. The next step is to analyze the audience so that the message can be adapted to fit their views and needs. It may be helpful to picture the recipient and think about which areas of the message they might find positive or negative, interesting or boring, pleasing or displeasing. After that, the sender must choose the ideas to include and collect all the necessary facts. The next step involves organizing the message, since a poorly organized message will fail to elicit the required response. It may be helpful to prepare an outline beforehand, paying particular attention to the beginning and ending portions. Finally, before transmitting the message it is important to edit and proofread.

Communications Technologies

Advances in technology over the last 20 years have dramatically changed the way in which business communications take place. In fact, in many ways communication technologies have changed the way in which business is done. The expanded use of electronic mail and of the Internet generally have enabled businesses to more easily move work from one location to another, establish remote and mobile offices, even to create virtual offices. New communication technology has also speeded up the turn-around time for decision making and blurred the line between work hours and personal hours. All of these developments challenge companies to adapt to a faster business environment. This is both an opportunity for companies to become more productive and efficient and a test of their adaptability.

Although changes in electronic communication technology are occurring at a phenomenal pace, they are not radical changes in the basic forms of communication. They are, rather, enhancements to traditional communication techniques. These technologies have made two basic enhancements in how we can communicate.

Mobility and Reach

Wireless and cellular technology have greatly expanded the places from which we can communicate and the distance over which we communicate easily. A manager on the way to work anywhere in the U.S. can easily call and chat with a colleague or supplier in Singapore as she makes her way home in the evening there.

Speed and Power

High-speed fiber optic phone lines and reasonably priced high-speed satellite transmissions have created a situation in which it is as easy to transfer large data files from one department to another in a single building as it is to transfer those files to a location anywhere in the world.

Both of these enhancements to communications have influenced how business is done. They each have upsides and downsides. The ease with which colleagues can stay in touch with one another is helpful in coordinating a company's activities. Staying in close contact with suppliers is also beneficial. For a particular employee, however, being available at any time may also be a burden.

Cell phones, lap top computers, and hand-held messaging devices of various kinds are all valuable tools for business communications. They enhance our ability to communicate and stay in touch but to benefit from their potential a company must use them wisely and efficiently and establish rules that prevent the devices from becoming burdensome to the user. With ease may also come complacency. For example, just because a sales representative can call Joan in production—easily, quickly, and from almost anywhere—to clarify and answer questions about a sloppily placed order does not mean that making and answering many calls about the order is efficient. An emphasis on clear and accurate communications is needed for efficiency, regardless of the ease or speed with which communication devices operate.

Internal Communications

Intranets, or internal organizational computer networks, have become the media of choice for most companies when it comes to keeping employees informed. The company intranet can be used like an electronic bulletin board and when paired with e-mail can serve to disseminate information quickly and efficiently.

Since an intranet may be used to easily connect people working in various locations, it can help to establish or maintain a sense of community in an organization that is geographically dispersed. In fact, intranets make it possible for groups of people to work together closely in what is known commonly as a virtual office. Many small service businesses are started as virtual offices in which each person within the group works at his or her own home or place of choosing. What unites the group are two things: a common goal, and a computer network of some sort through which information and software tools are shared.

External Communications

The growth of the Internet has made it almost essential for a business to have an online presence, simple though it may be. On a simple Internet Web site a company can provide potential customers, clients, employees, and investors with contact information and a picture of the company. For those wishing to use the Internet as a sales and marketing vehicle, a more sophisticated (and expensive) site can be developed. Often called e-Commerce Web sites, these sites are used for advertising, displaying merchandise, taking and processing orders, tracking orders, and performing many customer service tasks.

Small businesses may have a unique opportunity for benefiting from a Web presence. The outreach that is possible through a well-marketed Web site is much greater than would be possible through any other media at a similar cost. According to some analysts, for businesses one of the most powerful aspects of an interactive medium like the Internet is the ability to develop a true two-way conversation with clients and customers. The Internet is a powerful communications tool and one that businesses of all sizes now use regularly.

Informal Communications

Informal methods of communication, such as rumors and "the company grapevine," can be outside of management's control. The grapevine is a bottom-up form of communication in which employees try to understand what is happening around them when there is no official word from management. When management is silent, employees fill the void with guesses about what is happening. Although there is no way the grapevine can be stopped, it can be influenced. When dealing with questions that cannot, or should not, be answered, managers should take the initiative before negative rumors get started. If it is obvious to employees that the company will soon undergo major changes, for example, management should confirm that it will. Employees should be informed that management recognizes they have legitimate concerns, which will be addressed when possible. If official talk would damage the company, that should be made clear to the employees.

The Importance of Good Communication

All forms of communication, even the lack of it, can have a significant impact on business dealings. A stiffly-worded, official-sounding memo to employees telling them not to talk to the press about impending litigation could be interpreted as admitting that the company did something wrong. Management's repeated "no comments" to employees and the press on a rumored merger may launch dozens of informal discussions about company suitors, how much the company will sell for, and how many employees will be laid off.

In order to avoid the negative effects of such scenarios, small business owners should make it a practice to communicate as much and as openly as possible. They should think twice before eliminating the company newsletter as a cost-saving measure, keep electronic bulletin boards up-to-date, and hold meetings in which employees can ask questions of management. In addition, they should develop their skills so that all business communications are easily understandable. Management terms and jargon, stiff or flowery language may contribute to the impression among employees that management is talking down to them. It is also helpful to obtain and analyze feedback. Asking employees if they feel informed or not and what would make them feel more informed about the company can open valuable channels of communication.

Interpersonal Communication

Communication is the heart of any business regardless of what you do, how many employees you have and to whom you sell. The process of interpersonal communication in business involves sending and receiving messages with colleagues, managers, partners, customers and other business stakeholders. Effective interpersonal communication happens when the message is understood as it was intended.

Interpersonal communication is the procedure by which people swap information, feelings and impart through verbal and non-verbal messages. This definition underlines the crucial fact that interpersonal communication is not only apprehensive about 'what' is pronounced, i.e., the language employed, but 'how' it is pronounced, e.g., the nonverbal messages sent, such as tone of voice and facial expressions. Hartley defines interpersonal communication as having the following characteristics:

- Communication from one person to another.
- Communication which is face-to-face.

- Both the form and the content of the communication reflect the personal characteristics of the individuals as well as their social roles and relationships.

When two or more people are in the same place and are aware of each other being there, then communication is said to be taking place, no matter how subtle or inadvertent it may be. Even without vocalizations, an onlooker may be using prompts of stance (posture), facial manifestation, and garb to impact other's role, poignant situation, persona or intents. Even though no communication may be aimed at, people receive messages through forms of non-verbal conduct. This is a significant thrust for those working in people-centered vocations, who require to foster an awareness of the assortment of prompts entailed in interpersonal communication. Hartley suggests that interpersonal communication includes the following aspects: non-verbal communication, reinforcement, questioning, reflecting, opening and closing, explanation, listening and self-disclosure.

Although interpersonal communication can include oral, written, and non-verbal forms of communication, the term is by and large related to spoken communication that takes place between two or more individuals in person. Some of the types of interpersonal communication that are generally used within a business organization comprise staff meetings, formal project discussions, employee performance reviews, and informal chit-chats. Interpersonal communication with those outside the business organization can be in various forms, too counting client meetings, employment interviews, or sales visits. So as to comprehend the principles of effective interpersonal communication, it is beneficial to look at the fundamental process of communication.

The basic process of communication initiates when a fact is perceived or an idea devised by a single person. That person (the sender) chooses to decipher the perception into a message, and subsequently conveys the message through some communication medium to another person (the receiver). The receiver then must construe the message and supply feedback to the sender indicating that the message has been comprehended and fitting action taken.

Regrettably, errors can be instituted during any stage of the communication process. For instance, misunderstandings can crop up when the sender does not have an apparent idea of the message he or she is attempting to communicate, or has a clear idea but is unable to articulate it perfectly. However, errors can also take place when the receiver does not take note warily, deduces a sense other than what was meant by the sender, or does not provide feedback. Eventually, blurred, imprecise, or thoughtless business communication can squander precious time, estrange employees or customers, and obliterate goodwill toward management or the business on the whole.

Role of Non-verbal Communication in Interpersonal Communication

Non-verbal communication is also required in Interpersonal communication. At times, we don't need words. When words are not enough or we are not able to speak with entire comprehension, non-verbal communication works visually. Signs or emotions or body language can be termed as different non-verbal communication tools. A person uses non-verbal communication several times in his daily life. Emotions are of special importance in non-verbal communication because they have more meanings in them.

Facial emotions can be interpreted differently by every person. A word has a common meaning for everybody but each facial emotion has its own meaning and message and every receiver takes the message in a different way. There are basic emotions that we can see in a written communication. A person can express feelings in many different ways. Body language is the most important part of non-verbal communication. Moving head up and down means 'yes' while shaking it right to left means 'no' or shaking hand means 'hello' and so on. These non-verbal communication kinds are used by everyone everyday. The reason for using this non-verbal communication tools is that they provide sense to words or messages that one wants to send, and at the same time manage our conversations.

Fundamentals of Interpersonal Communication

Scores of researchers have split interpersonal communication into numerous rudiments so that it can be more easily comprehended. These are explained below:

Communicators

For any communication to take place there ought to be at least two people involved. Conventionally, communication is seen as involving a sender and a receiver of a message. Nevertheless, the problem with this way of seeing a relationship is that it presents communication as a one-way process, i.e., one person sends the message and the other receives it, which is a lateral process. Today, it is acknowledged that communications are roughly always complex, two-way processes, with people sending and receiving messages to and from each other, in any interaction.

Message

Message not only means the speech used or information communicated, but also the non-verbal messages swapped such as facial expressions, tone of voice, gestures and body language. Non-verbal behavior can transmit supplementary information about the message vocalized. Particularly, it can divulge more about emotional attitudes which may underlie the substance of discourse.

Noise

Noise has a unique connotation in the theory of communication. It refers to anything that deforms the message, so that what is received is dissimilar from what is proposed by the speaker. Even as physical 'noise' (sounds) can meddle with communication, things like the use of intricate jargon, unsuitable body language, negligence and cultural disparities can be considered 'noise' in the context of interpersonal communication. Thus, misrepresentations or discrepancies that might crop up during an effort to communicate are capable of being termed as noise.

Response

Response/feedback comprises messages the receiver replaces, which allows the sender to know how accurately the message has been received, along with the receiver's reaction. The receiver may also reply to the unintentional message in addition to the intentional one. The various types of feedback range from direct verbal statements, to subtle facial expressions or changes in posture which might point to the sender that the receiver experiences discomfort with the message. Response/feedback permits the sender to regulate, acclimatize or restate his/her message to facilitate communication.

Background

All communication is influenced by the background in which it takes place. However, apart from looking at where the interaction takes place, i.e., the situational background (room, office, etc.), the social background needs to be referred to, i.e., the roles, responsibilities and rank of the participants. The emotional setting and participants' expectations of the interaction will also affect the communication.

Channel

It refers to the physical means by which the message is transported from one person to another. In the case of inter-personal communication, the channels considered are speech and vision.

Communication Channels

Communication channels are the media chosen to convey the message from sender to receiver. Communication channels can be categorized into two main categories: Direct and indirect channels of communication.

- Direct channels are those that are apparent, and can be easily recognized by the receiver. They are also under direct control of the sender. In this category lie the verbal and non-verbal channels of communication. Verbal communication channels are those that employ words in some way, such as written communication or spoken communication. Non-verbal communication channels, on the other hand, are those that do not demand words, such as certain explicit facial expressions, controllable body movements (like that made by a traffic police to control traffic), color (red for danger, green means go, etc.), sound (alarms, sirens, etc.).

- Indirect channels are those channels that are recognized spontaneously and unintentionally by the receiver, and are not under the direct control of the sender. This includes kinesics or body language that reflects the inner emotions and motivations rather than the actual delivered message. It also includes such vague terms as 'instincts', 'hunches', 'premonitions', or 'intuitions'.

Types of Interpersonal Communication

Interpersonal communication is subdivided into dyadic communication, public speaking, and small-group communication. Dyadic communication is simply a method of communication that involves only two people such as a telephone conversation or even a set of letters sent to and received from a pen friend. In this communication process, the sender can instantly receive and appraise feedback from the receiver so that, it permits more specific couture of the message and more personal communication than do numerous other media.

Uses of Interpersonal Communication

Interpersonal communication can be used to:

- Furnish and gather information.

- Influence the stances and conduct of others.

- Develop acquaintances and preserve relationships.
- Formulate sense of the planet and our experiences in it.
- Utter personal desires and understand the desires of others as well.
- Bequeath and take delivery of emotional joist.
- Make decisions and solve problems.
- Try to anticipate and envisage behavior.

Good interpersonal communication knack support of such processes like intimate relationship, counselling, management, selling, conflict management and others.

Barriers to Effective Interpersonal Communication

Sentiments

At times when people communicate an idea, the receiver can feel how the sender perceives the subject matter. Very often messages are construed differently by different people. Intense emotions are most likely to encumber effective communication because the idea or message maybe misconstrued. It's advisable to avoid reacting to the subject matter when one is upset or irate because it is then that one is not able to think rationally.

Filtering

At this juncture, the sender manipulates the information that he communicates to the receiver. The purpose is that sometimes people tend to shape the message so as to make it sound favorable to the receiver. Sifting (filtering) information may deceive the receiver into thinking, into something favorable and the disappointment may be upsetting if it's found out that information has been sifted.

Message Crammed with Information

Excessive information about the same subject matter may be perplexing. For example, you have 20 e-mails on the same theme, each e-mail contains some part of the theme. Instead, it would be better to have a single e-mail from the sender which focuses in lucid form only the information you want. By and large, the human brain can only take in required information to process, and hence overloading it with irrelevant information will exceed the human processing capacity, and the receiver would often miscomprehend or not comprehend at all what the sender is conveying to him/her.

Defensiveness

Human beings are likely to decline a mutual understanding when they feel that they are being threatened or are put in a difficult position. Defensiveness normally comprises assaulting what the sender tells you, putting out sardonic remarks, questioning their motives or being excessively judgmental about the topic.

Cultural Difference

Our culture, at times, may be a colossal encumbrance for effective interpersonal communication. When two people with different cultures communicate, they often do not comprehend each other's cultures and might misinterpret the true meaning of what each other is trying to convey through such a sense.

Argot

Not all and sundry understand each other's argot/jargon words. Therefore, argot is best avoided when talking to someone who one is not familiar with personally or within one's organization.

Overcoming the Barriers of Effectual Interpersonal Communication

Simplify Language: By structuring your language to clear, uncomplicated sentences, the receiver would be able to effortlessly understand what the sender is saying.

Control Emotions: Constrain emotions at the time of discussing a certain sensitive issue. Articulating in a neutral manner allows mutual understanding to take place and for both sender and receiver to communicate rationally.

Listen Ardently: Often, when the sender says something, the receiver normally hears but does not listen. Place yourself in the sender's position and try to comprehend exactly what they are trying to convey to you. The receiver is trying to comprehend fully what the sender is trying to say, so putting the receiver in the sender's point of view makes understanding much easier.

Use Feedback: This is done by the sender, as a symbol of confirmation by using closedended questions such as "Did you understand what I have just said?" or "Is what I said clear to you?", or using an open-ended question to have the receiver recapitulate the message. This results in the sender knowing that the receiver has completely recognized what is being communicated.

Interpersonal Communication Styles

Generally, interpersonal communication can be categorized as either one-way or two-way. One-way communication takes place when the sender conveys information in the form of direction, without expecting any feedback. For instance, a manager may halt briefly by an employee's desk to inform him that a certain project would be due the subsequent day. One-way communication is quicker and simpler for the sender— because he or she does not have to deal with possible questions or discord from the receiver—but it is likely to be overused in business contexts.

On the contrary, two-way communication involves sharing of information between two or more participants in a productive exchange. For instance, a manager may hold a staff meeting in order to establish the due dates for a number of projects. Engaging in a two-way communication shows that the sender is amenable to feedback and eager to supply a response. Even though it is complex and time-consuming for the sender as compared to the one-way communication, it also ascertains a more precise comprehension of the message.

Apart from being classified as one-way or two-way, interpersonal communication can also be fragmented into a variety of styles. Bateman and Zeithaml identified six core styles of interpersonal communication that are used in business settings: controlling, egalitarian, structuring, dynamic, relinquishing, and withdrawal. "Different individuals use different communication styles", the authors observed. "A communicator should realize that some styles are more effective than others in certain situations."

The controlling style is a form of one-way communication that is used to direct others and gain their compliance. Managers using this style usually do not want feedback, and they tend to employ power and even manipulation to reinforce their message. Although the controlling style can be effective when it is used on occasion by respected individuals, particularly in times of crisis, it can also alienate workers. In contrast, the egalitarian style is a form of two-way communication that involves sharing information rather than directing behavior. It is used to stimulate others to express their ideas and opinions in order to reach a mutual understanding. In most situations—particularly when cooperation is needed—it is more effective than the controlling style.

The structured style of interpersonal communication is used to establish schedules imposed by the organization. Managers using this style would likely cite company standards or rules. Though the structuring style may be necessary to inform others of goals or procedures when complex tasks must be performed by a group, it should usually be counterbalanced with the egalitarian style. The dynamic style is a high-energy approach that uses inspirational pleas to motivate another person to take action. This style can be effective in crisis situations, but it is generally ineffective when the receivers do not have enough knowledge or experience to take the required action.

The relinquishing style of interpersonal communication is deferential rather than directive. It is highly receptive to the ideas of others, to the point of shifting responsibility for communication to the receiver. For example, a manager employing this style might allow her staff to discuss and develop the final solution to a problem while making little comment. This style is particularly effective when the receivers have the knowledge, experience, and willingness to assume responsibility. The withdrawal style is more like a lack of communication. Managers using this style try to avoid using their influence and may indicate a disinterest or unwillingness to participate in the discussion.

Finally, an often overlooked element of interpersonal communication is being a good receiver, which involves developing listening skills. Good listening skills can be vital in finding a solution to grievances or even in making sales calls. Listening involves showing an interest in the speaker, concentrating on the message, and asking questions to ensure understanding. One useful listening technique is reflection, or attempting to repeat and clarify the other person's message rather than immediately responding to it with a message of your own. Used correctly, reflection can allow managers to view issues from their employees' point of view. Some other keys to effective listening include: keeping an open mind rather than allowing emotions to intervene; finding a part of the subject that may have application to your own experience; and resisting distractions such as the speaker's mannerisms or clothing. It also helps to be prepared for the discussion, to take notes as needed, and to summarize the speaker's statements.

Strong interpersonal communication skills, utilizing a variety of styles and techniques, are particularly important for small business owners who must supervise the work of others.

Bateman and Zeithaml described some of the characteristics of supervisors who receive high marks from their employees. First, these managers tend to communicate more than other managers, explaining the reasons behind decisions and providing advance warning of changes. Second, they tend to employ an egalitarian rather than controlling style when communicating with subordinates, asking for instead of demanding their compliance. Third, they tend to take others' needs and feelings into account when communicating. Finally, most effective managers are good listeners, giving careful consideration to employee concerns and taking the time to respond to questions and complaints.

Effects of Interpersonal Communication in an Organization

When interpersonal communication in the workplace is effective, it makes operations more efficient and teamwork not only possible but also easier.

Whether it is carried out correctly or not, interpersonal communication has a direct and indirect impact on many areas of business. Here are some of the effects of interpersonal communication in business:

Effect on Management

When a manager has poor interpersonal communication skills, they can expect to irritate and confuse both the employees and clients of the business. In fact, there is a greater need for a manager to work on his or her interpersonal skills than there is for the average employee.

Managers are in charge of a lot of important things, including ensuring that staff members cooperate on tasks that help the organization to achieve its business goals. They are supposed to build the trust of the staff members in the organization and in each other while also holding them accountable for their role in the achievement of the goals of the organization.

With all of these responsibilities, if the manager is incapable of precise communication, they are likely to waste the time of the employees because they will often need to revisit issues that they had already communicated earlier but had not done so properly.

Effect on Sales

Sales are all about communication. The ability to sell is contingent upon the ability to influence others and that all ultimately boils down to the ability to communicate. There are lots of roles that sales personnel and business leaders as a whole play that are intensive in the sales aspect. These include communicating with the clients, the employees, and even each other.

Whenever communication is happening in an organization, sales are involved. It doesn't have to be actual sales of the product or service that the organization deals in; it could be some intangible quality, such as a vision or project idea. When management is trying to convince the employees to work harder to achieve the goals of the organization, they are selling the business' vision and goals to the employees; when employees are trying to convince management to accept their proposals, whether for a pay rise, or a project, or paid leave, they are selling management on something.

When the organization is trying to get outside investment or trying to build its brand with customers, it is selling itself to the outside world.

Role of Communications in Sales

Ultimately, sales cannot occur without communication, and there is a maxim to be respected in this respect, if communication can fail, then sales can fail. Another important point to remember is that if a message is ambiguous enough to be potentially understood in multiple ways, then it is most likely that it will be understood in the most harmful way. It is therefore imperative to ensure communication is stable, so that it does not fail, and also to ensure that the messages being sent out to the other party are specific enough that the number of ways in which they can be understood is strictly limited.

When the communication skills in an organization are poor starting from the top all the way to the bottom, then the impact on the bottom can be very large.

Effect on Training

While employees coming into the organization are expected to have a certain minimum level of training as evidenced by their academic qualifications, they will still have to undergo significant training while in the organization in order to be acquainted with the company operations, specific company-centric skills, and the organizational culture of the company.

This internal training is, yet again, predicated on communication. That communication will happen in a variety of formal and informal ways and will be done by the management, supervisors, and various skilled and experienced employees.

Good Interpersonal Communication Skills

These instructors need to have good interpersonal communication skills if they're going to do their job well. They need to be able to pass on the right skills to the employees that will enable them to perform the technical tasks they need to perform to achieve business goals as well as gain the soft skills necessary for them to productively do their work at the organization.

Perhaps the most important skill the trainers will have to pass on to trainees is the ability to communicate with others. This is one of the most important skills the employees will have to acquirein order to be able to collaborate with each other and work well in teams. The trainers will not be able to teach the trainees this skill if they do not possess it themselves.

Effect on Conflict Resolution

Conflict is normal at the workplace, and the fact is that employees won't always be able to resolve conflict in the most amicable, timely manner. When conflicts of this nature arise, interpersonal communication can come to the rescue. With interpersonal communication skills, the employees will be able to harness their ability to communicate with each other to arrive at an amicable resolution to the conflict.

Conflict management cannot happen without effective interpersonal communication. In fact, all conflict management strategies that use communication to diffuse hostile situations in stressful environments, are not possible without interpersonal communications.

Importance of Interpersonal Communication in Business

Sharing Information Effectively and Solving Problems

Interpersonal communication helps organizations to come up with solutions to ensure the business runs smoothly. Interpersonal communication examples include:

- Speaking on the phone with a supplier.
- Having a staff meeting with all employees.
- Helping a customer in the store.
- Emailing instructions to a colleague.
- Chatting on instant messaging with a peer.

During interpersonal communication, employees share information, provide updates, clarify misunderstandings, offer solutions and introduce new ideas. Effective interpersonal communication helps to ensure everyone in the business is aligned.

For example, when the human resources manager shares new health and safety rules with employees, he is communicating vital information that helps them to do their jobs more effectively. Doing so helps to avoid risk and reduce workplace issues for everyone involved.

Becoming more Aware of Nonverbal Communication

Interpersonal communication helps employees to focus on nonverbal communication. Sometimes, it is not just what is being said that matters but how it is being said. Nonverbal communication includes tone of voice, eye contact, body posture, hand gestures, facial expressions and physical contact. By tuning in to nonverbal communication signals, employees can better understand the message being sent.

For example, if a customer service representative asks a customer who is browsing in the store whether she needs any help, the customer may respond by saying she is OK. However, if her facial expression looks confused, then she may just be too shy to ask for help. Through effective interpersonal communication, the employee can let the customer know he is available anytime to help her find the right product.

Building a Culture of Employee Engagement

Interpersonal communication in business helps to create an open andhonest work culture where employees feel they have the ability to communicate with all levels of the organization. Strong interpersonal skills help to make people more relatable to others, which is an important quality in the workplace.

A new employee may feel out of place or nervous about interacting with others. Through effective interpersonal communication with colleagues and management, the new employee can begin to open up and feel more at ease in the workplace.

Increasing Customer Satisfaction

Interpersonal communication in business is vital for keeping customers happy. Interpersonal communication includes negotiation, conflict resolution, relationship nurturing and other skills that are required to successfully communicate with customers.

Ensuring all customer-facing employees have the training and knowledge they need to effectively communicate with customers results in higher customer satisfaction. Focusing on interpersonal communication also shows customers that the business values its relationship with them and puts in the effort to ensure it can share information effectively.

Respect and Empathy through Interpersonal Communication in Business

The importance of interpersonal skills in business is that they help individuals to show respect for one another. Whether you are dealing with colleagues, customers or partners, showing respect is not only courteous, but it helps to build trust, credibility and confidence.

Interpersonal communication in business also helps to show empathy. This can boost employee morale and create loyalty in the workplace. For example, if an employee is having trouble with his car and is not able to get to work on time, you can offer him the ability to work from home for a day while he gets his car fixed. This helps to foster a sense of community in the workplace, where people take care of one another.

Intrapersonal Communication

Business leaders spend a lot of time and money developing strong communications skills to help them inspire and lead the company. But if they aren't accentuating these skills with interpersonal skills, they may be missing effective methods that help them relate to others. Intrapersonal communication is the communication you have with yourself, including your self-concept and how your internal dialogue becomes part of your external communication.

Communicating with yourself is the definition of intrapersonal communication. It expands beyond the basic chat you might have while talking yourself through a task. It is the foundation of your communication ability with all external resources, because how you view your position in your surroundings will always affect how you interact with them. The mutterings under your breath or your vision of yourself as a leader fall into the realm of intrapersonal communication. At the foundation of intrapersonal communication is self-awareness, taking in the various stimuli from our internal and external surroundings and assessing the situation.

A lot of intrapersonal communication is not consciously driven – meaning our internal thoughts and judgments are often based on years and years of conditioning. The way your family, teachers and early coaches and mentors spoke to you contributed to the self-image you have and how you ultimately communicate with yourself. This conditioning can be good or bad, depending on the ultimate self-concept and self-talk. When the result is negative, mindset experts seek to help change internal narratives to help individuals achieve greater success both at work and in personal endeavors.

Intrapersonal Relationships for Success

Self-awareness helps a person see where she is performing well and where she is not in relation to her surroundings. There may be emotional reactions, judgments and choices happening that differ from scenario to scenario. An executive might be very calm in dealing with a problem with another executive, but might explode if a subordinate makes an error. Self-awareness through intrapersonal communication helps the executive understand how she is reacting in different situations and then direct a change of action that will be inspiring rather than demoralizing to her team.

Because a large chunk of your self-concept is developed as you mature, it is important to consider the influences of past experiences, the input of family, friends and colleagues, and the role as a leader you play within your own life. By adjusting reactions, self-talk and self-concepts, a person is able to build greater personal models for success.

Developing Intrapersonal Skills

Improving and developing greater intrapersonal skills takes three primary components: self-awareness, self-regulation and motivation. Self-awareness uses personal assessment tools to monitor reactions. It requires the confidence to understand that this is the first step to growth. It isn't enough to merely be aware of an explosive reaction to one group versus another. One must learn to curb what has become conditioned responses that seem like natural reactions. This is why self-awareness progresses to self-regulation. To achieve success requires the right motivation to change internal thoughts, behaviors and self concepts.

A leader seeking to improve leadership skills must then learn to regulate his habitual adverse reactions. Those who begin to master self-regulation demonstrate higher levels of integrity, reliability and adaptability. These are competencies of great leaders who understand their role is much greater than delegating tasks. But even self-regulation isn't enough. There has to be a motivating factor that generates enough internal drive to make the changes long-lasting. An analogy is quitting smoking; a person may quit for a period of time, but when stressed will go right back to smoking unless he has the motivation to stay away – maybe a newborn baby or significant health issue.

Importance of Intrapersonal Communication in Business

Self-awareness: It allows the person to be aware of every aspect of their own personality. Through introspection, the person becomes aware of the qualities that help shape his personality which in turn makes him aware of his motivations, aspirations, and expectations from the world. If one's understanding of self is absolute, it would help in easily communicating his wants and needs to others.

Self-confidence: A self-aware state makes one secure and increases confidence.

Self-management: The fact that one is conscious of the indwelling strengths and shortcomings, it equips him to manage his daily affairs efficiently using his strengths to the maximum which in turn compensates for his weaknesses.

Self-motivation: The absolute knowledge of what one wants out of life will enable the person to strive to achieve those aims and goal while continuously motivating themselves.

Focused: The qualities of self-motivation and self-management will help develop deeper concentration and direct his focus towards the task at hand.

Independence: Self-awareness allows the person to be independent.

Adaptability: The person is highly adaptable to his surroundings as the knowledge of his own qualities allows him to confidently and calmly take decisions and change his approach accordingly in response to situational stimuli.

Corporate Communication

Corporate communication is a set of activities involved in managing and orchestrating all internal and external communications aimed at creating favourable point of view among stakeholders on which the company depends. It is the messages issued by a corporate organization, body, or institute to its audiences, such as employees, media, channel partners and the general public. Organizations aim to communicate the same message to all its stakeholders, to transmit coherence, credibility and ethics.

Corporate communication helps organizations explain their mission, combine its many visions and values into a cohesive message to stakeholders. The concept of corporate communication could be seen as an integrative communication structure linking stakeholders to the organisation.

Methods and Tactics

Three principal clusters of task-planning and communication form the backbone of business and the activity of business organizations. These include management communication, marketing communication, and organizational communication.

- Management communication takes place between management and its internal and external audiences. To support management communication, organizations rely heavily on specialists in marketing communication and organizational communication.
- Marketing communication gets the bulk of the budgets in most organizations, and consists of product advertising, direct mail, personal selling, and sponsorship activities.
- Organizational communication consists of specialists in public relations, public affairs, investor relations, environmental communications, corporate advertising, and employee communication.

The responsibilities of corporate communication are:

- To promote the profile of the "company behind the brand" (corporate branding).
- To minimize discrepancies between the company's desired identity and brand features.
- To delegate tasks in communication.
- To formulate and execute effective procedures to make decisions on communication matters.

- To mobilize internal and external support for corporate objectives.
- To coordinate with international business firms.

A Conference Board Study of hundreds of the US's largest firms showed that close to 80 percent have corporate communication functions that include media relations, speech writing, employee communication, corporate advertising, and community relations. The public is often represented by self-appointed activist non-governmental organizations (NGOs) which identify themselves with a particular issue.

Most companies have specialized groups of professionals for communicating with different audiences, such as internal communication, marketing communication, investor relations, government relations and public relations.

Components

Corporate Branding

A corporate brand is the perception of a company that unites a group of products or services for the public under a single name, a shared visual identity, and a common set of symbols. The process of corporate branding involves creating favourable associations and positive reputation with both internal and external stakeholders. The purpose of a corporate branding initiative is to generate a positive halo over the products and businesses of the company, imparting more favourable impressions of those products and businesses.

In more general terms, research suggests that corporate branding is an appropriate strategy for companies to implement when:

- There is significant "information asymmetry" between a company and its clients; customers are much less informed about a company's products than the company itself.
- Customers perceive a high degree of risk in purchasing the products or services of the company.
- Features of the company behind the brand would be relevant to the product or service a customer is considering purchasing.

Corporate and Organizational Identity

There are two approaches for identity:

- Corporate identity is the reality and uniqueness of an organization, which is integrally related to its external and internal image and reputation through corporate communication.
- Organizational identity comprises those characteristics of an organization that its members believe are central, distinctive and enduring. That is, organizational identity consists of those attributes that members feel are fundamental to (central) and uniquely descriptive of (distinctive) the organization and that persist within the organization over time (enduring)".

Four types of identity can be distinguished:

- Perceived identity: The collection of attributes that are seen as typical for the continuity, centrality and uniqueness of the organization in the eyes of its members.
- Projected identity: The self-presentations of the organization's attributes manifested in the implicit and explicit signals which the organization broadcasts to internal and external target audiences through communication and symbols.
- Desired identity (also called "ideal" identity): The idealized picture that top managers hold of what the organization could evolve into under their leadership.
- Applied identity: The signals that an organization broadcasts both consciously and unconsciously through behaviors and initiatives at all levels within the organization.

Corporate Responsibility

Corporate responsibility (often referred to as corporate social responsibility), corporate citizenship, sustainability, and even conscious capitalism are some of the terms bandied about the news media and corporate marketing efforts as companies jockey to win the trust and loyalty of constituents.

Corporate responsibility (CR) constitutes an organization's respect for society's interests, demonstrated by taking ownership of the effects its activities have on key constituencies including customers, employees, shareholders, communities, and the environment, in all parts of their operations. In short, CR prompts a corporation to look beyond its traditional bottom line, to the social implications of its business.

Corporate Reputation

Reputations are overall assessments of organizations by their stakeholders. They are aggregate perceptions by stakeholders of an organization's ability to fulfill their expectations, whether these stakeholders are interested in buying the company's products, working for the company, or investing in the company's shares.

In 2000, the US-based Council of PR Firms identified seven programs developed by either media organizations or market research firms, used by companies to assess or benchmark their corporate reputations. Of these, only four are conducted regularly and have broad visibility:

- "America's Most Admired Companies".
- The "Brand Asset Valuator" by Young & Rubicam.
- "RepTrak" by Reputation Institute.
- "Best Global Brands" by Interbrand.

Crisis Communication

Crisis communication is sometimes considered a sub-specialty of the public relations profession that is designed to protect and defend an individual, company, or organization facing a public challenge to its reputation. These challenges may come in the form of an investigation from a government agency, a criminal allegation, a media inquiry, a shareholders lawsuit, a violation of environmental regulations, or any of a number of other scenarios involving the legal, ethical, or financial standing of the entity. The crisis for organizations can be defined as follows:

> "A crisis is a major catastrophe that may occur either naturally or as a result of human error, intervention, or even malicious intent. It can include tangible devastation, such as the destruction of lives or assets, or intangible devastation, such as the loss of an organization's credibility or other reputational damage. The latter outcomes may be the result of management's response to tangible devastation or the result of human error. A crisis usually has significant actual or potential financial impact on a company, and it usually affects multiple constituencies in more than one market."

Internal Communication

As the extent of communication grows, many companies create an employee relations (ER) function with dedicated staff to manage the numerous media through which senior managers can communicate among themselves and with the rest of the organization. Internal communication in the 21st century is more than the memos, publications, and broadcasts that comprise it; it's about building a corporate culture on values that drive organizational excellence. ER specialists are generally expected to fulfill one or more of the following four roles:

- Efficiency: Internal communication is used primarily to disseminate information about corporate activities.
- Shared meaning: Internal communication is used to build a shared understanding among employees about corporate goals.
- Connectivity: Internal communication is used mainly to clarify the connectedness of the company's people and activities.
- Satisfaction: Internal communication is used to improve job satisfaction throughout the company.

Investor Relations

The investor relations (IR) function is used by companies which publicly trade shares on a stock exchange. In such companies, the purpose of the IR specialist is to interface with current and potential financial stakeholders-namely retail investors, institutional investors, and financial analysts.

The role of investor relations is to fulfill three principal functions:

- Comply with regulations.
- Create a favorable relationship with key financial audiences.
- Contribute to building and maintaining the company's image and reputation.

Public Relations: Issues Management and Media Relations

The role of the public relations specialist, in many ways, is to communicate with the general public in ways that serve the interests of the company. PR therefore consists of numerous specialty areas that convey information about the company to the public, including sponsorships, events, issues management and media relations. When executing these types of activities, the PR Specialist must incorporate broader corporate messages to convey the company's strategic positioning. This ensures the PR activities ultimately convey messages that distinguish the company vis-à-vis its competitors and the overall marketplace, while also communicating the company's value to target audiences.

Issues Management

A key role of the PR specialist is to make the company better known for traits and attributes that build the company's perceived distinctiveness and competitiveness with the public. In recent years, PR specialists have become increasingly involved in helping companies manage strategic issues – public concerns about their activities that are frequently magnified by special interest groups and NGOs. The role of the PR specialist therefore also consists of issues management, namely the "set of organizational procedures, routines, personnel, and issues". A strategic issue is one that compels a company to deal with it because there is "a conflict between two or more identifiable groups over procedural or substantive matters relating to the distribution of positions or resources".

Media Relations

To build better relationships with the media, organizations must cultivate positive relations with influential members of the media. This task might be handled by employees within the company's media relations department or handled by a public relations firm.

Spokesperson Profiling

These "public faces" are considered authorities in their respective sector/field and ensure the company/organization is in the limelight.

- Managing content of corporate websites and other external touch points.
- Managing corporate publications – for the external world.
- Managing print media.

Written Communication

The Written Communication refers to the process of conveying a message through the written symbols. In other words, any message exchanged between two or more persons that make use of written words is called as written communication.

The written communication is the most common and effective mode of business communication. In any organization, the electronic mails, memos, reports, documents, letters, journals, job descriptions, employee manuals, etc. are some of the commonly used forms of written communication.

Such communication is used when the information to be transmitted is lengthy and includes some complex terms that cannot be explained verbally. Also, the organizations maintain their documents in writings such that these can be used as a reference and evidence of any transaction anytime in the future. Thus, it is essential for every business organization to develop effective writing skills and inculcate this in all its employees.

The effectiveness of written content depends on the correct choice of words, their organization into correct sentence sequence and the cohesiveness in the sentences. The information in writing is considered more legal and valid than the spoken words. Also, people rely more on the written content than what has been said orally. But, however, unlike verbal communication the feedback of written communication is not immediate since it is not spontaneous and requires time to get into the understandable form.

Characteristics of a Good Written Communication

Characteristics of a good written communication are discussed below:

- Easy language: Easy language should be used in written communication. The sentences of written communication must be understandable to the reader.
- Structure: Definite structure must be followed in drafting any written document. Every written form has its own structure.
- Accurate and precise: A well written document must be accurate and precise. Written communication insists on greater accuracy and precision.
- Direct speech: Direct speech should be used in written communication. Indirect and passive sentences must be avoided.
- Paragraph design: A good written communication bears a paragraph design. Paragraphing is also important to clear communication.
- Error-less: A well written document must be free from error in both grammar and language.
- You-attitude: There must be your attitude in written communication. The reader can be impressed for this.
- Personal and organizational images: A good written communication bears the personal image of the writer. It also increases the organizational image as a whole.

Types of Written Communication

Written business communication has several purposes. In most business settings, there are four types of written communication: transactional, persuasive, informational and instructional.

Transactional Forms of Written Communication

One of the most common forms of written communication in business is transactional content. The purpose of this kind of communication is results oriented, as you are trying to achieve a specific goal with transactional content.

Examples of written communication that is transactional include emails, instant messages, invoices, short memos, forms and letters. This kind of business communication is for day-to-day use and is generally short and direct and requires action from the reader.

For example, if you need to ask your colleague a quick question about a customer, you can use a team collaboration software such as Slack to send him a real-time message. The software notifies the recipient, who can then send you a short answer to your question.

Persuasive Business Writing

Written communication in business also includes persuasive content. The goal of this kind of material is to provide the reader with a unique value proposition about your business and encourage them to respond. Depending on the kinds of written materials used, the responses can be to make a sale or further a relationship.

Examples of persuasive business writing include marketing and promotional content such as ads, brochures, press releases, emails, newsletters and direct mail campaigns. Sales decks and proposals to prospects are also persuasive business writing, as are cover letters and resumes.

One of the key elements to consider when writing persuasively is to not focus on the business too much. Instead, it's important to focus on what the *audience* wants and the kinds of problems they are trying to solve.

Informational Business Documents

One of the most common forms of written communication in business is informational material. The goal of this kind of written communication is to provide a reference or a record of specific areas of the business. Informational writing doesn't necessarily require an action from the reader, unlike transactional and persuasive content.

Examples of informational business communication include quarterly financial reports, meeting minutes, employee handbooks and annual departmental overviews. An FAQ page on a website is also an example of informational content. This kind of writing is direct and thorough, covering a wide range of content with the goal of keeping the reader up to date on specific aspects of the business.

Informational business communication enables the company to predict future performance, record previous performance and meet legal or regulatory obligations.

Instructional Business Materials

Written communication in business also includes instructional business writing. The goal of this kind of material is to provide step-by-step detailson how to complete a specific task. Similar to transactional and persuasive content, instructional content usually requires the reader to take some kind of action either now or in the future.

Examples of instructional communication in business include user manuals, job description handbooks, technical specifications and instructional memos. This kind of writing is clear and direct, often written in short sentences that follow a chronological order.

Instructional content needs to take into account how much the reader knows about the topic at hand and provide the missing information. If the instructional content is for multiple people with varying levels of understanding, then the material needs to first cover the basics and then move on to the specific tasks that need to be completed.

Advantages of Written Communication

- Written communication helps in laying down apparent principles, policies and rules for running of an organization.
- It is a permanent means of communication. Thus, it is useful where record maintenance is required.
- It assists in proper delegation of responsibilities. While in case of oral communication, it is impossible to fix and delegate responsibilities on the grounds of speech as it can be taken back by the speaker or he may refuse to acknowledge.
- Written communication is more precise and explicit.
- Effective written communication develops and enhances an organization's image.
- It provides ready records and references.
- Legal defenses can depend upon written communication as it provides valid records.

Disadvantages of Written Communication

- Written communication does not save upon the costs. It costs huge in terms of stationery and the manpower employed in writing/typing and delivering letters.
- Also, if the receivers of the written message are separated by distance and if they need to clear their doubts, the response is not spontaneous.
- Written communication is time-consuming as the feedback is not immediate. The encoding and sending of message takes time.
- Effective written communication requires great skills and competencies in language and vocabulary use. Poor writing skills and quality have a negative impact on organization's reputation.
- Too much paper work and e-mails burden is involved.

Oral Communication

Oral communication describes any type of interaction that makes use of spoken words, and it is a vital, integral part of the business world, especially in an era dubbed the information age. The types of oral communication commonly used within an organization include staff meetings, personal discussions, presentations, telephone discourse, and informal conversation. Oral communication with those outside of the organization might take the form of face-to-face meetings, telephone calls, speeches, teleconferences, or videoconferences.

Conversation management skills are essential for small business owners and managers who often shoulder much of the burden in such areas as client/customer presentations, employee interviews, and conducting meetings. For oral communication to be effective, it should be clear, relevant, tactful in phraseology and tone, concise, and informative. Presentations or conversations that bear these hallmarks can be an invaluable tool in ensuring business health and growth. Unclear, inaccurate, or inconsiderate business communication, on the other hand, can waste valuable time, alienate employees or customers, and destroy goodwill toward management or the overall business.

Oral Presentations

The public presentation is generally recognized as the most important of the various genres of oral business communication. As is true of all kinds of communication, the first step in preparing a public speech or remarks is to determine the essential purpose/goal of the communication. Business presentations tend to have one of three general purposes: to persuade, to inform or instruct, or to entertain. Out of the purpose will come the main ideas to be included in the presentation. These ideas should be researched thoroughly and adapted to the needs of the audience.

The ideas should then be organized to include an introduction, a main body or text, and a summary or conclusion. Or, as the old adage about giving speeches goes, "Tell them what you're going to tell them, tell them, and tell them what you told them." The introduction should grab the listener's interest and establish the theme of the remainder of the presentation. The main body should concentrate on points of emphasis. The conclusion should restate the key points and summarize the overarching message that is being conveyed.

Visual aids can be a useful component of some presentations. Whether they are projected from a PC, displayed on chalkboards, dry-erase boards, or flip charts visual aids should be meaningful, creative, and interesting in order to help the speaker get a message across. The key to successful use of visual aids is that they should support the theme of the presentation, aid in its transmittal but do so without detracting by being sloppy, complicated, or even too entertaining.

Once the presentation has been organized and the visual aids have been selected, the speaker should rehearse the presentation out loud and revise as needed to fit time constraints, and to assure thorough coverage of the main points. It may help to practice in front of a mirror or in front of a friend in order to gain confidence. A good oral presentation will include transitional phrases to help listeners move through the material, and will not be overly long or technical. It is also important for the speaker to anticipate questions the audience might have and either include that information in the presentation or be prepared to address them in a Q&A session at the end of the presentation. Professional and gracious presentation is another key to effective communication, whether the setting is a conference, a banquet, a holiday luncheon, or a management retreat. "Recognize that when you speak at a business event, you represent your company and your office in that company," stated by Steve Kaye. "Use the event as an opportunity to promote good will. Avoid complaints, criticism, or controversy. These will alienate the audience and destroy your credibility quickly. Instead, talk about what the audience wants to hear. Praise your host, honor the occasion, and compliment the attendees. Radiate success and optimism."

Oral presentations can be delivered extemporaneously (from an outline or notes); by reading from a manuscript; or from memory. The extemporaneous approach is often touted as a method that allows the speaker to make eye contact and develop a rapport with the audience while simultaneously conveying pertinent information. Reading from a manuscript is more often utilized for longer and detailed communications that cover a lot of ground. Memorization, meanwhile, is usually only used for short and informal discussions.

The delivery of effective oral presentations requires a speaker to consider his or her vocal pitch, rate, and volume. It is important to incorporate changes in vocal pitch to add emphasis and avoid monotony. It is also helpful to vary the rate of speaking and incorporate pauses to allow the listener to reflect upon specific elements of the overall message. Finding the appropriate volume is crucial to the success of a presentation as well. Finally, speakers should be careful not to add extraneous words or sounds—such as "um," "you know," or "okay"—between words or sentences in a presentation.

Nonverbal elements such as posture, gestures, and facial expressions are also important factors in developing good oral communication skills. Your outward appearance mirrors your inner mood. "Thus good posture suggests poise and confidence; stand neither at rigid attention nor with sloppy casualness draped over the podium, but erect with your weight about equally distributed on each foot." Some movement may be helpful to hold listeners' attention or to increase emphasis, but constant shifting or pacing should be avoided. Likewise, hand and arm gestures can be used to point, describe, or emphasize, but they should be varied, carefully timed, and adapted to the audience. Finally, good speakers should make frequent eye contact with the audience, let their facial expression show their interest in the ideas they are presenting, and dress in a way that is appropriate for the occasion.

Small business owners reflect the general population in that their enthusiasm for public speaking varies considerably for individual to individual. Some entrepreneurs enjoy the limelight and thrive in settings that call for public presentations (formal or informal). Others are less adept at public speaking and avoid being placed in such situations. But business consultants urge entrepreneurs to treat public presentations and oral communication skills as a potentially invaluable tool in business growth. You may consider hiring a presentation coach or attending a workshop on business presentations. "These services can show you how to maximize your impact while speaking. In fact, learning such skills serves as a long-term investment in your future as an effective leader."

Oral communication offers different advantages that are not available with other communication system. In some situations oral communication is more effective than any other communication. Following are the circumstances where oral communication is more effective:

- Immediate Communication: Oral communication is more effective when it is necessary to communicate with someone immediately. In some situations, people can make phone calls to others due to emergency.

- Immediate Response: In oral communication the response of the receiver can be received instantly. So, when immediate response is required by the sender, oral communication is most preferred.
- Oral Explanation: In some cases detailed explanation is required to understand any message clearly. In such case, oral communication is more effective.
- Maintaining Secrecy: In oral communication only the sender and the receiver know the message, nobody else. Moreover, no record of oral message is kept for future. So, the secrecy of the message can best be maintained in oral communication. Hence, oral communication is mostly preferred where the secrecy of the message is to be maintained strictly.
- Developing Direct Relation: Oral Communication helps to develop direct and strong relation between the sender and receiver. Here both the parties get the opportunity to develop informal relation also. So, when it is necessary to develop direct relation between the sender and the receiver, oral communication is preferred.
- Illiterate Communicators: It is not possible to communicate with illiterate people by written message. Oral communication is the only way to communicate with the illiterate people and other communication methods are ineffective here.
- Face-to-Face Communication: Oral Communication is the only method of communication when face-to-face conversation is essentially required.
- Time Saving: If the communicators want to save their time, oral communication is preferred. Because written communication consumes huge time.
- Avoiding Bureaucratic Complexities: Bureaucratic complexities delay the process of written communication. But in oral communication, there are no bureaucratic complexities, thus information flows here rapidly.
- Reaching to Large Audience: When the sender needs to reach a large audience, it is better to select oral communication instead of others.

Principles of Oral Communication

The principles of oral communication are discussed below:

- Clear pronunciation: Clear pronunciation of message sender in the main factor or oral communication. If it is not clear, the goal of the message may not be achieved.
- Preparation: Before communicating orally the speaker should take preparation both physically are mental.
- Unity and integration: The unity an integration of the speech of the message sender is a must for successful oral communication.
- Precision: Precision is needed to make oral communication effective. The meaning of the words must be specific.

- Natural voice: The speakers must not fluctuate at the time of oral communication. On the other hand, the artificial voice must be avoided.
- Planning: Organized plan is a must for effective oral communication. The speaker should take a proper plan for delivering speech.
- Simplicity: The speaker should use simple understandable words in oral communication. It should be easy and simple.
- Legality: The speaker's speech should be legal and logical at the time of oral communication.
- Avoiding emotions: At the time of oral discussion, excessive emotions can divert a speaker from main subject. So, the speaker should be careful about emotion. The speech must be emotionless.
- Acting: Many people lose concentration after listening for a few minutes. So speech must be emotionless.
- Efficiency: Speaker's efficiency and skill is necessary for effective oral communication.
- Vocabulary: Words bear different meanings to different people in different situations. In oral communication, a speaker should use the most familiar words to the receiver of the message to avoid any confusion in the meaning of the words.

Importance of Oral Communication in Business

Communication is perhaps the most essential component in business. Without communication, companies cannot interact with their customers. Internally, confusion will arise and slow productivity. Without well-defined oral communication skills, a worker will not likely advance in his or her career and may even be terminated.

Internal Oral Communication

Internal oral communication is important for both the individual and organization. Internal oral communication can be defined as the language and verbal exchanges within a company. For the individual employee, effective oral communication is necessary to be a good manager because a good manager must relay instructions and interact with junior employees. Oral communication is also valuable to the employee while speaking with his or her superiors.

If the employee cannot communicate effectively, his or her needs may go unnoticed and he or she may be blamed for miscommunication and not following instructions. If an organization does not have employees with a well-defined skill set for oral communication, loss of productivity, along with internal confusion, can be a problem.

Customer Service Communication Skills

Any customer who has dealt with a customer service representative who lacks effective oral communication skills or conversational English skills has undoubtedly found it frustrating. Customer service representatives, sales staff and any front-line workers must be well versed in oral communication, and it is essential for them to speak the native language fluently. Customers want to communicate their needs to these employees; they may need a certain product or question answered. If the employee does not understand or cannot effectively communicate the right information the customer, that customer may take his or her business elsewhere.

Complexities of Technical Knowledge

Things become more complex with industry-specific or technical knowledge. Not only are basic language skills required for the interaction, advanced language skills may be required to translate technical knowledge into layman's terms. This is a difficult enough task for a person with average oral communication skills.

For example, internally, communication with an engineer or product specialist may require an in-depth discussion to discuss a new product. This information must then be translated into the language a salesperson or manager can understand--they may not care about how it works but rather about the benefits they can tell consumers about.

Importance of Communicating Ideas

Ideas may be very clear in the mind of the person who comes up with them. However, if that person cannot translate the idea into words his or her colleagues can understand, the idea is useless. If a person does manage to get his or her idea out, but his or her communication is so poor the idea is misinterpreted and dismissed, both the company and the individual lose out.

Efficiency and Productivity

There is a tangible benefit or loss for organizations based on their overall level of oral communication competency. Efficiency can be enhanced if instructions do not need to be repeated because communication was complete the first time. This increases productivity and creates a culture of understanding, in which employees can foster new ideas because they know the company values communication and sharing information.

Advantages of Oral Communication

- There is high level of understanding and transparency in oral communication as it is interpersonal.
- There is no element of rigidity in oral communication. There is flexibility for allowing changes in the decisions previously taken.
- The feedback is spontaneous in case of oral communication. Thus, decisions can be made quickly without any delay.
- Oral communication is not only time saving, but it also saves upon money and efforts.
- Oral communication is best in case of problem resolution. The conflicts, disputes and many issues/differences can be put to an end by talking them over.
- Oral communication is an essential for teamwork and group energy.

- Oral communication promotes a receptive and encouraging morale among organizational employees.
- Oral communication can be best used to transfer private and confidential information/ matter.

Disadvantages/Limitations of Oral Communication

- Relying only on oral communication may not be sufficient as business communication is formal and very organized.
- Oral communication is less authentic than written communication as they are informal and not as organized as written communication.
- Oral communication is time-saving as far as daily interactions are concerned, but in case of meetings, long speeches consume lot of time and are unproductive at times.
- Oral communications are not easy to maintain and thus they are unsteady.
- There may be misunderstandings as the information is not complete and may lack essentials.
- It requires attentiveness and great receptivity on part of the receivers/audience.
- Oral communication (such as speeches) is not frequently used as legal records except in investigation work.

Listening

Listening is a highly complex, interactive process "by which spoken language is converted to meaning in the mind". As this definition suggests, listening is more than just hearing, although these two terms are often used synonymously. Hearing is only an important component of listening. Listening is a specialized form of hearing and is the primary function of the ear. The most crucial part of the listening process is thinking or converting to meaning what one hears.

Hearing is a passive process. It is merely the detection of sounds around us. Normally, we come across 'hearing' in certain situations.

Listening: It is an active process. It involves the conscious desire to determine the meaning of what is heard. While listening, one is engaged in processing the date, reconstructing the data and also giving meaning to the data.

Types of Listening

Discriminative Listening

As the name itself suggests, discriminative listening is the most basic type of listening, whereby the difference between the sounds is identified. If you cannot hear differences, then you cannot grasp the meaning that is expressed by such differences.

Comprehension Listening

When the discrimination between sounds is achieved, one should learn to make sense of the perceived sound. To comprehend the meaning, one requires a lexicon of words and all rules of grammar and syntax by which one can understand what others are saying.

Evaluative Listening

Evaluative listening is also called 'critical listening' because we make judgments about what the other person is saying. We seek to assess the truth of what is being said, We also judge what they say about our values, assessing them as good or bad, worthy or unworthy.

Empathetic Listening

When we listen empathetically, we seek to understand the beliefs, moods, emotions and goals of other people. This requires excellent discrimination and close attention to the nuances of emotional signals.

Herapeutic Listening

In therapeutic listening, the listener has a purpose of not only empathizing with the speaker but also to use this deep connection in order to help the speaker understand, change or develop in some way.

Dialogic Listening

The word 'dialogue' stems from the words 'dia', meaning 'through' and 'logos' meaning 'words'. Thus dialogic listening means learning through conversation. Dialogic listening is also known as 'relational listening' because with the help of exchange of ideas while listening, we also indirectly creation a relation.

Active Listening

Active listening is technique that is used in counseling, training, and solving disputes or conflicts. It requires that the listener fully concentrate, understand, respond and then remember what is being said. This is opposed to other listening techniques like reflective listening and empathic listening. Reflective listening is where the listener repeats back to the speaker what they have just heard to confirm understanding of both parties.Empathic listening is about giving people an outlet for their emotions before being able to be more open, sharing experiences and being able to accept new perspectives on the troubled topic that is the reason of emotional suffering. Listening skills may establish flow rather than closed mindedness, negative emotions include stress, anger and frustration.

Comprehending

Comprehension is a shared meaning between parties in a communication transaction. This is the first step in the listening process. The second step is being able to take breaks between discernible words, or talking segmentation.

Retaining

Retaining is the second step in the process. Memory is essential to the listening process because the information retained when a person is involved in the listening process is how meaning from words is created. Because everyone has different memories, the speaker and the listener may attach different meanings to the same statement. Memories are fallible, things like cramming may cause information to be forgotten.

Responding

Listening is an interaction between speaker and listener. It adds action to a normally passive process.

Tactic

Active listening involves the listener observing the speaker's behavior and body language. Having the ability to interpret a person's body language lets the listener develop a more accurate understanding of the speaker's message. Having heard, the listener may then paraphrase the speaker's words. It is important to note that the listener is not necessarily agreeing with the speaker—simply stating what was said.

Individuals in conflict often contradict each other. Ambushing occurs when one listens to someone else's argument for its weaknesses and ignore its strengths. This may include a distortion of the speaker's argument to gain a competitive advantage. On the other hand, if one finds that the other party understands, an atmosphere of cooperation can be created.

Use

Active listening is used in a wide variety of situations, including public interest advocacy, community organizing, tutoring, medical workers talking to patients, HIV counseling, helping suicidal persons, management, counseling and journalistic settings. In groups it may aid in reaching consensus. It may also be used in casual conversation or small talk to build understanding, though this can be interpreted as condescending.

A listener can use several degrees of active listening, each resulting in a different quality of communication.

The proper use of active listening results in getting people to open up, avoiding misunderstandings, resolving conflict, and building trust. In a medical context, benefits may include increased patient satisfaction, improved cross-cultural communication, improved outcomes, or decreased litigation.

Active listening can be lifted by the active listening observation scale.

Barriers to Active Listening

Some barriers are due to hunger or fatigue of the listener, making them irritated and less inclined to listen to the speaker. Sometimes it is due to the language the speaker uses—such as high sounding and bombastic words that can lead to ambiguity. Other barriers include distractions, trigger words, vocabulary, and limited attention span. Listening barriers may be psychological (e.g., emotions) or physical (e.g., noise and visual distraction).

Shift Response

Shift response is the general tendency of a speaker in a conversation to affix attention to their position. This is a type of conversational narcissism—the tendency of listeners to turn the topic to themselves without showing sustained interest in others. A support response is the opposite of a shift response; it is an attention giving method and a cooperative effort to focus the conversational attention on the other person. Instead of being me-oriented like shift response, it is we-oriented. It is the response a competent communicator is most likely to use.

Understanding of Non-verbal Cues

Ineffective listeners are unaware of non-verbal cues, though they dramatically affect how people listen. To a certain extent, it is also a perceptual barrier. Up to 93 percent of people's attitudes are formed by non-verbal cues. This should help one to avoid undue influence from non-verbal communication. In most cases, the listener does not understand the non-verbal cues the speaker uses. A person may show fingers to emphasize a point, but this may be perceived as an intent by the speaker to place their fingers in the listener's eyes. Overuse of non-verbal cues also creates distortion, and as a result listeners may be confused and forget the correct meaning.

Overcoming Listening Barriers

The active listening technique is used to improve personal communications in organizations. Listeners put aside their own emotions and ask questions and paraphrase what the speaker says to clarify and gain a better understanding of what the speaker intends to say. Judging or arguing prematurely is a result of holding onto a strict personal opinion. This hinders the ability to be able to listen closely to what is being said. Eye contact and appropriate body languages are seen as important components to active listening. The stress and intonation may also keep them active and away from distractions.

Workplace Listening

Workplace listening is a type of active listening that is generally employed in a professional environment. Listening skills are imperative for career success, organizational effectiveness, and worker satisfaction. Workplace listening includes understanding the listening process (i.e. perception, interpretation, evaluation, and action) and its barriers that hamper the flow of that process. Like other skills, there are specific techniques for improving workplace listening effectiveness. Moreover, it is imperative to become aware of the role of nonverbal communication in communicating in the workplace, as understanding messages wholly entails more than simple verbal messages.

Appreciative Listening

Appreciative listening is a type of listening behavior where the listener seeks certain information which they will appreciate, for example that which helps meet his/her needs and goals. One uses appreciative listening when listening to good music, poetry or maybe even the stirring words of a great leader.

It involves listening to music that one enjoys, people the listener likes to listen to because of their style and the choices the listener make in the films and television he/she watches, radio programmes and plays and musicals in the theatre. Unlike informative listening or relationship listening, appreciative listening does not rely on the message from the speaker it is how one responds as a listener. Our appreciation of what we hear will vary depending on our individual tastes, but will also be affected by three different factors:

Presentation

There are many different factors that encompass presentation including the medium, the setting and the style and personality of a presenter. Of course this works both ways and equally you will have been entranced by others because of the force of their personality and their delivery style.

The environment can also impact your appreciation of the presentation. Seating, temperature, clarity and volume of sound will all impact on whether it's a good or poor experience.

Perception

Perception is an important factor in appreciative listening. As one is exposed to different experiences his/her perceptions can change. For example: individual's taste in music. We need to listen to various types of music to have a preference over other types and appreciate them. An individual's expectations also affects our perception.

An individual's perception and expectations are driven by his/her attitudes which determine how he/she reacts to and interact to the world in which he/she lives.

Previous Experience

Some of our perceptions are clearly influenced by our previous experience and impact on whether or not we enjoy listening to something, or whether we are even willing to listen. Whether our memories evoke pleasant or unpleasant reminders will affect our appreciation. However, it's important to remain open to new experiences. We can develop our appreciative listening skills.

Reflective Listening

Reflective listening is a communication strategy involving two key steps: seeking to understand a speaker's idea, then offering the idea back to the speaker, to confirm the idea has been understood correctly. It attempts to "reconstruct what the client is thinking and feeling and to relay this understanding back to the client". Reflective listening is a more specific strategy than the more general methods of active listening. It arose from Carl Rogers' school of client-centered therapy in counseling theory. Empathy is at the center of Rogers' approach.

Dalmar Fisher developed a model for Reflective Listening that includes the following elements:

- Focusing upon the conversation by reducing or eliminating any kind of distraction.
- Genuinely embracing the speaker's perspective without necessarily agreeing with it. By engaging in a non-judgmental and empathetic approach, listeners encourage the others to speak freely.

- Mirroring the mood of the speaker, reflecting the emotional state with words and nonverbal communication. This requires the listener to quiet his mind and focus fully upon the mood of the speaker. This mood will become apparent not just in the words used but in the tone of voice, posture and other nonverbal cues given by the speaker. The listener will look for congruence between words and mood.
- Summarizing what the speaker said, using the speaker's own words rather than merely paraphrasing words and phrases, thereby mirroring the essential concept of the speaker.
- Responding to the speaker's specific point, without digressing to other subjects.
- Repeating the procedure for each subject, and switching the roles of speaker and listener, if necessary.
- During the reflective listening approach, both client and therapist embrace the technique of thoughtful silence, rather than to engage in idle chatter.

Reflective listening has been found to be effective in a therapeutic setting. Subjects receiving reflective listening from a counselor have reported better therapeutic relationship and more disclosure of feelings.

Cognitive content is one of the two main options that a counselor has for reflecting the client's previous communication in the counseling session. This form deals with people, places, problems, situations, and things. Cognitive content can play a role in help with problem solving. Incorporating cognitive content in problem solving makes it easier for clients to identify and work through issues. If neither the counselor nor the client can identify a problem that the client has, there is no need to problem solve and there is no need for counseling. Similar to problem solving where one initially identifies the quandary, counseling calls for identification of the fundamental issue in order to successfully change the client's behaviors or thought patterns.

Informational Listening

The process of informational listening focuses on the ability of an individual to understand a speaker's message. It is a huge part of everyday life, and failing to understand the concept of informational listening can be very detrimental to one's quality of life and to their contribution to society. Much of the listening people engage in on a regular basis falls under the blanket of listening for information. In the office, people listen to their superiors for instructions about what they are to do. At school, students listen to teachers for information that they are expected to understand for quizzes and tests. In all areas of life, informational listening plays a huge role in human communication.

Potential Hindrances

When listening to a person's message, it is common to overlook aspects of the conversation or make judgments before all of the information is presented. This lack of effective comprehension is detrimental to communication and is illustrated effectively by several specific obstacles. Chief among these obstacles are confirmation bias and the vividness effect, both of which distort the speaker's message by severely affecting the perception of a particular topic.

Confirmation Bias

Confirmation bias is the tendency to pick out aspects of a conversation that support one's own beliefs and values. This psychological process proves to have a detrimental effect on communication for several reasons.

First, confirmation bias tends to become involved in conversation before the speaker finishes his/her message. As a result, an opinion is formed without first obtaining all pertinent information. This, in turn, leads to uneducated thinking and fallacious judgments that could later affect others.

Second, confirmation bias detracts from a person's ability to be open-minded. For example, when listening to a statement, an individual may hear something at the beginning of the conversation that arouses a specific emotion. Whether this is anger or frustration or anything else, it could have a profound impact on that person's perception of the rest of the conversation. If they were to become angry about a statement the speaker made early in the conversation, they would likely be averse to accepting arguments presented later in the discourse.

To combat this bias and its consequences, an individual must be aware of it and its effects. With this knowledge, an individual can learn to critically judge both sides of an argument before coming to a conclusion.

Vividness Effect

The vividness effect explains how vivid or highly graphic and dramatic events affect an individual's perception of a situation. This phenomenon has been amplified by the media in recent decades. With the use of media technology, graphic images can be used to portray an event. While this makes the process of receiving news easier and more enjoyable, it can also blow a situation out of proportion. One year after the Columbine High School massacre, about 60 percent of the people who responded to a survey said that they felt a shooting was likely at their own school. The reality was much different; in fact, the likelihood of a school shooting is negligibleacross America.

The vividness effect was only amplified by the media. It existed long before the advent of television or radio. When observing an event in person, an individual is automatically drawn toward the sensational or vivid aspects. Thus, a person becomes quick to believe that all aspects of an event are bad if they only remember the vivid parts that offended them. To counter this, an individual must be aware of and deal with the inclination to the dramatic and offensive, act accordingly. One must resist the temptation to jump to conclusions and instead weigh all facts before judging.

Effective Listening

In addition to avoiding the two major mistakes listed above, there are things one must do to be a competent informational listener.

Memory

To understand what is said in the present, one must remember what has been said before; and for the message to have impact, one must remember at least parts of it at some point in the future.

The most obvious memory aid is simply taking notes, but it is also helpful to create a mental outline of the message as it is being heard.

Identification

Identify the main point that the speaker is trying to bring across. When the main point has been deduced, one can begin to sort out the rest of the information and decide where it belongs in the mental outline. Before getting the big picture of a message, it can be difficult to focus on what the speaker is saying, because it is impossible to know where any particular piece of information fits.

Questions

It is usually helpful to ask oneself questions about the speaker's message. If the listener is mentally asking questions about what is being said, it is a good sign that he/she is actively involved in effective informational listening.

7 C's of Business Communication

The 7 C's of effective communication, also known as the seven principles of communication are a useful way to ensure good business communication. The 7 C's of Effective Communication provide a useful check list as a result of which both written and verbal communication pass off in a clear, plain, target group-oriented and well-structured manner. These are as follows:

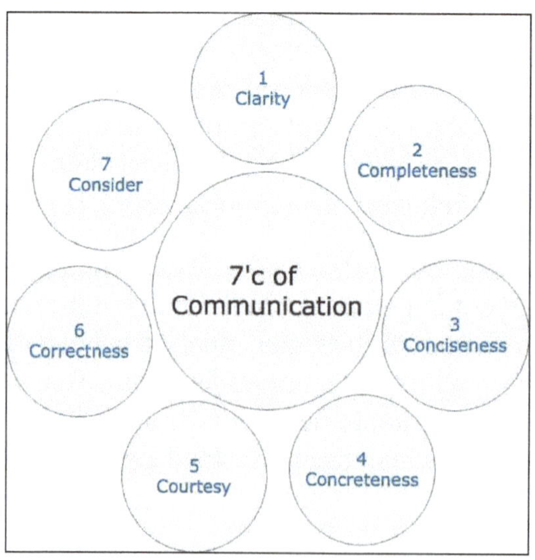

Clarity

A firm needs to be clear on the message being put a crossed, whether formal or informal. An organization is made up of different people, and everyone has an idea of how a project should be done. By establishing a common mission, vision, or project the employees and staff will work toward achieving it.

However, a communication about these factors needs to reach all the employees. The directive should start from the top management. Later the same message must trickle down to the lower, and middle management. This gives the employees a sense of belonging, and the goal can be easily achieved. Clarity also ensures that one goal is completed before embarking on another.

Features

- A clear message grantees understanding among the employees and consumers.
- Makes use of concrete and appropriate words.
- It also enhances the meaning of the message.

Complete

The particular principle requires excellent communication. This means the message sent within the firm or outside needs to have all the required details. Figures or graphs can be included if need be and no information should be left out.

When a section of the message is omitted, it is termed incomplete, and these leave the employees and consumer imagining. Later their imagination turns into doubt, and this affects production and sales. Therefore, information sent to the employees or consumer has to have additional information if need be. This wins their trust, and the quality of products and sales will increase.

Features

- It gives complete information to the employees or consumers, and nothing is left out of the message.
- Completeness of messages develops the company's image hence increasing the market share. It cuts cost since you won't have to print out or send additional information that was left out in the previous notice.
- Complete information about a product persuades the consumer into buying the product. This is because they trust. that the product being offered to serve a particle need. This in turn, improves sales.

Concise

It's also part of the seven C's of business communication; this dictates that the information sent to the relevant parties should use fewer words. However, that doesn't mean excluding the other seven C's of communication. The message sent should not have vague words. This ensures the information submitted by the firm is straight to the point and easy to comprehend.

Features

- Incorporating this form of communication about products saves time and money.
- It is not repetitive, which grasps the attention of the consumer when placed on an advert.

- The message is usually short and precise, highlighting the main points in fewer words. This makes it easy for an employee to understand regardless of their educational background.

Concrete

Firms need to be clear on the information that they give to the public. This is where concreteness comes in as part of the seven C's of business communication. It implies that the messages conveyed to the consumers or staff has to be factual. Nothing should be assumed and should be backed up with figures.

For example, if the firm is selling a product, and they claim that it helps in satisfying a need. There has to be proof of such claims, but when the consumer learns all this is just claims. The organization will lose a large percentage of its market share to other companies.

What a consumer desires is truth about the product or services be used. If a firm chooses to lie about its products then this will automatically decrease the sales. On the other hand, the consumer can also sue for damages since the information given is false. This affects the firm's reputation as well.

Features

- It contains specific facts and figures.
- The words used are usually clear and also builds the reputation of the company.

Courteous

Consumers want to feel appreciated and respected after and before purchasing product. This gives them a sense of belonging. Therefore, businesses need to show these emotions when communicating with them. A courteous message should show sincerity, politeness, and enthusiasm when he or she reads it.

This paints a picture that you have taken into consideration his\ her feelings before selling to them. A good business also ensures that the information sent to the employees' reflects the same. This guarantees that they will remain loyal to the company. Hence, this increases product quality and profit margin.

Features

- Such information sent to the consumers or employees is not biased.
- The words used to craft the message are polite and positive.
- The message sent by the firm from the top management should incorporate the views of the employees.

Correct

The correctness of information ensures there is an understanding between the management and the employees, investors or consumers. Hence no grammatical error as expected. For example, if the firm is looking for an investor to finance their projects.

They should ensure the ideas and thoughts being pitched to the investors are correct and arrange in the right manner. This gives the investors' confidence to have their money in the project. But when the idea is pitch incorrectly, that means it isn't clear cannot be understood. Therefore the investor is likely to work away.

Features

- It as contains figures, graphs, and specific facts.
- The impact of the message is significant because there is an understanding between the management, staff and the investors.
- There is the use of a correct and appropriate language in the message.

Consideration

Consideration is something a firm should look into when communicating with its employees. The message has to be logical and in line with the topic. For, example, when it comes to the mission, values and goals of the firm. It has to be sensible and achievable.

If a construction firm is undertaking a project that takes a span of four years. The employees are supposed to be aware of this. Not that the company reduces the time frame of the project and increases the working hours without proper communication. This affects the employees, and the output will be of low quality.

Features

- The message should concentrate more on the employees or consumer and not the company.
- Present the employees with logical projects that can be achieved and not straining them.

Ethics in Business Communication

Ethical issues of business communication is the way by which individuals or groups of people exchange information between them.From end-to-end the process, effective communicators try as clearly and accurately to pass on their ideas, intentions and, objectives to their receiver. Communication is successful only when both the sender and the receiver understand the same information.Nowadays business world, effective communication skills are necessary due to the highly informational and technological era,Which has made it easier for exchanging of information between the parties.

Despite of the context, communication is all about choice, reflects values, and has consequences. For better communication, understanding the obvious and the subtle issues relating to communication is necessary. Any company that aims to be socially and ethically responsible must make a priority of ethical communication both inside the company and in its interactions with the public. In theory, many consumers prefer to do business with companies they believe are ethical which gives those ethical businesses an advantage in the market.

Some of the vital characteristics of ethical communication are discussed below:

- Conveying the point without offending the audience: While communicating with the audience, expressing the desired message to them in a significant manner is of primary importance.Strong conversation skills can make a big difference in the workplace. Knowing how to share an attentive, friendly discussion will give you more confidence and help you build better relationships. As you improve your skills, you'll become a more thoughtful listener, give sharper responses, and learn how to handle common mistakes. For instance, the employees in a company can be asked to increase their efficiency in a demanding manner whereas managers and executives will feel offended if the same tone is used on them. There are different ways to explain the exact things to them in a much smoother manner.

- Maintain a relationship with the audience: Maintaining the same wavelength with the audience is very important for a communicator to ensure the audiences feel at home. Experienced communicators immediately build a relationship based on trust with the audience as soon as they start speaking. As the audience shares, ask relevant questions to give them further chances to express themselves. For instance, if they're talking about a tough presentation they just gave, ask how they felt when they finished.

- Avoid withholding crucial information: In the modern era, information is vital for all decision. Hence, it is essential for any organization to be cautious when communicating with titanic. The related information should be absolute, and all crucial information must be passed on appropriately. Purposely withholding crucial information might result in the public conceiving a bad image.

- Well organized value system: In order to ensure that this concept is successfully practiced and understood in an organization, a well-organized value system must be established throughout the organization by the top management.If an organization functions on the base of value systems common to both the top management and the employees, mutual respect between them will be present. A sound and healthy value system can make way for ethical communication.

- Accuracy of information is necessary: Any information that is to be passed on must be true and accurate. Communicating without checking the truth of the information can be highly dangerous for the organization. Identification of the source and testing the information is necessary before communicating it.

The work of an organizational communication professional consists in developing communication plans that seek to restore trust, not only in the organization but the leaders and in all the people who work for it, in verbally promoting ethical behaviors and generating spaces of communication that help support institutional values.

In this way, both managers and employees will be "on the same page," employees will feel heard and respected and will treat customers in the same way. Also, this will generate more loyalty on the part of the client and, therefore, more business. In addition, a business that communicates internally with ethics will most likely project that image in the business community, will seek to maintain good relations with the government and its most successful businesses. Without the distractions and negative effects that can have the legal implications of running a business " ethically debatable," the organization will be able to concentrate its efforts on its employees, its products, and its clients.

Barriers to Effective Communication

The process of communication has multiple barriers. The intended communique will often be disturbed and distorted leading to a condition of misunderstanding and failure of communication. The barriers to effective communication could be of many types like linguistic, psychological, emotional, physical, and cultural etc.

Linguistic Barriers

The language barrier is one of the main barriers that limit effective communication. Language is the most commonly employed tool of communication. The fact that each major region has its own language is one of the Barriers to effective communication. Sometimes even a thick dialect may render the communication ineffective.

As per some estimates, the dialects of every two regions changes within a few kilometers. Even in the same workplace, different employees will have different linguistic skills. As a result, the communication channels that span across the organization would be affected by this.

Thus keeping this barrier in mind, different considerations have to be made for different employees. Some of them are very proficient in a certain language and others will be ok with these languages.

Psychological Barriers

There are various mental and psychological issues that may be barriers to effective communication. Some people have stage fear, speech disorders, phobia, depression etc. All of these conditions are very difficult to manage sometimes and will most certainly limit the ease of communication.

Emotional Barriers

The emotional IQ of a person determines the ease and comfort with which they can communicate. A person who is emotionally mature will be able to communicate effectively. On the other hand, people who let their emotions take over will face certain difficulties.

A perfect mixture of emotions and facts is necessary for effective communication. Emotions like anger, frustration, humour, can blur the decision-making capacities of a person and thus limit the effectiveness of their communication.

Physical Barriers to Communication

They are the most obvious barriers to effective communication. These barriers are mostly easily removable in principle at least. They include barriers like noise, closed doors, faulty equipment used for communication, closed cabins, etc. Sometimes, in a large office, the physical separation between various employees combined with faulty equipment may result in severe barriers to effective communication.

Cultural Barriers of Communication

As the world is getting more and more globalized, any large office may have people from several parts of the world. Different cultures have a different meaning for several basic values of society. Dressing, Religions or lack of them, food, drinks, pets, and the general behaviour will change drastically from one culture to another.

Hence it is a must that we must take these different cultures into account while communication. This is what we call being culturally appropriate. In many multinational companies, special courses are offered at the orientation stages that let people know about other cultures and how to be courteous and tolerant of others.

Organisational Structure Barriers

As we saw there are many methods of communication at an organizational level. Each of these methods has its own problems and constraints that may become barriers to effective communication. Most of these barriers arise because of misinformation or lack of appropriate transparency available to the employees.

Attitude Barriers

Certain people like to be left alone. They are the introverts or just people who are not very social. Both these cases could become a barrier to communication. Some people have attitude issues, like huge ego and inconsiderate behaviours.

These employees can cause severe strains in the communication channels that they are present in. Certain personality traits like shyness, anger, social anxiety may be removable through courses and proper training. However, problems like egocentric behaviour and selfishness may not be correctable.

Perception Barriers

Different people perceive the same things differently. This is a fact which we must consider during the communication process. Knowledge of the perception levels of the audience is crucial to effective communication. All the messages or communique must be easy and clear. There shouldn't be any room for a diversified interpretational set.

Physiological Barriers

Certain disorders or diseases or other limitations could also prevent effective communication between the various channels of an organization. The shrillness of voice, dyslexia, etc are some examples of physiological barriers to effective communication. However, these are not crucial because they can easily be compensated and removed.

Technological Barriers and Socio-religious Barriers

Other barriers include the technological barriers. The technology is developing fast and as a result, it becomes difficult to keep up with the newest developments. Hence sometimes the technological advance may become a barrier. In addition to this, the cost of technology is sometimes very high.

Most of the organizations will not be able to afford a decent tech for the purpose of communication. Hence, this becomes a very crucial barrier. Other barriers are socio-religious barriers. In a patriarchal society, a woman or a transgender may face many difficulties and barriers while communicating.

References

- Communication-systems, encyclopedia: inc.com, Retrieved 20 January, 2019
- Importance-interpersonal-communication-business- 6460060: bizfluent.com, Retrieved 16 June, 2019
- Effects-interpersonal-communication-organization-18338: smallbusiness.chron.com, Retrieved 14 July, 2019
- Effective-intrapersonal-communication-36895: smallbusiness.chron.com, Retrieved 08 April, 2019
- Importance-of-intrapersonal: englishflair123.blogspot.com, Retrieved 19 May, 2019
- What-is-written-communication: thebusinesscommunication.com, Retrieved 17 August, 2019
- Written-communication: managementstudyguide.com, Retrieved 23 July, 2019
- What-is-oral-communication: thebusinesscommunication.com, Retrieved 16 May, 2019
- Barriers-in-communication, business-correspondence-and-reporting-communication: toppr.com, Retrieved 19 June, 2019

3

Levels in Business Communication

Business communication has been divided into different levels for effective communication. It involves organizational communication, internal communication, external communication, upward communication, lateral communication, etc. This chapter discusses these different levels of business communication in detail.

Organizational Communication

Organizational communication is the exchange of information, ideas, and views within and outside the organization. Organizational communication indicates communication not only in business but also in hospitals, churches, government agencies, military organization, and academic institutions. Every organization whether business or non-business has some specific goals and stakeholders. Attainment of those goals depends on successful communication with the respective stakeholder groups.

Therefore, communication is considered as the part and parcel of any organization.

Organizational communication is the exchange of formation with the internal and external stakeholders of an organization. It is not only concerned with the effectiveness of the individual communication, but with the role of communication in contributing to the effective functioning of the organization. Organizational communication entices communication in all types of organizations.

Importance of Organizational Communication

The various points that highlight the importance of organizational communication are:

Leading

William Neher identifies the five primary functions of business communication as leading, rationalizing, problem-solving, conflict management and compliance gaining. The function of leading is important to enable management to issue instructions in a clear, specific manner so that workers are able to follow them without difficulty. This is generally downward communication.

Rationalizing

This function enables management to explain the reasons for instructions in a way that workers can understand. In this context, it is downward communication; however, rationalizing is also important for enabling workers to bring issues to the attention of management, using upward communication to do so. If a worker identifies a motivation problem, for example, he may communicate this upward formally to management and use rationalization to highlight the potential impact of the problem on profitability.

Problem-solving

Most companies hold regular meetings to discuss issues such as production cycles, delivery times, price margins and other areas where unusual situations could arise that may affect the performance of a business. In these meetings, organizational communication plays an important role in tabling problems, brainstorming potential responses and finalizing solutions. In this way, a company obtains maximum benefit from the abilities of those involved in the communication, which flows horizontally and often informally.

Conflict Management

Conflict in the workplace can lead to the loss of talented employees, the lodging of grievances and possibly lawsuits. Managing conflict by bringing all parties together to discuss their differences in a safe, moderated environment is an important function of organizational communications. This type of communication usually involves all three directions of communication, and, although discussions may be informal, the final decisions are usually communicated formally.

Gaining Compliance

Gaining the compliance of employees is necessary for them to adhere fully to instructions. To do this, management needs to listen to feedback from the staff and to take account of their ideas and comments. Feedback or two-way communication can be both upward and downward or horizontal and may be formal or informal, but it is important for a company to enable open communication channels to motivate and achieve the best performance from employees.

Direction of Communication Flow in an Organization

Within organizations, there are three directions in which communications flow: downward, upward and laterally (horizontal).

Downward Communication

Downward communication involves a message travelling to one or more receivers at the lower level in the hierarchy. The message frequently involves directions or performance feedback. The down ward flow of communication generally corresponds to the formal organizational communications system, which is usually synonymous with the chain of command or line of authority. This system has received a great deal of attention from both managers and behavioural scientists since it is crucial to organizational functioning.

Upward Communication

In upward communication, the message is directed toward a higher level in the hierarchy.

It is often takes the form of progress reports or information about successes and failures of the individuals or work groups reporting to the receiver of the message. Sometimes employees also send suggestions or complaints upward through the organization's hierarchy.

The upward flow of communication involves two distinct manager-subordinate activities in addition to feedback:

- The participation by employees in formal organizational decisions.
- Employee appeal is a result against formal organization decisions. The employee appeal is a result of the industrial democracy concept that provides for two-way communication in areas of disagreement.

Stimulating Upward Communication

Although most managers agree on the need for upward communication, it is often not clear what actions can be taken to stimulate it. Given this situation, it is important to develop ways to stimulate upward communication. Planty and Machaver give the following suggestions.

If properly utilized, upward communication is potentially one of the most useful managerial practices. Upward communication keeps managers aware of how employees feel about their jobs, co-workers and the organization in general. Managers also rely on upward communication for ideas on how things can be improved.

Lateral Communication

When takes place among members of the same work group, among members of work groups at the same level, among managers at the same level or among any horizontally equivalent personnel, we describe it as lateral communications. In lateral communication, the sender and receivers are at the same level in the hierarchy. Formal communications that travel laterally involve employees engaged in carrying out the same or related tasks.

The messages might concern advice, problem solving, or coordination of activities. The direction of communication in organizations explained above is summarized.

Directions of Communication in Organization

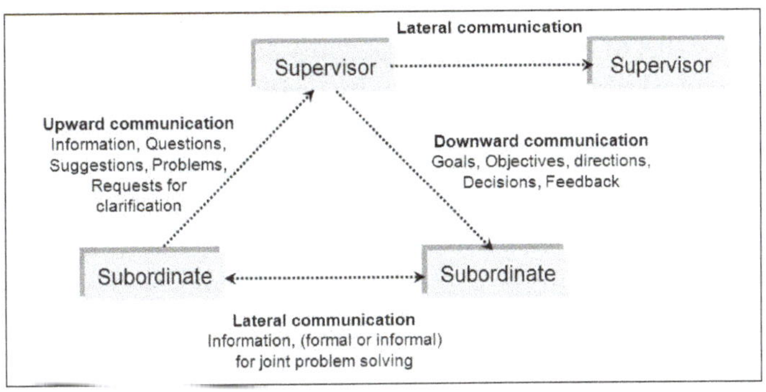

Internal Communication

Internal communications (IC) is the function responsible for effective communications among participants within an organization. The scope of the function varies by organization and practitioner, from producing and delivering messages and campaigns on behalf of management, to facilitating two-way dialogue and developing the communication skills of the organization's participants.

Filming a day's work for the US Armed Forces
Network Television Services, an internal communication channel.

Modern understanding of internal communications is a field of its own and draws on the theory and practice of related professions, not least journalism, knowledge management, public relations (e.g., media relations), marketing and human resources, as well as wider organizational studies, communication theory, social psychology, sociology and political science.

Role of IC in the organization

The purpose that a formally appointed IC manager or IC team will serve within a given organization will depend on the business context. In one, the IC function may perform the role of 'internal marketing' (i.e., attempting to win participants over to the management vision of the organization); in another, it might perform a 'logistical' service as channel manager; in a third, it might act principally as strategic adviser.

There is a practical distinction to make between managed communication and regular interactions among teams or between managers and subordinates. Minzberg talks about the fact that communicating is intrinsic to the work of a manager - especially so in an information society. Interpersonal communications in the workplace are explored by writers such as Phillip Clampitt.

There are a number of reasons why organisations should be concerned with internal communication. Employees are the heart and soul of an organization, thus it's critical to pay attention to their needs. An engaged and committed employee work force increases and drives business results. Employee engagement encourages higher employee performance, results in lower turnover and offers competitive advantage. Even in a difficult economy, companies need to inspire and retain high performers.

Importantly, there is commonly a legal requirement for organizations to communicate with their workers. In Europe, for example, the EU has made very specific provision about workers' rights to be informed and consulted with Directive 94/45/EC (Works Council).

Effective internal communications is commonly understood by practitioners to improve employee engagement and therefore to add significant value to organizations on metrics from productivity to customer research.

As noted in Quirke: "Traditionally, internal communications has focused on the announcement of management conclusions and the packaging of management thinking into messages for mass distribution to the 'troops'". Research indicates a limit to the value of this 'broadcasting' model of IC. Without feedback loops and harnessing the active involvement and mediation skills of frontline supervisors or team leaders, broadcasting tends to be more effective at influencing senior and middle managers than frontline employees.

As the IC function matures within the organization, then, it may come to play a wider role in facilitating conversations "upwards", "downwards" and "across" the organization. Organizations increasingly see IC as playing a role in external reputation management. This trend reaches its full potential with the arrival of new 'norms' and customer expectations around social media, for example in the work of Scoble and Israel. Market researchers MORI have likewise highlighted the effects of employee advocacy on an organisation's external reputation.

IC managers try to get senior leaders to think strategically about how management decisions can be perceived internally and externally. The focus of IC is often to ensure that employees can support a decision and understand how it impacts their work. An engaged employee is someone who is fully involved in, committed, and enthusiastic about his or her work. It's the extent to which employees put discretionary effort into their work. Involvement of hearts as well as minds. The ability to work as a team across disciplines and functions. The understanding and commitment to achieving company goals and business context. Employee engagement speaks to the level of trust in leadership, a belief that decisions are made in the best interests of the organization and its employees, and the level to which employees feel valued and appreciated. The more engaged, committed and inspired an employee is, the higher the employee performance, and the more impact on the bottom line.

Internal Communication Strategy

There are two sides to strategy in internal communications. In the first instance there is the organization's strategy — what it hopes to achieve and how it plans to go about achieving it. That strategy will be supported and, to some extent, delivered through effective internal communications.

In this context internal communication can help on several different levels:

- Tell: Simply informing people of the direction, non-negotiable.
- Sell: Anticipating some form of backlash, requiring some persuasion.
- Consult: Seeking specific areas of input to the decision-making process.
- Involve: Seeking varying degrees of involvement and co-creation.

Secondly, and more importantly, internal communications needs a strategy of its own. It should be positioned more than a simple plan of tactical interventions in support of business activities. The strategy should consider the following:

- Market: What does the organization know about its audiences' needs? How should its audiences be segmented?
- Message: What is it the organization's message is trying to achieve? In what tone should it be conveyed?
- Media: Which channels work best for the different audience segments? How will it maximize reach and cut-through? Are there clear editorial guidelines for each?
- Measurement: Are there clearly defined success criteria? What are the leading and lagging measures? As well as informing all of the other three M's, it should be used to demonstrate value and measures of performance (ROI, message penetration, hit rates, quality of feedback, etc.)

The strategy will inform the best way to organize effective communications.

Five general modes of IC practice are itemised below, ranked loosely according to their position along a spectrum from *tactical* to *strategic* activities.

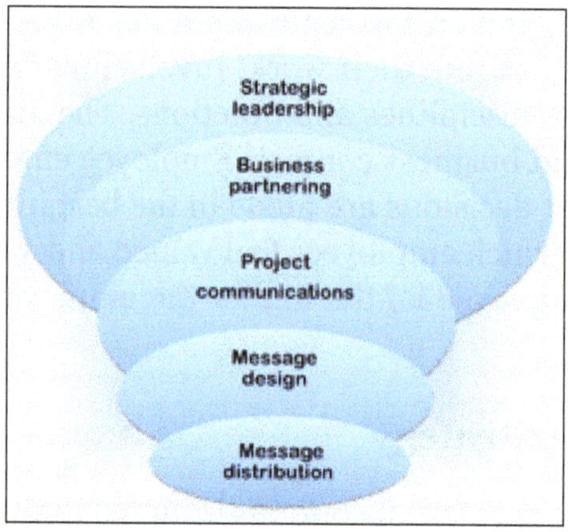

The modes of IC practice, arranged along a spectrum from the tactical to the strategic.

Message Distribution

Formal channels typically fall into one of four broad categories:

- Electronic: Communications that are delivered and/or accessed electronically, either by computer, telephone, television or other devices. Examples include email, intranet, video and webcasts, DVD, electronic newsletters, podcasts, blogs, voicemail, conference calls, SMS text messaging, screensaver messaging, desktop news feeds, internal social media tools and team chat tools.
- Print: Paper-based communications. Examples include magazines, newsletters, brochures, postcards and other 'desk drops', posters, memos, communication packs or 'toolkits' for line managers, etc.
- Face-to-face: One-to-one and one-to-many forums where people are physically present. Examples include a 'cascade' of team meetings or briefings, conferences, site visits, 'back to the floor', consultation forums, 'brown bag' lunches, round-table discussions, 'town meetings', etc.
- Workspace: The working environment. Examples include notice boards, plasma and LCD screens, accessories (e.g.: mousemats), window decals, etc.

Informal channels reflect the non-linear dynamics of a social network and can be as influential, if not more so, than official channels, often more likely to stimulate and create discussion and dialogue. The channels may manifest themselves via the rumour-mill, water-cooler conversations, social networking, graffiti, spoof newsletters, etc.

Selecting Channels

One of the key challenges any internal communicator will face is how to select the right channels - and the right mix of channels - for both the audience and the message.

The practical considerations are:

- Availability: what channels either already exist within the organisation or can be introduced effectively?

- Audience: who are they, where are they based, how do they prefer to access information and how effective will the proposed channel be in reaching them and engaging them?
- Objectives: what does the organisation want people to learn, think, feel or do as a result of the message?
- Content: what is the context and substance of the message? (for example, sensitive messages may need to be communicated face-to-face, rather than by text message).
- Timing: how urgent is the message? (for example, communications in times of crisis which require quick dissemination of important messages).

Traffic Control

A typical large organisation IC function will be concerned to monitor and limit the *quantity* of information flowing through each internal channel, prioritising according to the relevance of a given message to the audience implicated in that channel, as well as the urgency and impact of the message. Such organisations typically face a risk that channels (such as intranet news, or email) are over-used for inappropriate, low value messages, causing vital audience groups to filter them out.

Channel Development and Administration

IC teams will often (but not always) hold responsibility for the administration and development of several of the organisation's communications channels. The range of media available is wide - and growing fast with new electronic media. Initially, IC tends to focus on the existing resources of the organization, typically an intranet, email distributions, and newsletters.

One common element of channel development and administration involves managing supplier relationships - agencies external to the organization typically specialise in one main channel area, such as audiovisual, or print production.

Line Manager Cascade

Sending information down the line to local supervisors, expecting them to deliver it without any corruption, interpretation or deviation has long been the main focus of 'cascaded' internal communications (for example, UK guidance from The Industrial Society, now the Work Foundation, focused on giving managers very clear instructions about what to say and how to say it). However, in recent years thinking has evolved and literature now concentrates on empowering managers to facilitate discussion rather than cascade management of messages which will have little authority or impact. This is a particularly strong theme in the writing of TJ and Sandar Larkin. Clampitt lists three approaches managers use to communicate with their employees.

Employee communication is an important skill for all line managers, irrespective of their seniority. Like any skill it requires training and development. Often, organisations do not invest the appropriate amount of time and effort in developing managers' communications skills. Too often this leads to managers abdicating responsibility for communications to their 'internal communications department' and a lack of confidence in facilitating discussion in their teams. This raises debate around the following issues:

- The nature of supervisory relationships and organisational communication.
- The potency of managers as a channel of official communications.
- How best to support managers in their roles.

FitzPatrick and Valskov argue that strong manager communication systems attempt to address five essential issues:

- Do managers understand that communication is part of their role - in general and on specific occasions or topics?
- Do managers have access to more detailed background or context - rather than just be supplied with the same material as their teams?
- Have managers received training or development to support their role?
- Are manager supplied with materials to make their task easier?
- What attention is given to their feedback?

Social Media

Social media is becoming increasingly discussed in the field of internal communication. However, there is little documented, academic evidence of where it is being used successfully as part of a planned campaign of employee communications, and it is often confused with digital media.

Other Collaborative Software

Since 2012, several communication technologies usually classified as workplace group chat apps or collaborative software have emerged.

Message Design and Production

Basic IC services to an organization begin with editorial services - either fine-tuning messages drafted by participants in the organization, or drafting new material on their behalf. IC practitioners might simply correct basic grammar, etc., especially in organisations where many participants may be operating in their second or third language. Or they might re-work it to conform to house style or its branded equivalent, 'tone of voice'. The skillset involved relates closely to media professions such as journalism, copywriting and film or print production. Message design may be iterative, or involve a range of participants in an approvals process.

Project Communications

IC practitioners may be seconded to a specific project team, to support the stages of the project that carry a communications or engagement component. Project communicators might produce a schedule of communication objectives and milestones for the project; a map of vital stakeholders (senior individuals or large groups / segments of the overall population); and a message framework to guide project participants towards a single, coherent message about their work. They might also contribute to the project's aggregate risks 'log' on the reputational risks, and work-up contingency plans covering unintended situations.

Change Communications

Most writers on the subject of communications talk about the idea of change. Most intentional communication takes place with the aim of effecting some kind of change or another. However, many practitioners in internal communications make a distinction between change and transformation.

Drawing on the work of writers such as William Bridges, practitioners talk of 'change' as the act of altering something within an organisation (such as the introduction of a new IT system or the closure of an office) and they describe 'transition' as the process through which an individual passes as part of the process of coping with change. The use of the two terms interchangeably causes some confusion. Communicators who specialise in change communications tend to be interested in behaviour change and will draw heavily on psychological models.

Crisis Communications

Organizations occasionally face unplanned reputational crises which can destroy brand value or even finish the organization. At such moments, the support of the internal constituency becomes especially valuable, as employees' friends and relatives seek their account of events, and as talented and motivated participants consider whether or not to remain with the organization.

As with media relations and PR, the role IC plays in a crisis can be decisive for the success or failure of an organization, as it responds to a critical challenge. Organizations with a mature IC function may have contingency planning in place, ready to be tailored to the particulars of the situation. They are also more likely to have 'well flexed', well-rehearsed line management communications capability, making crisis communications more effective. Less mature IC functions may find it difficult to bring senior leaders' attention to the internal audience, when critical stakeholders such as investors or customers appear more likely to desert the organization.

Although unplanned and usually under-resourced, the quality of an IC function's response in a crisis often has a decisive impact in the maturing of an IC function within an organization. Effective responses bring IC up the list of priorities for senior leaders, following the crisis.

Internal Communication Roles

In recent years the practice of internal communications has professionalised.

In common with the Ulrich model for human resources practice, IC may be delivered via a 'business partnering' relationship, acting as adviser to a given function or unit on IC issues relevant to the delivery of their strategic plans and projects. As a representative of the audiences with a stake in the developments under discussion, this can be both an awkward and a privileged position to occupy, requiring skills of diplomacy and objectivity.

External Communication

Communication with people outside the company is called "external communication". Supervisors communicate with sources outside the organization, such as vendors and customers. External communication comprehends all information developed by the company, which is related to its activity that is released in the press, for public knowledge. Such information is crucial in order to promote the company's image.

When it comes to business communication, or for that matter, any aspect, the most important thing is the customer. We need to ensure that we deliver what the customer wants. Even when it comes to things like marketing or advertising, we need to show what the customer appreciates and likes. Different customers accept different kinds of marketing. It all depends on us to ensure that via business communication, we are able to cater to the choices of a wide range of people. If we are able to master the art of impressing many people by various means, we will be able to take our business to the top.

However, merely enticing our customer by showing them certain things is not good business. Good business means getting a quality product together and then marketing for it wisely so that people accept it. Just promising our customers a lot and then delivering nothing will only get our business into a soup. So gauge our products and services and then embark upon advertising and marketing. Internal business communication is the key to get all our people together and then inspiring them to deliver the best.

If we want to create a world class product, the first thing that we need to do is believe in yourself. This is where internal business communication comes in. It helps we get all our employees together and tell them that we can pull it off with élan. If there is a lot of positive thinking and bursting enthusiasm in our camp, the good spirit will show in our product. Our employees are an integral part of the company, so keeping them happy and making them believe in the company and themselves is very important.

External Communication is used for:

- Through ensuring the information flow from various stakeholders to the organization, they help to meaningfully define the organization's environmental policy, targets, as well as operational performance, environmental condition and management performance indicators.
- Through ensuring the information flow from the organization to various stakeholders they promote the credibility of the organization.
- Image management is one of the company's most relevant concerns, not only because of its own presentation, but also because it is considered to bea success-factor.

It is commonly assumed that the most importantimage is the perception image,as far as impression formation is concerned.However, this company bets on an aesthetical and a visual approach so as to foment a constant reflection flow on what is seen and how it is seen.

In this context, and contrary to the majority of companies, the organization demonstrates a collective motivation in constantly synchronizing its external image to the accessible products.

Another way to divulge its image is to provide the media with information on the company's relevant events and areas of intervention.

- Public relations include ongoing activities to ensure the organization has a strong public image. Public relations activities include helping the public to understand the organization and its products. Similar to effective advertising and promotions, effective public relations often depends on designing and implementing a well-designed public relations plan. The plan often includes description of what you want to convey to whom, how you plan to convey it, which is responsible for various activities and by when, and how much money is budgeted to fund these activities. Similar to advertising and promotions, a media plan and calendar can be very useful, which specifies what media methods that are used and when.

Key Principles of External Environmental Communications

External communication should be interactive and work in both ways.

External communication should be sensitive to the needs of both the organization and its stakeholders with whom the organization intends to communicate. External communications should not discriminate different audiences based on their language, technical skills, race or other factors. Thus, the content and form of external communications should be developed in a participatory manner.

External communications should be objective, use sound data sources, be clear and accessible to its intended audiences.

The Scope of Guidance on External Communications

There is a need for several kinds of guidance on external communication: process-oriented as well as product-oriented. The former guidance should focus on the process of developing and implementing an external communication program (for example, in relation to EMS introduction and implementation, certification, environmental labeling etc.). The latter may involve specific advice on information products, such as environmental reports, which constitute such a program. It is also possible that both types of guidance are combined in a single document.

Process-oriented Guidance

Guidance of this type may cover the main principles and the essential elements (stages) of the process of external communication accompanying certain organization's activities such as:

- Identifying the objectives and audiences of the external communication program.
- Identifying the existing information which may serve these information needs and any related issues of confidentiality.
- Identifying the types of information to be communicated (these may be, for example, performance indicators of different types as appropriate to the needs of the audiences), in which form it should be communicated (what should be the information products?).
- Setting up responsibilities for external communication (including data collection, analysis, validation (if necessary by a third party) and dissemination).

- Monitoring the quality, performance and effectiveness of external communications and adjusting them if and as necessary.

Guidance should emphasize that all these elements of the communication strategy should be performed in consultation with key stakeholders, such as the local community, government regulators, and other interested parties.

Additionally, such guidance should also define 'environmental information' which should be included in external communications.

Product-oriented Guidance

This type of guidance covers the content and format of particular information products used in external communication, such as periodic environmental statements, environmental reports, or Internet sites, etc. It is possible that several types of guidance might be needed depending on particular information products. For example, guidance on producing a validated Environmental Statement may follow the principles outlined in EMAS.

Essential Content and Elements of External Communication

The form and the content of the external communications should be appropriate to its objectives and serve the needs of the intended audiences. Ideally, the objectives and the audience of the external communications should be clear from its content. Other key elements of external communications may be the following:

- Methods of obtaining data and arriving at conclusions should be acknowledged as well as any external data sources.
- External communication should use widely recognized frameworks for assembling and presenting the data, such as, for example, the one defined in ISO 14031.
- Care should be taken in the presentation of information to make sure that it is accessible to the non-specialist. The layout of the communications should enable the reader to find and assimilate data easily and quickly.
- Unnecessarily technical or obscure language should be avoided. Technical terms, acronyms and initials should be defined.
- Information should be presented without bias and receive the emphasis appropriate to its importance in the context of the EMS. Prominence and emphasis should be given to potentially significant environmental issues. Adverse impacts should not be disguised.

Possible forms of External Communication

External communication can take a variety of forms depending on their purpose and intended audiences. If external communications are considered as essentially a two-way activity, then the following forms of communication may be useful:

- Production of special printed or electronic documents and disseminating them to concerned audiences (or making them publicly available e.g. through libraries or Internet sites); such reports might be validated by a third party to increase their credibility;

- Establishing more open access procedure for existing documents and information;
- Organizing public hearing, public meetings, "open door" events, exhibitions, seminars, etc. where communication is occurring more interactively;
- Setting up hot-lines and other services for disseminating information and collecting stakeholders' comments; conducting surveys for the latter purpose.

There is no 'most effective' form of external communications – it is not a particular form, but the process of determining it which defines the success of a communication strategy.

Some Techniques for External Communication

In the field of external communication we want to start by stating your opinion clearly, and making sure your message doesn't sound too complicated. It is very important for us to follow this step; never do we want a misunderstanding since we may lose the customer or client's interest. If we happen to have an external conversation through the phone make sure we aren't speaking too loud as we don't want to speak too low either.

If we speak too loud we can easily cause irritation to the client and the client may soon feel annoyed. Speaking too soft or too low is also irritating, try your best to speak at a moderate tone so the client may hear us clearly, and if possible try to stay away from noise pollution so we may hear with clarity.

When we are present with the client, the steps are somewhat similar as if we were talking to the client over the phone, but the only difference is that we want to make good eye-contact. Obviously through the phone we can't make good eye-contact with a client, but we can make good eye-contact when we are present with the client, so then it is important we do so, since it proves we are interested on what the client is saying and we demonstrate a sign of respect towards the client.

Superior-subordinate Communication

In an organization, communication occurs between members of different hierarchical positions. Superior-subordinate communication refers to the interactions between organizational leaders and their subordinates and how they work together to achieve personal and organizational goals Satisfactory upward and downward communication is essential for a successful organization because it closes the gap between superior and subordinates by increasing the levels of trust, support, and the frequency of their interactions.

Downward Communication

In a workplace environment, orders being given from superiors to subordinates is the most basic form of downward communication. These are usually done via manuals and handbooks, oral communication, and/or written orders. Two other forms of downward communication are when a customer gives orders to a supplier and when shareholders instruct management to do certain things.

- Implementation of goals, strategies, and objectives: This type of communication involves transmitting new information that will keep subordinates on the same page and mindset of their superiors, as well as the organization. This helps provide a direction for subordinates to take to help achieve organizational goals and targets.
- Job instructions and rationale: The first purpose is to provide subordinates with what the organization would like to achieve or reach, while this second purpose is to help give subordinates a successful way to accomplish the tasks. Coordinating both the individual goals and department goals, helps individuals understand their company's aspirations. Procedures and practices: This type of communication includes the most basic conception of downward communication. Superiors communicate the company's prewritten policies, procedures, restrictions, and compensation packages. The overall purpose is to create a sense of expectations and requirements in the subordinate's mind.
- Performance feedback: In order for the procedures and practices to help formulate uniformity along organizational boundaries; progress reports for both individuals/departments and appraisals help communicate subordinates overall performance with the organizations standards.
- Socialization: The last purpose of downward communication is to communicate a sense of belonging to subordinates to promote them to become a part of the organization's culture. This may include motivating subordinates to attend special events that are sponsored by the organization.

In a study conducted by John Anderson and Dale Level, the following were cited to be benefits of effective downward communication:

- Better coordination.
- Improved individual performance through the development of intelligent participation.
- Improved morale.
- Improved consumer relations.
- Improved industrial relations.

In order for downward communication to be effective, the superior should remain respectful and concise when giving orders, they should make sure the subordinate clearly understands instructions, and they should give recognition for admirable performance.

Openness in Communication

Open communication between superior and subordinate organizational members is an effective way to establish trust within the company. The most effective way to implement open communication is for management to engage in regular face-to-face conversations with employees in order to express their level of care for the work being done. It is important for management to ensure that each employee is being praised for his/ her individual contributions to the organization and to provide ample feedback on things he/ she is doing well and things he/ she can improve upon. This line of open communication makes employees feel more comfortable disclosing any personal issues they are experiencing within the organization. Employees who have an open communication with their superiors have been found to be more satisfied with their jobs than those who do not have this. Openness in communication requires both openness in message sending and openness in message receiving between superiors and subordinates. Achieving openness in message sending requires complete honesty whether the news is good or bad. Certain types of messages facilitate open communication better. Supervisory messages are preferable for both superiors and subordinates when they are encouraging or reciprocating, rather than responses that are either neutral or negative. Openness in message receiving requires a willingness to listen to the message without jumping to conclusions even when the message is not what you wanted to hear. An open communication relationship differs from a closed by the reactions and types of feedback given, not the message itself. Subordinates in a closed communication relationship with their superior are more likely to respond negatively to the superior's feedback than those who have more open communication with their superior.

Scanlon Plan

It has been proposed that those who perform specific tasks at work on a daily basis are more effective at determining how to improve things in an organization than upper-level management who rarely deals with daily tasks at the company. Everyone in the organization benefits from the Scanlon Plan via profit sharing methods. This plan allows for all employees to be more open-minded about decisions being proposed within an organization by giving them a say in how things are run.

Relationship Maintenance

Maintaining the relationship between superior and subordinate will differ greatly, depending on the expectations of the individual parties. Some will settle for nothing less than a close friendship with their superior. Others may be primarily focused on maintaining a professional relationship. Those may not get along with their superiors may be focused on just maintaining a civil relationship. The unusual relationship between superior and subordinates requires specific maintenance strategies since some typical ones, like avoidance, are unacceptable. There are four common types of relationship maintenance strategies for this variation of relationship. First there are informal interactions, such as joking and non-work related conversations that emphasize creating a friendship. There are also formal interactions, such as politeness and respect for the superior's authority, that help to create a professional superior-subordinate relationship. There are also tactics that allow a subordinate to appear impressive to the superior, such as a hesitancy to deliver bad news or showing enthusiasm. The final relationship maintenance strategy includes open discussion about the relationship with the superior, including explicitly telling them how they want to be treated in the workplace.

Feedback

Feedback allows for growth in a variety of areas for both superiors and subordinates. Using Feedback as a relational tool allows for a variety of positive outcomes.

For Subordinates:

- Promotion/Raise.
- Skill development.
- Improved communication with the boss.
- More Motivation to perform well and improve.
- Self identification with the organization.

For Superior:

- To review selection processes, training, promotion requirements, etc.
- Look at employees potential benefit to the organization.
- Influencing positive employee work habits.

Effective Feedback should be big picture focused, behavioral, specific, and both positive and negative.

Upward Communication

Upward Communication is the process of information flowing from the lower levels of a hierarchy to the upper levels. This type of communication is becoming more popular in organizations as traditional forms of communication are becoming less popular. The more traditional organization types such as a hierarchy, places people into separate ranks.

Upward communication helps employees to express their requirements, ideas, and feelings. For the top management, upward communication is an important source of information for business decisions. It helps in alerting top management about the requirement of changes in an organisations. Upward contribution is the core contributor of business process reengineering in many organisations.

Upward communication is widely used as part of whistleblowing policy in many large organisations. Under whistle blowing policy, each employee is permitted to directly communicate with top management about matters requiring examination on vigilance angle. Hence it is used as a fraud prevention tool as well.

Upward communication keeps managers aware of how employees feel about their jobs, policies and procedures, and the business in general. It consists of methods like Feedback from employees, helps in bringing Mutual Trust and helps the organization to determine, implement or decide upon new policies. It keeps the organization updated or prone to upcoming challenges.

Upward communication is not free from disadvantages too. It suffers from problems like information can be changed during transmission, unwillingness to participate, fear of inefficiency, bypassing and flattery too. Sometimes top level executives discourage the upward flow of information and neglect the constructive suggestions and opinions about the work related issues of the organization. It is a time taking process and is comparatively slow too.

Lateral Communication

Lateral communication is, "the exchange, imparting or sharing of information, ideas or feelings between people within a community, peer groups, departments or units of an organization who are at or about the same hierarchical level as each other for the purpose of coordinating activities, efforts or fulfilling a common purpose or goal".

Communities communicate and store collective knowledge through lateral communication and is an essential ingredient in making hierarchies work, by compensating for errors in vertical information flows.

In an organization, lateral communication is communication between different individuals/departments at the same organizational level.

The term lateral communication can be used interchangeably with horizontal communication. Horizontal communication is defined as, "the flow of messages across functional areas at a given level of an organization". People at the same level, "communicate directly without going through several levels of organization". Given this elasticity, members of an organization have an easier time with, "problem-solving, information sharing across different work groups, and task coordination between departments or project teams". The use of lateral or horizontal communication in the workplace "can also enhance morale and afford a means of resolving conflicts.

Other research asserted, "lateral communication involves not only the movement of information from the upper levels to the lower levels of the organizational hierarchy but also is defined primarily as the quality of information sharing among peers at similar levels. Specifically, lateral communication occurs among coworkers, during staff meetings and informational presentations, throughout shift changes, and among employees regardless of peer types. In short, lateral communication's purpose is to keep organizational personnel informed of all current practices, policies, and procedures".

"Communicating effectively laterally involves the exchange of information between and among all organizational members. While we may perceive that organizational information flows vertically or from top to bottom, in reality, information moves laterally. In other words, as information directives are communicated from an upper to a lower position on the hierarchy, peers at each hierarchical level should quickly interpret and communicate these directives between and among peers at similar hierarchical levels. Thus, it is critical for an organization to understand its structure and culture, which are the two major determinants of the quality of lateral communication.".

Quality: Structure and Culture

Structure

- Mechanistic structure – "A mechanistic or hierarchical organizational structure emphasizes specialization in position. Examples include healthcare and governmental organizations where information is communicated based on a chain of command. This organizational structure type is not conducive to lateral communication and, in fact, discourages it. Since direction and coordination are achieved through upper hierarchical levels, peer information sharing is limited. Overall, a mechanistic structure promotes vertical communication or top-down communication with strict alignment and unity of command within the organization".

- Organic structure – "An organic organizational structure is built upon an entrepreneurial concept. Here, the decisions made are decentralized and coordinated by mutual adjustment rather than command and control. Examples include a small business or a manufacturing facility where communication is promoted at all levels of the organization. This organizational structure allows for greater autonomy, promotes individual initiative, and allows employees to be involved in the decision-making process thus enabling employee decision-making to contribute to or detract from organizational goals. In short, an organic organizational structure can encourage and facilitate lateral communication".

Culture/Climate

Organizational culture refers to the organization's shared visions, values, beliefs, goals, and practices. Deals and Kennedy have connected culture with effective communication. Strong cultures and effective communication result in employees who are more productive because they know exactly what is expected of them in organizational settings. Gilsdorf has implied that the more employees perceive a positive or strong organizational culture, the more productive they will be. Poole has contended that an organization's quality of communication is summed-up in its culture. In many cases, a strong positive organizational culture or climate can encourage employees to communicate effectively laterally when sharing achievements and disappointments. Thus, as Comer has asserted, managers should actively encourage employees to communicate effectively laterally with their peers. In sum, lateral communication allows for a spirit of collaboration and teamwork by empowering employees at every level of the organizational hierarchy to work effectively together.

Challenges

Although laterl communication can be effective, "horizontal communication problems occur because of territoriality, rivalry, specialization, and simple lack of motivation." In addition to these problems and in general, "organizations that traditionally have functioned under rigid authority structures with fixed lines of communication may find that the values and expectations that members have acquired under such systems inhibit attempts at horizontal communication."

Other problems with this form of communication can happen between multinational corporations. "Horizontal communication between subsidiaries of the same multinational corporation (MNC) is a problem faced by staff as the demands for communicating across borders are pushed downwards in the organizational hierarchy."

Territoriality

Territoriality often occurs when members of an organization "control task-related activity within a defined and fixed jurisdictional area" and as a result "regard others' involvement in that area as territorial encroachment." "Departments value their turf and strive to protect it. This problem may be compounded by interdepartmental rivalries that arise from win/lose the competition for rewards and resources".

Rivalry

Rivalry within organizations occurs for example when different groups at a given organization level fail to cooperate. For example, Papa gives an example of "corporate executives in a national department store chain" who "encountered territorial rivalry when they discovered that local stores within each of the company's major sales districts refused to cooperate with one another on sales promotions"."Stores within the same sales region literally were in competition with one another as well as with other department store chains."

Specialization

Specialization can inhibit communication when organizations do not have uniformity within departments. Specialization can occur within procedures or jargon used by different departments. For example, when "different specialties use the same terms in different ways", this can create confusion and miscommunication. When this occurs organizations have trouble functioning properly and do not run smoothly.

Motivation

"Horizontal communication often fails simply because organization members are unwilling to expend the additional effort that it requires." "Horizontal communication may require contact with people in units that are well removed from our own. The channels and rules of interaction may be unclear. We do not really know these people. The need to communicate with them makes us uneasy or takes too much time, so we avoid or ignore it".

Personal Communication

Communication that occurs for exchanging personal information, ideas and feelings rather than business related information are termed as personal communication. Not all communication that occurs in business is personal.

Whenever people come in contact with each other, they engage in personal communication.

Personal communication is a crucial part of organizational communication. Although such form of communication does not deal with operational plans, it influences the attitudes of the employees regarding those operational plans.

Therefore, every organization must recognize personal communication as part of its overall organizational communication.

Interpersonal communication is all about the exchange of thoughts and ideas between individuals using a variety of methods, including words, tonal variation, facial expressions, gestures, and body language. Interpersonal communication and the skills to relate with others aren't just important for an individual, but they happen to be at the core of the success of an organization. When interpersonal communication in the workplace is effective, it makes operations more efficient and teamwork not only possible but also easier.

The ability of the key functions of a business to operate more efficiently is directly founded on the ability of the people that carry out those functions to communicate efficiently with each other. These include such functions as the resolution of conflicts, sales, and management. Ultimately, the importance of interpersonal communication in an organization cannot be overstated.

Importance of Interpersonal Relationships at Workplace

No individual can work alone. Human beings, unlike machines, cannot work without occasionally needing someone with whom to share their thoughts and feelings. We are social creatures by nature, and so we are prone to be more anxious and stressed in an isolated environment. With the right kind of interpersonal relationships, employees can even end up being more productive than they would be if they worked alone because of the synergy that comes with teamwork.

Allowing People to Discuss Problems

A person working in isolation is incapable of solving all of the different types of problems they will encounter in the course of their work. Interpersonal relationships are necessary because they allow people to discuss problems and weigh the pros and cons of various alternative solutions before arriving at the optimal one. Brainstorming works best when it is done in a group or forum where everyone feels respected and free to share their ideas and views.

A Culture of Positivity and Synergy

Interpersonal relationships, especially when executed well, are important for an organizational culture to thrive. With good interpersonal relationships, the de facto organizational culture becomes one of positivity and synergy. With bad interpersonal relationships, the air becomes one of negativity, confusion, and constant conflict. This ultimately ruins the work environment, reduces the productivity of the staff members, and adversely affects the bottom line of the company.

Recognizing Good Work

Interpersonal relationships are also important for coaching. When employees have good interpersonal relationships with each other and with the manager, they are likely to recognize good work in each other and congratulate each other for it as well as help correct each other's mistakes. A simple pat on the back can go a long way when it comes to motivating an individual to do more and be more. Ultimately, some colleagues will cease to be mere colleagues and will eventually become mentors.

Effects of Communication on Business

Whether it is carried out correctly or not, interpersonal communication has a direct and indirect impact on many areas of business. Here are some of the effects of interpersonal communication in business:

Effect on Management: When a manager has poor interpersonal communication skills, they can expect to irritate and confuse both the employees and clients of the business. In fact, there is a greater need for a manager to work on his or her interpersonal skills than there is for the average employee.

Managers are in charge of a lot of important things, including ensuring that staff members cooperate on tasks that help the organization to achieve its business goals. They are supposed to build the trust of the staff members in the organization and in each other while also holding them accountable for their role in the achievement of the goals of the organization.

With all of these responsibilities, if the manager is incapable of precise communication, they are likely to waste the time of the employees because they will often need to revisit issues that they had already communicated earlier but had not done so properly.

Effect on Sales: Sales are all about communication. The ability to sell is contingent upon the ability to influence others and that all ultimately boils down to the ability to communicate. There are lots of roles that sales personnel and business leaders as a whole play that are intensive in the sales aspect. These include communicating with the clients, the employees, and even each other.

Whenever communication is happening in an organization, sales are involved. It doesn't have to be actual sales of the product or service that the organization deals in; it could be some intangible quality, such as a vision or project idea. When management is trying to convince the employees to work harder to achieve the goals of the organization, they are selling the business vision and goals to the employees; when employees are trying to convince management to accept their proposals, whether for a pay rise, or a project, or paid leave, they are selling management on something.

When the organization is trying to get outside investment or trying to build its brand with customers, it is selling itself to the outside world.

The Role of Communications in Sales

Ultimately, sales cannot occur without communication, and there is a maxim to be respected in this respect if communication can fail, then sales can fail. Another important point to remember is that if a message is ambiguous enough to be potentially understood in multiple ways, then it is most likely that it will be understood in the most harmful way. It is therefore imperative to ensure communication is stable, so that it does not fail, and also to ensure that the messages being sent out to the other party are specific enough that the number of ways in which they can be understood is strictly limited.

When the communication skills in an organization are poor starting from the top all the way to the bottom, then the impact on the bottom can be very large.

The Effect on Training

While employees coming into the organization are expected to have a certain minimum level of training as evidenced by their academic qualifications, they will still have to undergo significant training while in the organization in order to be acquainted with the company operations, specific company-centric skills, and the organizational culture of the company.

This internal training is, yet again, predicated on communication. That communication will happen in a variety of formal and informal ways and will be done by the management, supervisors, and various skilled and experienced employees.

Good Interpersonal Communication Skills

These instructors need to have good interpersonal communication skills if they're going to do their job well. They need to be able to pass on the right skills to the employees that will enable them to perform the technical tasks they need to perform to achieve business goals as well as gain the soft skills necessary for them to productively do their work at the organization.

Perhaps the most important skill the trainers will have to pass on to trainees is the ability to communicate with others. This is one of the most important skills the employees will have to acquirein order to be able to collaborate with each other and work well in teams. The trainers will not be able to teach the trainees this skill if they do not possess it themselves.

The Effect on Conflict Resolution

Conflict is normal at the workplace, and the fact is that employees won't always be able to resolve conflict in the most amicable, timely manner. When conflicts of this nature arise, interpersonal communication can come to the rescue. With interpersonal communication skills, the employees will be able to harness their ability to communicate with each other to arrive at an amicable resolution to the conflict.

Conflict management cannot happen without effective interpersonal communication. In fact, all conflict management strategies that use communication to diffuse hostile situations in stressful environments, are not possible without interpersonal communications.

Employee Relations

An organization can't perform only with the help of chairs, tables, fans or other non living entities. It needs human beings who work together and perform to achieve the goals and objectives of the organization.

The human beings working together towards a common goal at a common place (organization) are called employees. Infact the employees are the major assets of an organization.

The success and failure of any organization is directly proportional to the labour put by each and every employee.

The employees must share a good rapport with each other and strive hard to realize the goal of the organization. They should complement each other and work together as a single unit. For the employees, the organization must come first and all their personal interests should take a back seat.

Every individual shares a certain relationship with his colleagues at the workplace. The relationship is either warm, so-so or bad. The relationship can be between any one in the organization - between co workers, between an employee and his superior, between two members in the management and so on. It is important that the employees share a healthy relationship with each other to deliver their best performances.

An individual spends his maximum time at the workplace and his fellow workers are the ones with whom he spends the maximum hours in a day. No way can he afford to fight with his colleagues. Conflicts and misunderstandings only add to tensions and in turn decrease the productivity of the individual. One needs to discuss so many things at work and needs the advice and suggestions of all to reach to a solution which would benefit the individual as well as the organization.

No individual can work alone. He needs the support and guidance of his fellow workers to come out with a brilliant idea and deliver his level best.

Employee relations refer to the relationship shared among the employees in an organization. The employees must be comfortable with each other for a healthy environment at work. It is the prime duty of the superiors and team leaders to discourage conflicts in the team and encourage a healthy relationship among employees.

Life is really short and it is important that one enjoys each and every moment of it.Remember in an organization you are paid for your hard work and not for cribbing or fighting with each other. Don't assume that the person sitting next to you is your enemy or will do any harm to you. Who says you can't make friends at work, infact one can make the best of friends in the office. There is so much more to life than fighting with each other.

Observation says that a healthy relation among the employees goes a long way in motivating the employees and increasing their confidence and morale. One starts enjoying his office and does not take his work as a burden. He feels charged and fresh the whole day and takes each day at work as a new challenge. If you have a good relation with your team members you feel going to office daily. Go out with your team members for a get together once in a while or have your lunch together. These activities help in strengthening the bond among the employees and improve the relations among them.

An employee must try his level best to adjust with each other and compromise to his best extent possible. If you do not agree to any of your fellow worker's ideas, there are several other ways to convince him. Sit with him and probably discuss with him where he is going wrong and needs a correction. This way he would definitely look up to you for your advice and guidance in future. He would trust you and would definitely come to your help whenever you need him. One should never spoil his relations with his colleagues because you never know when you need the other person.

Avoid using foul words or derogatory sentences against anyone. Don't depend on lose talk in office as it spoils the ambience of the place and also the relation among the employees. Blame games are a strict no no in office.

One needs to enter his office with a positive frame of mind and should not unnecessarily make issues out of small things. It is natural that every human being can not think the way you think, or behave the way you behave. If you also behave in the similar way the other person is behaving, there is hardly any difference between you and him. Counsel the other person and correct him wherever he is wrong.

It is of utmost importance that employees behave with each other in a cultured way, respect each other and learn to trust each other. An individual however hardworking he is, cannot do wonders alone. It is essential that all the employees share a cordial relation with each other, understand each other's needs and expectations and work together to accomplish the goals and targets of the organization.

References

- Meaning-of-organizational-communication: thebusinesscommunication.com, Retrieved 23 August, 2019
- Importance-organizational-business-communication-23929: smallbusiness.chron.com, Retrieved 14 February, 2019
- Directions-of-communication-in-the-organization, principles-of-management-and-organisational-behaviour-tutorial -12760: wisdomjobs.com, Retrieved 16 May, 2019
- External-communication, essays-communications: ukessays.com, Retrieved 18 January, 2019
- Communication-forms: iedunote.com, Retrieved 19 August, 2019
- Effects-interpersonal-communication-organization-18338: smallbusiness.chron.com, Retrieved 13 March, 2019
- What-is-employee-relations: managementstudyguide.com, Retrieved 17 April, 2019

4

Technology in Business Communication

Business communication relies on several technologies for the development of business. A few of such technologies are email, Skype, messaging, business phones, video conferencing technology, etc. All these various technologies used in business communication have been carefully analyzed in this chapter.

Role of Technology in Business Communication

Technology in business communication has dramatically changed the workplace over the years and has been improving our daily operations since its existence. It has contributed to making our workplace and workflow more efficient, as well as increasing our productivity.

The digital revolution took place in late 1950s and the entire world noticed this transition from the industrial era. But since this initial transition, there have been hundreds of additional developments in both the technology and business industries. These developments have brought us what is known as technology in business communication; which has been increasing productivity among departments and companies all over the world.

5 Ways Technology in Business Communication has Improved the Workplace

Influential businesses around the globe are aware that technology has reshaped the way we work today. When the digital era first started, the process of adaptation took some time, nonetheless the reward was priceless. These are 5 benefits from technology used in business communications:

- Increased Communication: Do you remember a time at work when you had to send a hand-written letter to your boss who might have worked in a different located due to either travel meetings or important projects? The average respond time could have been days. Today, technology gives us the opportunity to communicate via email, messages, Skype or Face-Time, within minutes and most importantly, from any part of the world.
- Improved Level of Security and distribution: "Back in the day" we used to store piles of paperwork in a locked safety cabinet or safe. Today, technology allows businesses to save up to thousands and thousands of sensitive information and files, encrypt such files and store on a single PC, external hard drive or cloud drive. With a proper antivirus like Avira, and security tips to protect your devices from hacking, the appropriate departments have access to these files and can share among one another within seconds while keeping files safe.
- Visual Quality: Do you remember when you used to write your reports with a typewriter? And you had to do it carefully to keep paper quality? Nowadays, computers have software tools like Word, PowerPoint, and Excel, which can make your reports more visually attractive. As well as correct mistakes as many times as you would like without having to worry about paper issues or constantly restarting.
- Quick, accessible Information: The Internet is another technology used in business communication. Trips to this virtual library can take place within seconds! Getting the information you are looking for has never been easier and/or faster. Have you heard of a single company that doesn't use internet in their daily basis? That's right, today having Internet access is as important as having a computer, because of the accessible information you can get while using it at work, which can increase knowledge and substance different work reports.
- Increased Efficiency: Last but absolutely not least, efficiency. Here is a great example of how technology in business communications has increased efficiency: remember how credit cards used to be put under a carbon paper to get physical impression? We know what you're thinking, it was tedious and it took a while. Additional ways efficiency has increased are; computers are also a handy tool to process data, and employees are working faster than ever and this is making their workflow smoother.

The Development of the Cellular Phone

One of the biggest advancements in communication has been the development of the cellular phone. In the past, your only chance of reaching employees was when they were at their desks, prompting endless games of "phone tag" as people tried to connect during busy workdays. Now, workers are reachable no matter where they are, and even during non-work hours. The development of smartphones has also greatly expanded the types of business activities you can transact when out of the office, increasing productivity and extending the workday.

Other Communication Devices

Phones are not the only high-tech communication devices, of course. Computers come in a wide variety of configurations these days, including tablets, small-but-powerful laptops, 2-in-1 devices that serve as either a laptop or tablet, and other variations. These devices all have built-in wireless capabilities and can also be configured with mobile communications, making them, in essence, large cell phones. Whichever device a business person carries, it facilitates verbal, text and image communications.

Teleconferencing

High-speed data connections allow for the use of teleconferencing, virtual meetings held over audio and video links. Teleconferencing can save substantial amounts of money otherwise spent on travel by connecting important employees in far-flung branches together to share ideas and information. The use of virtual whiteboards, communal data-sharing platforms where remote users can interact as if around the same table, further increase the possibilities of the virtual workplace.

Image Scanning

Document and image scanners allow workers to convert paperwork, plans, diagrams and photos into electronic files quickly for storage and transmission. Instead of relying on hand delivery of important documents across town or across the country, employees can scan and send these files in a matter of seconds across the Internet. An architectural firm could, for instance, scan updates to a plan, transmit it to the client, receive changes and make alterations all before a messenger would have been able to make the first run across town.

Radio Frequency Identification Tags

The development of radio frequency identification (RFID) has substantially changed the field of business logistics and, paired with other business communication advancements, has the potential to increase a company's efficiency significantly. RFID tags are small chips that respond to radio waves with encoded information, allowing companies to tag and track items and materials. When an employee activates a scanning device, all RFID tags within range will respond with their coded information, allowing for quick updates of warehouse inventories and real-time tracking of shipments as they pass through the supply chain. Being able to access inventory on demand allows companies to take advantage of "just-in-time" shipping, providing products and material only when needed to reduce warehousing requirements and reduce the amount of excess stock stored at retail or office facilities.

Importance of Technology in Business

There are infinite reasons why technology is important in business. Whether we like it or not, the role of technology in business is expanding and will only keep growing in the future. Businesses owe it to their operations, employees, and bottom-line to utilize the new technological innovations. Businesses can no longer devalue the importance of technology in business, they must embrace the benefits of technology.

The various reasons for the importance of technology in business are:

Technology Improves Business' Communication

Businesses rely on several aspects of technology for communication such as email, Skype, instant messaging, business phones, video conferencing technology, etc. Communication breakdowns can lead to disasters for businesses and employees. Technology can assist in ensuring that you are prepared for even the most difficult communication obstacles.

Technology Increases Efficiency

It's no secret that there have been some awesome technological advancements in recent years. Advancements such as Lifesize's video conferencing technology and Zulty's VOIP phone cloud solution are strategically designed to improve efficiency and reduce lay time in the office.

New Innovations Protect Important Assets

Cyber attacks are growing at an alarming rate. So too are the amazing cyber-security defenses such as Sophos' Deep Learning technology. In an age where almost all important business assets are stored in the cloud or on endpoints, it is imperative that businesses employ security technology to protect those assets.

Employees Demand it

The role of technology in business is not new, but it is expanding. Employees expect their employers to provide them with the latest and greatest technology which will, in turn, help them be successful in fulfilling their job responsibilities. It is hard to compete against businesses that fully employ technology advancements when your own business is lagging in their technology.

With Technology, there are no Limitations

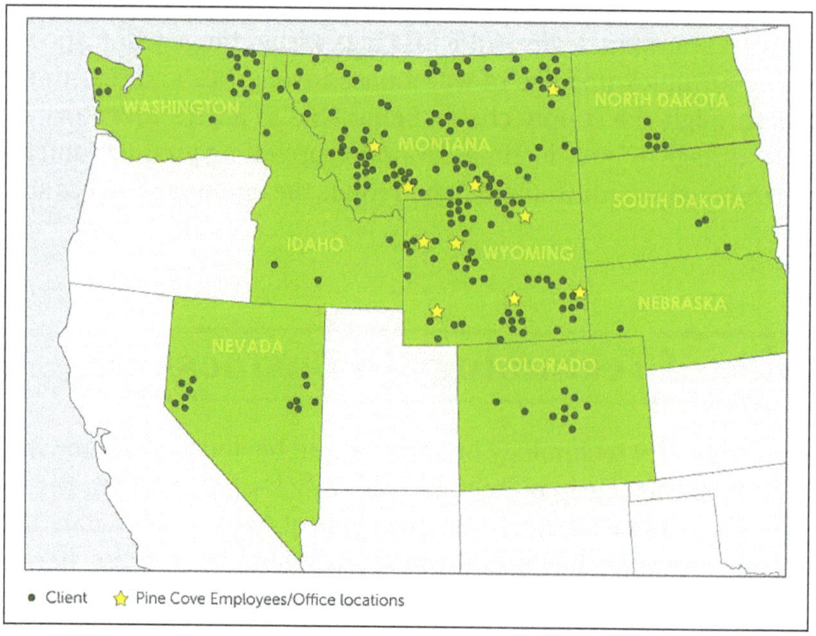

We know this principle is true from first hand experience. We are a company that has 20 employees stationed in 10 different locations across the Northwestern United States. If it wasn't for technology, we simply wouldn't be successful in coordinating all of the employees. Businesses across the nation are are diverse in needs, culture, and education. Advances in technology can help businesses address these differences unlike ever before. There is no limit to what can be accomplished by a business that employs a successful technology plan.

Technology keeps Employees Engaged

Technology keeps employees engaged in many different ways. It allows employees to telecommute to work. It encourages collaboration between coworkers in businesses through tools such as file sharing. It improves communication. It reduces stress by allowing you to schedule important deadlines and meetings on your electronic calendar. It also gives employees flexibility to perform work functions on your mobile device.

Tons of new Resources Exist that can Improve your Business

Technology is growing fast, prices are dropping, and new innovations are being rolled out constantly. If you haven't been consistently looking out for new technology to assist you business, chances are that you have missed something. For example, the Comfort Company implemented video conferencing technology that saved them time and costs while improving relationships and communication. Savage Public Schools discovered the need to totally revamp their technology and have since enjoyed an improved school system. There certainly are technology solutions out there that can improve your business.

Technology is Necessary to Succeed

Whether you like it or not, technology is essential to business success. Employees rely on it for day-to-day operations. Outside companies, clients, and prospective clients evaluate you on your use of technology. HR relies on technology to train and develop employees. Accounting employees rely on technology to complete payroll and execute necessary monetary management functions. Management relies on technology to communicate with those they supervise. Without technology, companies would almost certainly fail to accomplish all that there is to do.

Technology Increases the Capacity of Businesses

Technology allows businesses to reach more people in less time. For example, here at Pine Cove, we use a variety of technology mediums to communicate with our clients, potential clients, and experts in the industry. We use technology to host monthly webinars, to send out e-newsletters, and publish news and blogs. Technology also increases the capacity of businesses to work together through technology such as CRM's.

Technology Saves Time and Money

Lastly, technology now performs many of the mundane tasks that employees used to be expected to perform. This allows employees to focus their time elsewhere on more important duties. This can save money by cutting back on employee expenses and improving productivity.

If you ever find yourself wondering why is technology important? the answer is simple, the role of technology in business is to drive growth and improve operations, along with about a hundred other reasons.

5

Marketing Communication

Marketing communication consists of advertising, societal marketing, direct marketing, events and experiences, public relations and publicity, brand management, interactive marketing, personal selling, etc. This chapter closely examines the concepts under marketing communication to provide an extensive understanding of the subject.

Marketing

Marketing is a business term that experts have defined in dozens of different ways. In fact, even at company level people may perceive the term differently. Basically, it is a management process through which products and services move from concept to the customer. It includes identification of a product, determining demand, deciding on its price, and selecting distribution channels. It also includes developing and implementing a promotional strategy.

Marketing refers to the activities of a business related to buying and selling a product or service. It involves finding out what consumers want and determining whether it is possible to produce it at the right price. The company then makes and sells it.

Marketing covers a vast area of business, including:

- How you communicate,
- The brand,

- The design,
- Pricing,
- Market research,
- Consumer psychology,
- Measuring effectiveness.

At the core of marketing is an understanding of what customers need and value. A company's long-term success depends on learning what its customers' needs are. It then finds ways to add value through different approaches.

Business-to-business Marketing

This involves targeting other businesses. We also call it business-to-business or B2B marketing. It involves supplying other companies with products or services.

Physical products that companies sell to other businesses are *'industrial goods.'* Industrial goods may include raw materials for companies that make plastics, yarn for use in the textile trade. It also includes aircraft for airlines and the military.

In fact, the term 'industrial goods' refers anything a company or organization needs and buys.

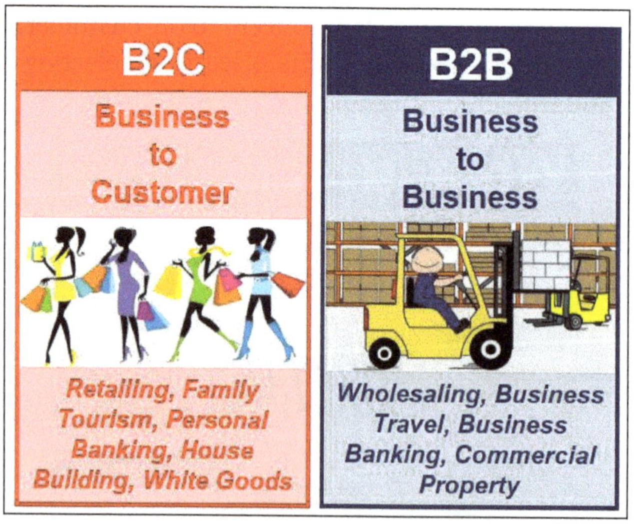

We can aim marketing at businesses (B2B) or individual consumers (B2C).

B2B services may include legal advice, management consultancy, tax consultancy, or training provision. IT services and the provision of temporary staff are also examples of B2B services. IT stands for Information Technology.

Marketing Directly to Consumers

We also call it B2C. The term refers to targeting the individual people who purchase products and use services. Specifically, people who bought for their own consumption.

This may include FMCGs (fast-moving consumer goods) such as food, beverages, and toiletries, or durable goods. For example, cars, televisions, refrigerators and other white goods are durable goods. 'White goods' are major appliances that traditionally have had a white enamel surface.

B2B + B2C Marketing

Most large corporations have an *integrated marketing approach.* In other words, they focus on both individual consumers and businesses at the same time.

The Coca-Cola company, for example, knows that its B2C marketing must succeed. Put simply; it has to persuade supermarkets and smaller stores – B2B – to provide shelf space.

Most makers of durable goods also have an integrated marketing approach. For example, The Haier Group focuses on individual consumers (B2C). However, it also focuses on supermarkets, department stores, and other retail outlets (B2B). The Haier Group is world's largest manufacturer of consumer electronics and home appliances.

Recruitment Marketing

Recruitment marketing includes all the tools and strategies that employers use to engage, attract, and eventually hire talented people. The aim is to encourage people to want to join the organization.

The practice takes advantage of data analytics, omnichannel communication, social media platforms, and other digital marketing strategies.

"Recruitment marketing is the process of trying to attract and hire talented people. It includes the strategies and tactics that employers use to attract, engage, and nurture talented personnel before they apply for a job."

Marketing Management

Marketing management is the process of planning & implementing the conception, pricing, promotion and distribution of products or services. It is a target-oriented process and an operational area of management.

Marketing management is basically an organizational discipline, which focuses on the practical usage of marketing orientation, techniques and methodologies in companies and organizations and on the management of a firm's marketing resources and activities.

The following are the main objectives of marketing management:

- To satisfy the clients' requirements and their objectives.
- To leverage the gain for the growth of business.
- To develop customer base for the business.
- To create an appropriate marketing mix.
- To raise the quality of life of people.

- To build a good image of the organization.
- To maintain the long-run concept.

Marketing Management - Process

Marketing process includes ways in which value can be created for the customers to satisfy their requirements. It is an endless series of actions and reactions between the customers and the companies making attempt to create value for and satisfy the needs of customers.

In marketing process, the situation is examined to identify opportunities, the strategy is formulated for a value proposition, tactical decisions are taken, plan is executed, and results are monitored.

The following four steps are involved in the marketing process:

Situation Analysis

Analysis of the situation in which the company finds itself serves as the basis for identifying chances to satisfy unfulfilled customer needs.

Situational and environmental analysis is done to identify the marketing options, to understand the company's own capabilities and to understand the surroundings in which the company is operating.

Marketing Strategy

After identifying the marketing options available, a strategic plan is developed to pursue the identified options. An analysis is done and the best available option is chosen; a plan or strategy is made for that option.

Marketing Mix Decisions

At this step, elaborated tactical decisions are made for the controllable parameters of the marketing mix. It includes decisions related to product development, product pricing, product distribution and product promotion.

Implementation and Control

Finally, the marketing plan is executed and the outputs of marketing efforts are monitored to adjust the marketing mix according to the market changes.

This being the final step, it transforms the written or planned strategy into action and the product is presented according to this process.

Marketing Management - Functions

We need to understand the major functions of marketing management in order to understand and groom our organization. The following are some of the major functions of marketing management –

- Selling,
- Buying and Assembling,

- Transportation,
- Storage,
- Standardization and Grading,
- Financing,
- Risk Taking,
- Market Information.

The marketing process performs certain activities as the products and services move from the producer to consumer. All these activities or jobs are not performed by every company.

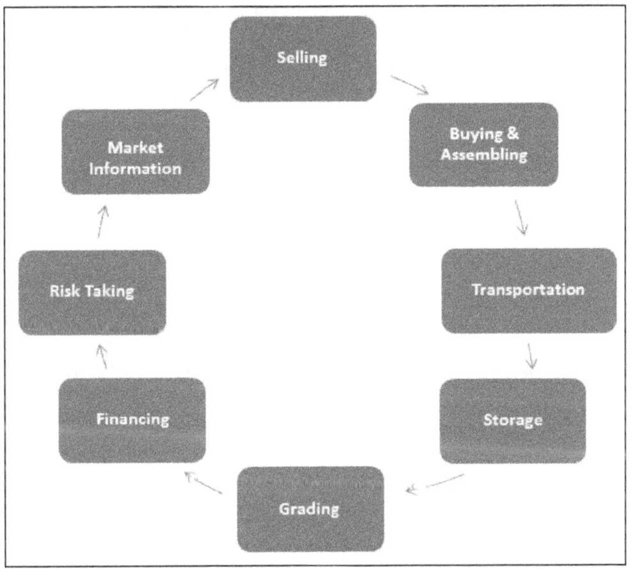

Nonetheless, it is recommended that they be carried out by any company that wants its marketing systems to function successfully.

Selling

Selling is the crux of marketing. It involves convincing the prospective buyers to actually complete the purchase of an article. It includes transfer of ownership of products to the buyer.

Selling plays a very vital part in realizing the ultimate aim of earning profit. Selling is groomed by means of personal selling, advertising, publicity and sales promotion. Effectiveness and efficiency in selling determines the volume of the firm's profits and profitability.

Buying and Assembling

It deals with what to buy, of what quality, how much from whom, when and at what price. People in business purchase to increase sales or to decrease costs. Purchasing agents are much tempted by quality, service and price. The products that the retailers buy for resale are selected as per the requirements and preferences of their customers.

Assembling means buying necessary component parts and to fit them together to make a product. 'Assembly line' marks a production line made up of purely assembly functions. The assembly operation includes the arrival of individual component parts at the work place and issuing of these parts for assembling.

Assembly line is an arrangement of employees and machines in which each individual has a particular job and the work is passed directly from one employee to the next until the product is complete.

Transportation

Transportation is the physical means through which products are moved from the places where they are produced to those places where they are needed for consumption. It creates locational utility.

Transportation is very important from the procurement of raw material to the delivery of finished products to the customer's places. Transportation depends mainly on railroads, trucks, waterways, pipelines and airways.

Storage

It includes holding of products in proper, i.e., usable or saleable, condition from the time they are produced until they are required by customers in case of finished products or by the production department in case of raw materials and stores.

Storing protects the products from deterioration and helps in carrying over surplus for future consumption or usage in production.

Standardization and Grading

Standardization means setting up of certain standards or specifications for products based on the intrinsic physical qualities of any item. This may include quantity like weight and size or quality like color, shape, appearance, material, taste, sweetness etc. A standard gives rise to uniformity of products.

Grading means classification of standardized items into certain well defined classes or groups. It includes the division of products into classes made of units possessing similar features of size and quality.

Grading is very essential for raw materials; agricultural products like fruits and cereals; mining products like coal, iron and manganese and forest products like timber.

Financing

Financing involves the application of the capital to meet the financial requirements of agencies dealing with various activities of marketing. The services to ensure the credit and money needed and the costs of getting merchandise into the hands of the final user are mostly referred to as the finance function in marketing.

Financing is required for the working capital and fixed capital, which may be secured from three sources — owned capital, bank loans and advance & trade credit. In other words, different kinds of finances are short-term, medium-term, and long-term finance.

Risk Taking

Risk means loss due to some unforeseen situations. Risk bearing in marketing means the financial risk invested in the ownership of goods held for an anticipated demand, including the possible losses because of fall in prices and the losses from spoilage, depreciation, obsolescence, fire and floods or any other loss that may occur with the passage of time.

They may also be due to decay, deterioration and accidents or due to fluctuation in the prices induced by changes in supply and demand. The different risks are usually termed as place risk, time risk, physical risk, etc.

Market Information

The importance of this facilitating function of marketing has been recently marked. The only sound foundation on which marketing decisions depend is timely and correct market information.

Societal Marketing

The societal marketing is a marketing concept that holds that a company should make marketing decisions not only by considering consumers' wants, the company's requirements, but also society's long-term interests.

The societal marketing concept holds that the organization's task is to determine the needs, wants, and interests of a target market and to deliver the desired satisfactions more effectively and efficiently than competitors in a way that preserves or enhances the well being of both the individual consumer and society in general. Therefore, marketers must endeavor to satisfy the needs and wants of their target markets in ways that preserve and enhance the well-being of consumers and society as a whole. It is closely linked with the principles of corporate social responsibility and of sustainable development.

Societal marketing can be defined as a "marketing with a social dimension or marketing that includes non-economic criteria". Societal marketing "concerns for society's long term interests". It is about "the direct benefits for the organization and secondary benefit for the community". Societal marketing distinguishes between the consumer's immediate satisfaction and longer term consumer and social benefits. Accordingly, Andreas Kaplan defines societal management as "management that takes into account society's overall welfare in addition to mere profitability considerations." It is a 3 dimensional concept of marketing – social welfare, individual welfare, company profits.

Objectives

Various attempts to define the objectives of societal marketing have been noted, such as:

- "Social responsibility implies that a business decision maker is obliged to take actions that also protect and enhance society's interests."
- "Business has the responsibility to help (the consumer). It is the duty of business to promote proper consumption values."
- "Business leaders are mandated to adopt roles of leadership in the advancement of our society to new levels of moral conduct."

Instruments

Kotler identified four categories of products, classified in terms of long term benefits and immediate satisfaction:

Cigarettes are typically classified as a *pleasing products* since they deliver immediate benefits with long-term social harm.

- Deficient products, which bring neither long-run or short term benefits.
- Pleasing products, which bring a high level of immediate satisfaction, but can cause harm to the society in the long run.
- Salutary products, which bring low short term satisfaction, but benefit the society in the long run.
- Desirable products, which combine long-run benefit and immediate satisfaction.

Kotler's concept of societal marketing suggested that for the well-being of society, deficient products should be eliminated from the market, pleasing and salutary products should go through a product modification process to acquire desirable status, by incorporating missing short term benefits into salutary products and long term benefits into pleasing products, and the companies' ultimate goal should be to develop desirable products. Rather than focusing on selling products, which can be good or bad for the consumers, companies should focus on consumer and society's well-being.

Examples:

Most companies recognize that socially responsible activities improve their image among customers, stockholders, the financial community, and other relevant publics. Ethical and socially responsible practices are simply good business, resulting not only in favorable image, but ultimately in increased sales.

- The Body Shop: The Body Shop International plc is the original, natural and cthical beauty brand. The company uses only plant-based materials for its products. It is against Animal testing, supports community trade, activate Self Esteem, Defend Human Rights, and overall protection of the planet. They have also their own charity, The Body Shop Foundation, to assist those working to achieve progress in the areas of human and civil rights, environmental and animal protection. Thus Body shop is really following the concept of Societal Marketing.
- AVON Product inc. has started an initiative known as Avon breast cancer awareness crusade in 1993 in partnership with National Alliance of breast cancer Foundation (NABCO). They started selling pink ribbon pins which depicts the international symbol for breast cancer for $2 and donates $1 to NABCO. Through the crusade, Avon sales representatives have raised billion of dollars for breast cancer education and access to early detection services for underserved women. In addition, Avon's 45,000 US salespeople have been trained to discuss breast cancer and the importance of early detection with their customers and distributed 80 million flyers on breast cancer detection.

Societal Marketing vs. Social Marketing

Societal marketing should not be confused with social marketing. Societal marketing is a philosophy or mindset that informs marketing decisions whereas social marketing is a distinct branch within the marketing discipline. Societal marketing is concerned with the consideration of the social and ethical aspects of marketing planning. Social marketing is concerned with facilitating social change. A key difference is that the greater 'social good' is the *principal* consideration in social marketing while social benefits are one of a number of considerations in societal marketing.

On the other hand, social marketing is a sub-branch of marketing that began in 1971 emphasising a planned approach to achieving social change. It is primarily concerned with encouraging pro-social behaviours (e.g. recycling, sun-safety, safe driving practices) and discouraging anti-social behaviours (e.g. littering, drink-driving). It is defined as an "adaptation of commercial marketing technologies to programs designed to influence the voluntary behavior of target audiences to improve their personal welfare and that of the society of which they are a part".

Social marketing uses more traditional commercial techniques and strategies, focusing on persuasion, to achieve goals for the greater social good. Its campaigns can either encourage merit goods, as for example fundraising for not-for-profit organizations or dissuade the use of demerit goods promoting society's well being, as non-smoking campaigns or promote the use of seat belts. Another characteristic of social marketing is that is planned to influence individual behaviour to improve well-being. It includes more than just advertising in traditional mass media, and may extend to educational programs and formal enforcement regimes in the case of road safety campaigns. It planned campaigns, implemented by governmental and non-governmental organisations. A clear example that differentiates societal from social marketing is a marketing campaign on non-smoking. A smoking cessation advertisement is an example of social marketing, but if the marketing strategies and techniques used in that campaign focus on increasing the well-being of society, that same campaign can be an example of societal marketing.

The societal marketing concept was a forerunner of sustainable marketing in integrating issues of social responsibility into commercial marketing strategies. In contrast to that, social marketing uses commercial marketing theories, tools and techniques to influence social change. Social marketing applies a "customer orientated" approach and uses the concepts and tools used by commercial marketers in pursuit of social goals like Anti-Smoking-Campaigns or fundraising for NGOs.

Corporate Social Responsibility (CSR)

Unlike societal marketing, CSR has existed for many years. Another difference is that CSR "focuses more in a corporate level and stakeholders", while societal marketing is more concerned about the consumer and their long term benefits. CSR social and environmental concerns are integrated into all business operations. CSR is mainly run by companies, while social marketing mainly by government or non-profit organizations. One example of CSR among companies is what Häagen-Dazs is doing with their "microsite" to raise awareness to the general public about the preservation of the honeybee.

Branding

Corporations are the one who are striving during the whole time for improvements. They are turning to all kind of forms of corporate societal marketing programs to help build and repair their brand images.

Corporate Social Marketing, or CSM, usually refers to marketing efforts that have at least one social related objective, such as charity founding, among its goals. Typical examples are releasing a certain percentage of the final sale product to a charity related to the product, or sponsoring events that encourage social well-being such as the Olympic Games. Corporate Social Marketing benefits a company in many ways, but its main goal is to improve the image the public has of the company. A company that appears committed to improving the lives of others, the environment or other worthy causes is seen in a better light than one who doesn't, and more and more business are hoping to benefit from that.

So, it can be so, that CSM programs are becoming extremely popular because the leaders believe that it is a good business to be viewed as a socially responsible company. However, even though past research suggests that CSM may be effective in improving brand equity and increasing market share, there are limits to the effectiveness of these initiatives.

An example of his is how corporate social initiatives adversely affected purchase intentions if consumers perceived that the company would forgo product quality in order to be socially responsible.

Depending on the nature of the CSM program, the intent of the corporation may not be as obvious to the consumers. This happens if the benefits to the corporation are not apparent or conflicts with what the consumer already believes about a specific firm or industry.

Since firms exist to make a profit, consumers may spend considerable energy in an attempt to infer motives related to the profit-oriented goals. As an example, a consumer may be suspicious of a tobacco company that undertakes a campaign to prevent underage smoking. If this is successful, the company would be affected and the cigarette sales will be lowered. So, in this situation, consumers' suspicions may lead them to infer motives that would actually protect the companies financial condition – as they are trying to improve their image to sell more cigarettes to adults. However, if a tobacco company undertook a CSM Campaign, that would sustain their business, consumers may be able to infer profit motives more easily and then have a more favorable attitude toward the partnership. Therefore, it can be concluded that the attitude of the consumers could be better if they knew more about the motives of the companies and they were more obvious.

Another aspect that may cause suspicion with consumers is the amount of harm that a company has already done, either because of unsafe products or harmful production practices. It is logical that consumers are more suspicious to companies that sell harmful products. Again examples are the tobacco companies and alcohol companies as well. They will meet resistance from consumers when they undertake socially-oriented campaigns aimed at mitigating the effects of their products. That is why when different industries are separated, two very general dimensions are used – the harmful nature of the products and the harmful nature of the production methods.

This classification can briefly show how consumers are influenced by the various CSM efforts. Companies that work in this "dangerous" industries are not that successful always, because the consumers may be suspicious of any societal efforts the company attempts to undertake. Consumers will infer less society-serving motives and more self-serving motives for corporate societal marketing programs undertaken by firms that operate in mixed or sin industries.

Based on how easily consumers could infer profit-driven motives, are classified the types of CSM campaigns: Positively tied to product sales, not directly tied to sales but aimed at sustaining the company's business, completely unrelated.

Direct Marketing

Direct marketing is a form of communicating an offer, where organizations communicate directly to a pre-selected customer and supply a method for a direct response. Among practitioners, it is also known as direct respo*nse marketing*. By contrast, advertising is of a mass-message nature.

Lester Wunderman, the founder of Wunderman, Ricotta & Kline, coined the phrase *Direct Marketing* in 1958.

Response channels include 800-numbers, reply cards, reply forms to be sent in an envelope, websites and email addresses.

The prevalence of direct marketing and the unwelcome nature of some communications has led to regulations and laws such as the CAN-SPAM Act, requiring that consumers in the United States be allowed to opt out.

A pile of advertising mail.

Intended targets are selected from larger populations based on vendor-defined criteria, including average income for a particular ZIP code, purchasing history and presence on other lists. The goal is "to sell directly to consumers" without letting others "join the parade."

A study by the Direct Marketing Association reports that in 2010, marketers—commercial and nonprofit—spent $153.3 billion on direct marketing, which accounted for 54.2% of all ad expenditures in the United States. Measured against total US sales, these advertising expenditures generated approximately $1.798 trillion in incremental sales. In 2010, direct marketing accounted for 8.3% of total US gross domestic product. In 2010, there were 1.4 million direct marketing employees in the US. Their collective sales efforts directly supported 8.4 million other jobs, accounting for a total of 9.8 million US jobs.

Benefits

Direct marketing is attractive to many marketers because its results, positive or otherwise, can be measured directly. For example, if a marketer sends out 1,000 solicitations by mail and 100 respond to the promotion, the marketer can say with confidence that campaign led directly to a 10% conversion. This metric is known as the 'response rate', and it is one of many clearly quantifiable success metrics employed by direct marketers. In contrast, general advertising uses indirect measurements, such as awareness or engagement, since there is no direct response from a consumer. Measurement of results is a fundamental element in successful direct marketing.

One of the other significant benefits of direct marketing is that it enables promoting products or services that might not be known to consumers. Products or service with a sound value proposition, matched with an attractive offer, supported with effective communication, delivered through a suitable direct marketing channel and targeting the relevant customer segment can result in a very effective cost of acquisition. Relative to other channels of distribution (say retailing) direct marketing as a practice principally relies on the proposition, offer, communication, choice of channel and the target customer and so less dependent on the brand strength. Despite the proven ability of direct marketing to generate measurable results, most companies continue to use general or branding advertising to market their products or services.

The Internet has made it easier for marketing managers to measure the results of a campaign. This is often achieved by using a specific website landing page directly relating to the promotional material. A call to action will ask the customer to visit the landing page, and the effectiveness of the campaign can be measured by taking the number of promotional messages distributed and dividing it into the number of responses. Another way to measure the results is to compare the projected sales or generated leads for a given term with the actual sales or leads after a direct advertising campaign. Some companies use conversion rate as a key metric while others use revenue as the key metric.

Role of Copywriters and other Creatives

Copywriters write the words that motivate the reader, listener, or viewer to take the action the marketer wants them to take. Copywriters in direct marketing are called direct response copywriters.

Although they have a specific skill-set based on proven direct marketing techniques, directed by the goal of motivating prospects to take a specific action, they also require a general and branding advertising focus on making current and potential customers feel a certain way about the product or service, and need the creativity shown in work such as "Don't treat your puppy like a dog" (Ralston Purina dog food) or the "Pick-UPS" portion of 1-800-PICKUPS.

Graphic designers, web developers, and other creatives also play a crucial role in successful direct marketing.

Challenges and Solutions

List brokers provide names and contact information, but their services need to be contrasted to expected "return on investment."

Success can vary based on factors such as:

- Offer (best offer may yield up to 3 times the response, as compared with the worst offer).
- Timing (best timing for the campaign may yield up to 2 times the response, as compared with the worst timing).
- Ease of response (best/multiple ways offered to respond may yield up to 1.35 times the response, as compared with not-so-friendly response mechanism/s).

- Creativity.
- Media employed: The medium/media used to deliver a message can have a significant impact on responses. It is difficult to truly personalize a DRTV or radio message. One can even attempt to send a personalized message via email or text message, but a high quality direct mail envelope and letter will typically have a better chance of generated a response in this scenario.

Some direct marketers use of individual "opt-out" lists, variable printing, and better-targeted list practices to improve success percentages. Additionally, in order to avoid unwanted mailings, members of the marketing industry have established preference services that give customers more control over the marketing communications they receive in the mail.

The term "junk mail", referring to unsolicited commercial ads delivered via post office or directly deposited in consumers' mail boxes, can be traced back to 1954. The term "spam," meaning "unsolicited commercial e-mail," can be traced back to March 31, 1993, although in its first few months it merely referred to inadvertently posting a message so many times on UseNet that the repetitions effectively drowned out the normal flow of conversation.

To address the concerns of unwanted emails or spam, in 2003, The US Congress enacted the Controlling the Assault of Non-Solicited Pornography and Marketing (CAN-SPAM) Act to curb unwanted email messages. Can-Spam gives recipients the ability to stop unwanted emails, and set out tough penalties for violations. Additionally, ISPs and email service providers have developed increasingly effective Email Filtering programs. These filters can interfere with the delivery of email marketing campaigns, even if the person has subscribed to receive them, as legitimate email marketing can possess the same hallmarks as spam. There are a range of email service providers that provide services for legitimate opt-in emailers to avoid being classified as spam.

Consumers have expressed concerns about the privacy and environmental implications of direct marketing. In response to consumer demand and increasing business pressure to increase the effectiveness of reaching the right customer with direct marketing, companies specialize in targeted direct advertising to great effect, reducing advertising budget waste and increasing the effectiveness of delivering a marketing message with better geo-demography information, delivering the advertising message to only the customers interested in the product, service, or event on offer. Additionally, members of the advertising industry have been working to adopt stricter codes regarding online targeted advertising.

Channels

Channels available include a variety of media: cell phone text messaging, email, websites, online adverts, database marketing, fliers, catalog distribution, promotional letters. Use of Television advertisements, newspapers, magazine advertisements, and outdoor advertising are not *direct*, although they may have a *direct response* aspect, such as an 800-number.

Email Marketing

Sending marketing messages through email or email marketing is one of the most widely used direct-marketing methods. One reason for email marketing's popularity is that it is relatively inexpensive to design, test, and send an email message. It also allows marketers to deliver messages around the clock, and to accurately measure responses.

Online Tools

With the expansion of digital technology and tools, direct marketing is increasingly taking place through online channels. Most online advertising is delivered to a focused group of customers and has a trackable response.

- Display Ads are interactive ads that appear on the Web next to content on Web pages or Web services. Formats include static banners, pop ups, videos, and floating units. Customers can click on the ad to respond directly to the message or to find more detailed information. According to research by eMarketer, Display Advertising, including Social Media display ads, was 45.9% of all ad spending in 2018, and is expected to grow to 60.5% of ad spending by 2023.
- Search: 49% of US spending on Internet ads goes to search, in which advertisers pay for prominent placement among listings in search engines whenever a potential customer enters a relevant search term, allowing ads to be delivered to customers based upon their already-indicated search criteria. This paid placement industry generates more than $10 billion for search companies. Marketers also use search engine optimization to drive traffic to their sites.
- Social Media Sites: Such as Facebook and Twitter, also provide opportunities for direct marketers to communicate directly with customers by creating content to which customers can respond.

Mobile

Through mobile marketing, marketers engage with prospective customers and donors in an interactive manner through a mobile device or network, such as a cellphone, smartphone, or tablet. Types of mobile marketing messages include: *SMS* (short message service)—marketing communications are sent in the form of text messages, also known as texting. *MMS* (multi-media message service)—marketing communications are sent in the form of media messages.

In October 2013, the Federal Telephone Consumers Protection Act made it illegal to contact an individual via cell phone without prior express written consent for all telephone calls using an automatic telephone dialing system or a prerecorded voice to deliver a telemarketing message (known as Robocall) to wireless numbers and residential lines. An existing business relationship does not provide an exception to this requirement.

Mobile Applications: Smartphone-based mobile apps contain several types of messages. Push Notifications are direct messages sent to a user either automatically or as part of a campaign. They include transactional, marketing, geo-based, and more. Rich Push Notifications are full HTML Push Notifications. Mobile apps also contain Interactive ads that appear inside the mobile application or app.

Location-Based Marketing: marketing messages delivered directly to a mobile device based on the user's location.

QR Codes (quick-response barcodes): This is a type of 2D barcode with an encoded link that can be accessed from a smartphone. This technology is increasingly being used for everything from special offers to product information.

Mobile Banner Ads. Like standard banner ads for desktop Web pages but smaller to fit on mobile screens and run on the mobile content network.

Telemarketing

Another common form of direct marketing is telemarketing, in which marketers contact customers by phone. The primary benefit to businesses is increased lead generation, which helps businesses increase sales volume and customer base. The most successful telemarketing service providers focus on generating more "qualified" leads that have a higher probability of getting converted into actual sales.

In the United States, the National Do Not Call Registry was created in 2003 to offer consumers a choice whether to receive telemarketing calls at home. The FTC created the National Do Not Call Registry after a comprehensive review of the Telemarketing Sales Rule (TSR). The do-not-call provisions of the TSR cover any plan, program, or campaign to sell goods or services through interstate phone calls.

The 2012 modification, which went into effect on October 16, 2013, stated that prior express written consent will be required for all autodialed and pre-recorded calls/texts sent/made to cell phone; and for pre-recorded calls made to residential land lines for marketing purposes.

Further, a consumer who does not wish to receive further prerecorded telemarketing calls can "opt out" of receiving such calls by dialing a telephone number (required to be provided in the prerecorded message) to register his or her do-not-call request. The provisions do not cover calls from political organizations or charities.

Canada has its own National Do Not Call List (DNCL). In other countries it is voluntary, such as the New Zealand Name Removal Service.

Voicemail Marketing

Voicemail marketing emerged from the market prevalence of personal voice mailboxes, and business voicemail systems. One particular form is known as Ringless voicemail. Voice-mail courier is a similar form of voice-mail marketing with both business-to-business and business-to-consumer applications.

Broadcast Faxing

Broadcast faxing, in which faxes are sent to multiple recipients, is now less common than in the past. This is partly due to laws in the United States and elsewhere which regulate its use for consumer marketing. In 2005, President Bush signed into law S.714, the Junk Fax Prevention Act of 2005 (JFPA), which allows marketers to send commercial faxes to those with whom they have an established business relationship (EBR), but imposes some new requirements. These requirements include providing an opt-out notice on the first page of faxes and establishing a system to accept opt-outs at any time of the day. Roughly 2% of direct marketers use fax, mostly for business-to-business marketing campaigns.

Couponing

Couponing is used in print and digital media to elicit a response from the reader. An example is a coupon which the reader receives through the mail and takes to a store's check-out counter to receive a discount.

Digital Coupons: Manufacturers and retailers make coupons available online for electronic orders that can be downloaded and printed. Digital coupons are available on company websites, social media outlets, texts, and email alerts. There are an increasing number of mobile phone applications offering digital coupons for direct use.

Daily Deal Sites offer local and online deals each day, and are becoming increasingly popular. Customers sign up to receive notice of discounts and offers, which are sent daily by email. Purchases are often made using a special coupon code or promotional code. The largest of these sites, Groupon, has over 83 million subscribers.

Direct Response Marketing

Direct Response Marketing is designed to generate an immediate response from consumers, where each consumer response (and purchase) can be measured, and attributed to individual advertisements. This form of marketing is differentiated from other marketing approaches, primarily because there are no intermediaries such as retailers between the buyer and seller, and therefore the buyer must contact the seller directly to purchase products or services. Direct-response marketing is delivered through a wide variety of media, including DRTV, radio, mail, print advertising, telemarketing, catalogues, and the Internet.

Direct Response Mail Order

Mail order in which customers respond by mailing a completed order form to the marketer. Mail order direct response has become more successful in recent years due to internet exposure.

Direct Response Television

Direct marketing via television (commonly referred to as DRTV) has two basic forms: long form (usually half-hour or hour-long segments that explain a product in detail and are commonly referred to as infomercials) and short form, which refers to typical 30-second or 60-second commercials that ask viewers for an immediate response (typically to call a phone number on screen or go to a website). TV-response marketing—i.e. infomercials—can be considered a form of direct marketing, since responses are in the form of calls to telephone numbers given on-air. This allows marketers to reasonably conclude that the calls are due to a particular campaign, and enables them to obtain customers' phone numbers as targets for telemarketing. One of the most famous DRTV commercials was for Ginsu Knives by Ginsu Products, Inc. of Rhode Island. Several aspects of ad, such as its use of adding items to the offer and the guarantee of satisfaction were much copied, and came to be considered part of the formula for success with short-form direct-response TV ads (DRTV).

Forms of direct response marketing on television include standard short form television commercials, infomercials and home shopping networks. Short-form direct-response commercials have time lengths ranging from 30 seconds to 2 minutes. Long form infomercials are typically 30 minutes long. An offshoot of the infomercial is the home shopping industry. In this medium, items can potentially be offered with reduced overhead.

Direct Response Radio

In direct response radio, ads contain a call to action with a specific tracking mechanism. Often, this tracking mechanism is a "call now" prompt with a toll-free phone number or a unique Web URL. Results of the ad can be tracked in terms of calls, orders, customers, leads, sales, revenue, and profits that result from the airing of those ads.

Direct Response Magazines and Newspapers

Magazine and newspaper ads often include a direct response call-to-action, such as a toll-free number, a coupon redeemable at a brick-and-mortar store, or a QR code that can be scanned by a mobile device—these methods are all forms of direct marketing, because they elicit a direct and measurable action from the customer.

By 1982, "the rising cost of an industrial sales call" (compared to 1971) led to business press outlets becoming a "primary reference for buying."

Other Direct Response Media

Other media, such as magazines, newspapers, radio, social media, search engine marketing and e-mail can be used to elicit the response. A survey of large corporations found e-mail to be one of the most effective forms of direct response.

Direct Mail

The term *advertising*, or *direct mail*, is used to refer to communications sent to potential customers or donors via the postal service and other delivery services. Direct mail is sent to customers based on criteria such as age, income, location, profession, buying pattern, etc. Direct mail includes advertising circulars, catalogs, free-trial CDs, pre-approved credit card applications, and other unsolicited merchandising invitations delivered by mail to homes and businesses. Bulk mailings are a particularly popular method of promotion for businesses operating in the financial services, home computer, and travel and tourism industries.

In many developed countries, direct mail represents such a significant amount of the total volume of mail that special rate classes have been established. In the United States and United Kingdom, for example, there are bulk mail rates that enable marketers to send mail at rates that are substantially lower than regular first-class rates. In order to qualify for these rates, marketers must format and sort the mail in particular ways—which reduces the handling (and therefore costs) required by the postal service. In the US, marketers send over 90 billion pieces of direct mail per year.

Advertisers often refine direct mail practices into targeted mailing, in which mail is sent out following database analysis to select recipients considered most likely to respond positively.

For example, a person who has demonstrated an interest in golf may receive direct mail for golf-related products or perhaps for goods and services that are appropriate for golfers. This use of database analysis is a type of database marketing. The United States Postal Service calls this form of mail "advertising mail" (admail for short).

In 1983, 15.1% of US postal revenue came from direct mail.

Insert Media

Another form of direct marketing, insert media are marketing materials that are inserted into other communications, such as a catalog, newspaper, magazine, package, or bill. Coop or shared mail, where marketing offers from several companies are delivered via a single envelope, is also considered insert media.

Out-of-home

Out-of-home direct marketing refers to a wide array of media designed to reach the consumer outside the home, including billboards, transit, bus shelters, bus benches, aerials, airports, in-flight, in-store, movies, college campus/high schools, hotels, shopping malls, sport facilities, stadiums, taxis—that contain a call-to-action for the customer to respond.

Direct Selling

Direct selling is the sale of products by face-to-face contact with the customer, either by having salespeople approach potential customers in person, or through indirect means such as Tupperware parties.

Grassroots/Community Marketing

Grassroots marketing involves advertising in the local community. The goal is to involve the community in discussions about the business through local events, meetings, and projects.

Ethical Conduct

The ICC Consolidated Code of Advertising and Marketing relates to all direct marketing activities in their entirety, whatever their form, medium or content. It sets the standards of ethical conduct to be followed by marketers, practitioners or other contractors providing services for direct marketing purposes or in the media.

The Offer

The fulfillment of any obligation arising from a direct marketing activity should be prompt and efficient.

Whenever an offer is made, all the commitments to be fulfilled by the marketer, the operator and the consumer should be made clear to consumers, either directly or by reference to sales conditions available to them at the time of the offer.

Presentation

When the presentation of an offer also features products not included in the offer, or where additional products need to be purchased to enable the consumer to use the product on offer, this should be made clear in the original offer.

High-pressure tactics which might be construed as harassment should be avoided, and, marketers should ensure that they respect local culture and tradition to avoid offensive questions.

Right of Withdrawal

Where consumers have a right of withdrawal (the consumer's right to resend any goods to the seller, or to cancel the order for services, within a certain time limit and thus annulling the sale), the marketer should inform them of the existence of this right, how to obtain further information about it, and how to exercise it. Where there is an offer to supply products to the consumer on the basis of "free examination", "free trial", "free approval" and the like, it should be made clear in the offer who will bear the cost of returning products and the procedure for returning them should be as simple as possible. Any time limit for the return should be clearly disclosed.

Identity of the Marketer

The identity of the marketer and operator and details of where and how they may be contacted should be given in the offer, so as to enable the consumer to communicate directly and effectively with them. This information should be available as a permanent reference which the consumer can keep, i.e. via a separate document offline, an online document, email or SMS; it should not, for example, appear only on an order form which the consumer is required to return. At the time of delivery of the product, the marketer's full name, address and telephone number should be supplied to the consumer.

Respecting Consumer Wishes

Where consumers have indicated the wish not to receive direct marketing communications by signing on to a preference service, or in any other way, this should be respected. Marketers who are communicating with consumers internationally should, where possible ensure that they avail themselves of the appropriate preference service in the markets to which they are addressing their communications and respect consumers' wishes not to receive such communications. Where a system exists, enabling consumers to indicate a wish not to receive unaddressed mail (e.g. mailbox stickers), this should be respected.

Responsibility

Overall responsibility for all aspects of direct marketing activities, whatever their kind or content, rests with the marketer. However, responsibility also applies to other participants in direct marketing activities and that needs to be taken into account. As well as marketers, these may include: operators, telemarketers or data controllers, or their subcontractors, who contribute to the activity or communication; publishers, media-owners or contractors who publish, transmit or distribute the offer or any other communication.

Interactive Marketing

Interactive marketing is a new direction of work with end-users, assuming direct participation of the consumer in the advertising campaign. Interactive marketing includes the enormous possibilities of Internet resources such as games, contests, social networks and other related services. By itself, interactive marketing is a form of direct marketing. However, taking into account its wide distribution in the world at present, it is fair to single out interactive marketing in an independent form of marketing communications. An important role of interactive marketing is the dissemination in the online space of a convincing brand image for consumers.

The Internet and search tools today make information search easy. And this means that any information can spread in the blink of an eye in a viral way everywhere. Therefore, today it is interactive marketing that becomes the central nervous system of many marketing campaigns. And it is online tools that have unprecedented speed and efficiency in determining the place of the campaign and its reputation in the market. The Internet is the channel that conveys consumer expectations and their sensitivity to brands.

Example of Interactive Marketing

With the growing popularity of social networks and mobile phones, there are many opportunities for the introduction of interactive marketing. This new trend can be illustrated by the example of world famous companies.

Coca-Cola: The campaign entitled "Share Coca-Cola with", in which the famous logo on the bottle was replaced by different names, is very popular all over the world. In fact, this is a viral action aimed at launching a new trend in social networks. In Instagram, the hashtag of the #shareacoke campaign has already been used more than 340,000 times, with 96% of the reviews either positive or neutral. Place in a profile photo with a bottle of Cola means not just enjoy a drink. It's about capturing the moment, and the name that flaunts on the bottle gives the moment a special importance.

Yoplait: Every year Yoplait donates 10 cents from the sale of specially labeled yogurts to the Fund for Breast Cancer of Susan G. Komen. Interaction with customers always benefits the company. If to give buyers a sense of involvement in a big business, they will be much more willing to recommend a product to their friends and acquaintances.

Jack Daniels: The world brand of whiskey Jack Daniels, developing its campaign called "The Few & Far Between" counted on the fact that everyone likes to hear a good story. Its essence lies in the fact that any person can share incredible stories about adventures in taverns around the globe. And the brand of Jack Daniels was not used in all the stories. As in the case of Coca-Cola, this company is not focused on immediate success - but nevertheless, it took a place in the memory of customers.

Benefits of Interactive Marketing

The relatively low cost of interactive marketing means that it can be used by both large and small companies. Interactive marketing also provides greater flexibility, allowing the seller to constantly make adjustments to their activities. Thus, the main benefits of interactive marketing include:

Selective impact:

- Identification of users;
- Activation of consumers;
- Using the effects of viral marketing;
- Reducing the cost of distributing advertising information.

Types of Interactive Marketing

Types of interactive marketing depend on the devices, technologies, and tools used.

The most important is the Internet and devices that provide access to it (computers, tablet PC's, smartphones, etc.) as a means of obtaining information, communication and self-realization tools.

Local networks. Internal computer networks of companies or urban areas, in fact, are self-sufficient information systems where users can communicate, play, exchange necessary information.

The next digital channel is mobile devices. Earlier brands delivered messages via SMS messages, now the installation of branded applications is popular.

Digital TV every year more and more confidently replaces the analog and gradually integrates with Internet applications. Already now it is possible using a TV set to go to a Facebook page, watch a video or find out the latest news.

Interactive screens, POS terminals. This is the kind of digital media that gradually replaces the standard outdoor advertising, because it allows companies to interact much more closely with the consumer and hook him with a message or, like POS terminals, help in making purchases.

Touchscreens, readers, and other devices. Special applications for them allow the user to get new knowledge, play, watch movies, go online and much more. For many people, a favorite tablet PC is part of a life from which information is consumed around the clock.

Digital gadgets are devices that can collect information and transfer it to other media. For example, smart watches, glasses, fitness bracelets and others.

Digital art is any kind of art where a computer is used to create or reproduce artwork. It can be a picture, sound, animation, video, game, website, algorithm, performance or installation. Many traditional forms of art integrate digital technologies, and as a result, the boundaries between traditional works of art and digital media become blurred.

Challenges of Interactive Marketing

The interactive marketing requires detailed study and constant monitoring since this form of marketing communications can have a significant negative impact on the image of the retailer. A website, for example, is an active, not a passive tool for interactive marketing, and a bad experience of using it leads to the spread of negative opinions about the brand, and it is also passed on to friends and acquaintances. If the consumer is satisfied with the goods of the company, then he can tell five friends about it. At the same time, an angry buyer will criticize a product for a much larger number of people.

In addition, interactive marketing has certain drawbacks:

- The limited access of some buyers to the Internet.
- The one-sidedness of demographic and psychological information about buyers, chaotic and information congestion of the network.
- The probability of penetration of thieves (hackers) Into a computer network in order to obtain secret information about the numbers of credit cards and bank accounts of customers.
- The risk of human rights violations in the process of creating data banks about buyers. But all these are shortcomings of growth. In the future, many of these problems will be solved with the help of certain legislative acts and reliable means of protecting the network.

Marketing Communication

The Marketing Communication refers to the means adopted by the companies to convey messages about the products and the brands they sell, either directly or indirectly to the customers with the intention to persuade them to purchase.

In other words, the different medium that company adopts to exchange the information about their goods and services to the customers is termed as Marketing Communication.

The marketer uses the tools of marketing communication to create the brand awareness among the potential customers, which means some image of the brand gets created in their minds that help them to make the purchase decision.

Marketing communication offer solutions to the following questions:

- Why shall the product be used?
- How can the product be used?
- Who can use the product?
- Where can the product be used?
- When can the product be used?

Marketing communication includes Advertising, Sales Promotion, Events and Experiences (sponsorship), Public Relations and Publicity, Direct Marketing, Interactive Marketing, Word-of-Mouth Marketing, Personal Selling. These tools of communication are collectively called as Marketing Communication Mix.

Elements of Marketing Communication Mix

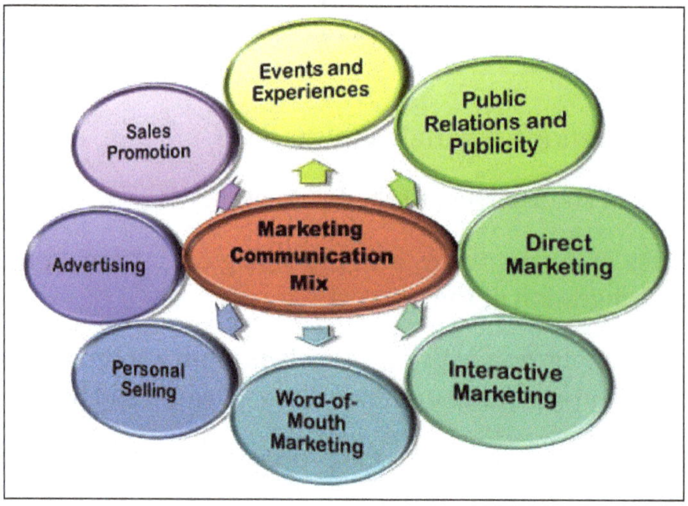

- Advertising: It is an indirect, paid method used by the firms to inform the customers about their goods and services via television, radio, print media, online websites etcAdvertising is one of the most widely used methods of communication mix wherein the complete information about the firm's product and services can be communicated easily with the huge target audience coverage.
- Sales Promotion: The sales promotion includes the several short-term incentives to persuade the customers to initiate the purchase of the goods and services. This promotion technique not only helps in retaining the existing customers but also attract the new ones with the additional benefits.Rebates, discounts, paybacks, Buy- one –get- one free scheme, coupons, etc. are some of the sales promotion tools.
- Events and Experiences: Several companies sponsor the events such as sports, entertainment, nonprofit or community events with the intention to reinforce their brand in the minds of the customers and create a long term association with them.

  The name of the firm sponsoring the event can be seen on the playground boundaries, player's jerseys, trophies, awards in the entertainment shows, hoardings on stage, etc.
- Public Relations and Publicity: The companies perform several social activities with a view to creating their positive brand image in the market. The activities that companies are undertaking such as, constructing the public conveniences, donating some portion of their purchase to the child education, organizing the blood donation camps, planting trees, etc. are some of the common moves of enhancing the Public Relations.
- Direct Marketing: With the intent of technology, the companies make use of emails, fax, mobile phones, to communicate directly with the prospective customers without involving any third party in between.
- Interactive Marketing: Interactive Marketing has recently gained popularity as a marketing communication tool, wherein the customers can interact with the firms online and can get their queries resolved online.

Amazon is one of the best examples of interactive marketing wherein the customers make their choice and can see what they have chosen or ordered in the recent past. Also, Several websites offer the platform to the customers wherein they ask questions and get the answers online such as answer.com.

- Word-of- Mouth Marketing: It is one of the most widely practiced method of communication tool wherein customer share their experiences with their peers and friends about the goods and services they bought recently.This method is very crucial for the firms because the image of the brand depends on what customer feels about the brand and what message he convey to others.
- Personal Selling: This is the traditional method of marketing communication wherein the salesmen approach the prospective customers directly and inform them about the goods and services they are dealing in. It is considered as one of the most reliable modes of communication because it is done directly either orally, i.e., face to face or in writing via emails or text messages.

Thus, marketing Communication mix refers to the different tools that a firm can adopt to inform, persuade, and remind the customer about the product and services it sells.

Advertising

Advertising is a marketing communication that employs an openly sponsored, non-personal message to promote or sell a product, service or idea. Sponsors of advertising are typically businesses wishing to promote their products or services. Advertising is differentiated from public relations in that an advertiser pays for and has control over the message. It differs from personal selling in that the message is non-personal, i.e., not directed to a particular individual. Advertising is communicated through various mass media, including traditional media such as newspapers, magazines, television, radio, outdoor advertising or direct mail; and new media such as search results, blogs, social media, websites or text messages. The actual presentation of the message in a medium is referred to as an advertisement, or "ad" or advert for short.

Commercial ads often seek to generate increased consumption of their products or services through "branding", which associates a product name or image with certain qualities in the minds of consumers. On the other hand, ads that intend to elicit an immediate sale are known as direct-response advertising. Non-commercial entities that advertise more than consumer products or services include political parties, interest groups, religious organizations and governmental agencies. Non-profit organizations may use free modes of persuasion, such as a public service announcement. Advertising may also help to reassure employees or shareholders that a company is viable or successful.

Modern advertising originated with the techniques introduced with tobacco advertising in the 1920s, most significantly with the campaigns of Edward Bernays, considered the founder of modern, "Madison Avenue" advertising.

A Coca-Cola advertisement.

Worldwide spending on advertising in 2015 amounted to an estimated US$529.43 billion. Advertising's projected distribution for 2017 was 40.4% on TV, 33.3% on digital, 9% on newspapers, 6.9% on magazines, 5.8% on outdoor and 4.3% on radio. Internationally, the largest ("Big Five") advertising-agency groups are Dentsu, Interpublic, Omnicom, Publicis, and WPP.

Classification

An advertisement for a diner. Such signs are common on storefronts.

Paying people to hold signs is one of the oldest forms of advertising, as with this human billboard.

Hot air balloon displaying advertising for *GEO* magazine.

A taxicab with an advertisement for Daikin in Singapore. Buses and other vehicles are popular media for advertisers.

A DBAG Class 101 with UNICEF ads at Ingolstadt main railway stationA Transperth bus with an advertisement on its side.

Advertising may be categorized in a variety of ways, including by style, target audience, geographic scope, medium, or purpose. For example, in print advertising, classification by style can include display advertising (ads with design elements sold by size) vs. classified advertising (ads without design elements sold by the word or line). Advertising may be local, national or global. An ad campaign may be directed toward consumers or to businesses. The purpose of an ad may be to raise awareness (brand advertising), or to elicit an immediate sale (direct response advertising). The term above the line (ATL) is used for advertising involving mass media; more targeted forms of advertising and promotion are referred to as below the line (BTL). The two terms date back to 1954 when Procter & Gamble began paying their advertising agencies differently from other promotional agencies. In the 2010s, as advertising technology developed, a new term, through the line (TTL) began to come into use, referring to integrated advertising campaigns.

Mobile Billboard in East Coast Park, Singapore.

Traditional Media

Virtually any medium can be used for advertising. Commercial advertising media can include wall paintings, billboards, street furniture components, printed flyers and rack cards, radio, cinema and television adverts, web banners, mobile telephone screens, shopping carts, web popups, skywriting, bus stop benches, human billboards and forehead advertising, magazines, newspapers, town criers, sides of buses, banners attached to or sides of airplanes ("logojets"), in-flight advertisements on seatback tray tables or overhead storage bins, taxicab doors, roof mounts and passenger screens, musical stage shows, subway platforms and trains, elastic bands on disposable diapers, doors of bathroom stalls, stickers on apples in supermarkets, shopping cart handles (grabertising), the opening section of streaming audio and video, posters, and the backs of event tickets and supermarket receipts. Any situation in which an "identified" sponsor pays to deliver their message through a medium is advertising.

Share of global adspend		
Medium	2015	2017
Television advertisement	37.7%	34.8%
Desktop online advertising	19.9%	18.2%
Mobile advertising	9.2%	18.4%
Newspaper#Advertising	12.8%	10.1%
Magazines	6.5%	5.3%
Outdoor advertising	6.8%	6.6%
Radio advertisement	6.5%	5.9%
Cinema	0.6%	0.7%

Television

Television advertising is one of the most expensive types of advertising; networks charge large amounts for commercial airtime during popular events. The annual Super Bowl football game in the United States is known as the most prominent advertising event on television – with an audience of over 108 million and studies showing that 50% of those only tuned in to see the advertisements. During the 2014 edition of this game, the average thirty-second ad cost US$4 million, and $8 million was charged for a 60-second spot. Virtual advertisements may be inserted into regular programming through computer graphics. It is typically inserted into otherwise blank backdrops or used to replace local billboards that are not relevant to the remote broadcast audience. More controversially, virtual billboards may be inserted into the background where none exist in real-life. This technique is especially used in televised sporting events. Virtual product placement is also possible. An infomercial is a long-format television commercial, typically five minutes or longer. The word "infomercial" is a portmanteau of the words "information" and "commercial". The main objective in an infomercial is to create an impulse purchase, so that the target sees the presentation and then immediately buys the product through the advertised toll-free telephone number or website. Infomercials describe, display, and often demonstrate products and their features, and commonly have testimonials from customers and industry professionals.

A television commercial being filmed in 1948.

Radio

Radio advertisements are broadcast as radio waves to the air from a transmitter to an antenna and a thus to a receiving device. Airtime is purchased from a station or network in exchange for airing the commercials. While radio has the limitation of being restricted to sound, proponents of radio advertising often cite this as an advantage. Radio is an expanding medium that can be found on air, and also online. Radio has approximately 241.6 million weekly listeners, or more than 93 percent of the U.S. population.

Online

Online advertising is a form of promotion that uses the Internet and World Wide Web for the expressed purpose of delivering marketing messages to attract customers. Online ads are delivered by an ad server. Examples of online advertising include contextual ads that appear on search engine results pages, banner ads, in pay per click text ads, rich media ads, Social network advertising, online classified advertising, advertising networks and e-mail marketing, including e-mail spam. A newer form of online advertising is Native Ads; they go in a website's news feed and are supposed to improve user experience by being less intrusive. However, some people argue this practice is deceptive.

Domain Names

Domain name advertising is most commonly done through pay per click web search engines, however, advertisers often lease space directly on domain names that generically describe their products. When an Internet user visits a website by typing a domain name directly into their web browser, this is known as "direct navigation", or "type in" web traffic. Although many Internet users search for ideas and products using search engines and mobile phones, a large number of users around the world still use the address bar. They will type a keyword into the address bar such as "geraniums" and add ".com" to the end of it. Sometimes they will do the same with ".org" or a country-code Top Level Domain (TLD such as ".co.uk" for the United Kingdom or ".ca" for Canada). When Internet users type in a generic keyword and add .com or another top-level domain (TLD) ending, it produces a targeted sales lead. Domain name advertising was originally developed by Oingo (later known as Applied Semantics), one of Google's early acquisitions.

Product Placements

Covert advertising is when a product or brand is embedded in entertainment and media. For example, in a film, the main character can use an item or other of a definite brand, as in the movie Min*ority Report*, where Tom Cruise's character John Anderton owns a phone with the *Nokia* logo clearly written in the top corner, or his watch engraved with the *Bulgari* logo. Another example of advertising in film is in *I, Robot*, where main character played by Will Smith mentions his *Converse* shoes several times, calling them "classics", because the film is set far in the future. *I, Robot* and *Spaceballs* also showcase futuristic cars with the *Audi* and *Mercedes-Benz* logos clearly displayed on the front of the vehicles. Cadillac chose to advertise in the movie *The Matrix Reloaded*, which as a result contained many scenes in which Cadillac cars were used. Similarly, product placement for Omega Watches, Ford, VAIO, BMW and Aston Martin cars are featured in recent James Bond films, most notably *Casino Royale*. In "Fantastic Four: Rise of the Silver Surfer", the main transport vehicle shows a large Dodge logo on the front. *Blade Runner* includes some of the most obvious product placement; the whole film stops to show a Coca-Cola billboard.

Print

Print advertising describes advertising in a printed medium such as a newspaper, magazine, or trade journal. This encompasses everything from media with a very broad readership base, such as a major national newspaper or magazine, to more narrowly targeted media such as local newspapers and trade journals on very specialized topics. One form of print advertising is classified advertising, which allows private individuals or companies to purchase a small, narrowly targeted ad paid by the word or line. Another form of print advertising is the display ad, which is generally a larger ad with design elements that typically run in an article section of a newspaper.

Outdoor

Billboards, also known as hoardings in some parts of the world, are large structures located in public places which display advertisements to passing pedestrians and motorists. Most often, they are located on main roads with a large amount of passing motor and pedestrian traffic; however, they can be placed in any location with large numbers of viewers, such as on mass transit vehicles and in stations, in shopping malls or office buildings, and in stadiums. The form known as street advertising first came to prominence in the UK by Street Advertising Services to create outdoor advertising on street furniture and pavements. Working with products such as Reverse Graffiti, air dancers and 3D pavement advertising, for getting brand messages out into public spaces. Sheltered outdoor advertising combines outdoor with indoor advertisement by placing large mobile, structures (tents) in public places on temporary bases. The large outer advertising space aims to exert a strong pull on the observer, the product is promoted indoors, where the creative decor can intensify the impression. Mobile billboards are generally vehicle mounted billboards or digital screens. These can be on dedicated vehicles built solely for carrying advertisements along routes preselected by clients, they can also be specially equipped cargo trucks or, in some cases, large banners strewn from planes. The billboards are often lighted; some being backlit, and others employing spotlights. Some billboard displays are static, while others change; for example, continuously or periodically rotating among a set of advertisements. Mobile displays are used for various situations in metropolitan areas throughout the world, including: target advertising, one-day and long-term campaigns, conventions, sporting events, store openings and similar promotional events, and big advertisements from smaller companies.

The *RedEye* newspaper advertised to its target market at North Avenue Beach with a sailboat billboard on Lake Michigan.

Point-of-sale

In-store advertising is any advertisement placed in a retail store. It includes placement of a product in visible locations in a store, such as at eye level, at the ends of aisles and near checkout counters (a.k.a. POP – point of purchase display), eye-catching displays promoting a specific product, and advertisements in such places as shopping carts and in-store video displays.

Novelties

Advertising printed on small tangible items such as coffee mugs, T-shirts, pens, bags, and such is known as novelty advertising. Some printers specialize in printing novelty items, which can then be distributed directly by the advertiser, or items may be distributed as part of a cross-promotion, such as ads on fast food containers.

Celebrity Endorsements

Advertising in which a celebrity endorses a product or brand leverages celebrity power, fame, money, popularity to gain recognition for their products or to promote specific stores' or products. Advertisers often advertise their products, for example, when celebrities share their favorite products or wear clothes by specific brands or designers. Celebrities are often involved in advertising campaigns such as television or print adverts to advertise specific or general products. The use of celebrities to endorse a brand can have its downsides, however; one mistake by a celebrity can be detrimental to the public relations of a brand. For example, following his performance of eight gold medals at the 2008 Olympic Games in Beijing, China, swimmer Michael Phelps' contract with Kellogg's was terminated, as Kellogg's did not want to associate with him after he was photographed smoking marijuana. Celebrities such as Britney Spears have advertised for multiple products including Pepsi, Candies from Kohl's, Twister, NASCAR, and Toyota.

Aerial

Using aircraft, balloons or airships to create or display advertising media. Skywriting is a notable example.

An Allegiant Air aircraft in the special Blue Man Group livery.

A Zeppelin NT (D-LZFN) of Friedrichshafen used for advertisement.

New Media and Advertising Approaches

A new advertising approach is known as advanced advertising, which is data-driven advertising, using large quantities of data, precise measuring tools and precise targeting. Advanced advertising also makes it easier for companies which sell ad-space to attribute customer purchases to the ads they display or broadcast.

Increasingly, other media are overtaking many of the "traditional" media such as television, radio and newspaper because of a shift toward the usage of the Internet for news and music as well as devices like digital video recorders (DVRs) such as TiVo.

Online advertising began with unsolicited bulk e-mail advertising known as "e-mail spam". Spam has been a problem for e-mail users since 1978. As new online communication channels became available, advertising followed. The first banner ad appeared on the World Wide Web in 1994. Prices of Web-based advertising space are dependent on the "relevance" of the surrounding web content and the traffic that the website receives.

In online display advertising, display ads generate awareness quickly. Unlike search, which requires someone to be aware of a need, display advertising can drive awareness of something new and without previous knowledge. Display works well for direct response. Display is not only used for generating awareness, it's used for direct response campaigns that link to a landing page with a clear 'call to action'.

As the mobile phone became a new mass medium in 1998 when the first paid downloadable content appeared on mobile phones in Finland, mobile advertising followed, also first launched in Finland in 2000. By 2007 the value of mobile advertising had reached $2 billion and providers such as Admob delivered billions of mobile ads.

More advanced mobile ads include banner ads, coupons, Multimedia Messaging Service picture and video messages, advergames and various engagement marketing campaigns. A particular feature driving mobile ads is the 2D barcode, which replaces the need to do any typing of web addresses, and uses the camera feature of modern phones to gain immediate access to web content. 83 percent of Japanese mobile phone users already are active users of 2D barcodes.

Some companies have proposed placing messages or corporate logos on the side of booster rockets and the International Space Station.

Unpaid advertising (also called "publicity advertising"), can include personal recommendations ("bring a friend", "sell it"), spreading buzz, or achieving the feat of equating a brand with a common noun (in the United States, "Xerox" = "photocopier", "Kleenex" = tissue, "Vaseline" = petroleum jelly, "Hoover" = vacuum cleaner, and "Band-Aid" = adhesive bandage). However, some companies oppose the use of their brand name to label an object. Equating a brand with a common noun also risks turning that brand into a generic trademark – turning it into a generic term which means that its legal protection as a trademark is lost.

From time to time, The CW Television Network airs short programming breaks called "Content Wraps", to advertise one company's product during an entire commercial break. The CW pioneered "content wraps" and some products featured were Herbal Essences, Crest, Guitar Hero II, CoverGirl, and Toyota.

A new promotion concept has appeared, "ARvertising", advertising on augmented reality technology.

Controversy exists on the effectiveness of subliminal advertising, and the pervasiveness of mass messages (propaganda).

Rise in new Media

With the Internet came many new advertising opportunities. Pop-up, Flash, banner, pop-under, advergaming, and email advertisements (all of which are often unwanted or spam in the case of email) are now commonplace. Particularly since the rise of "entertaining" advertising, some people may like an advertisement enough to wish to watch it later or show a friend. In general, the advertising community has not yet made this easy, although some have used the Internet to widely distribute their ads to anyone willing to see or hear them. In the last three quarters of 2009, mobile and Internet advertising grew by 18% and 9% respectively, while older media advertising saw declines: −10.1% (TV), −11.7% (radio), −14.8% (magazines) and −18.7% (newspapers). Between 2008 and 2014, U.S. newspapers lost more than half their print advertising revenue.

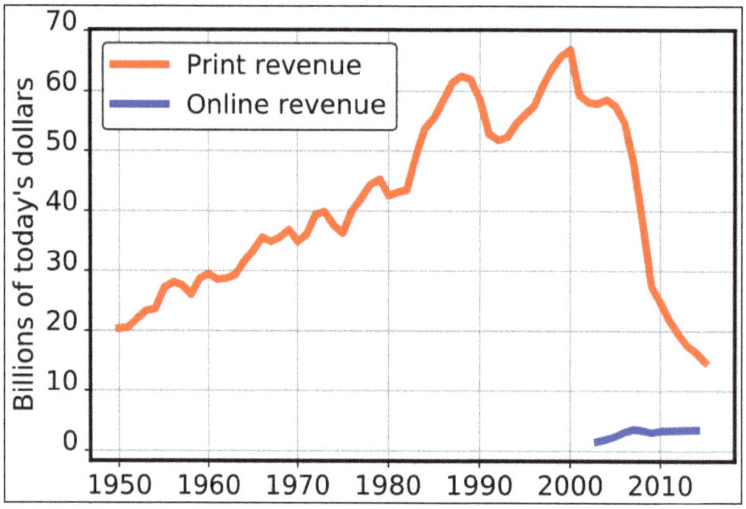

US newspaper advertising revenue, Newspaper Association of America published data.

Niche Marketing

Another significant trend regarding future of advertising is the growing importance of the niche market using niche or targeted ads. Also brought about by the Internet and the theory of the long tail, advertisers will have an increasing ability to reach specific audiences. In the past, the most efficient way to deliver a message was to blanket the largest mass market audience possible. However, usage tracking, customer profiles and the growing popularity of niche content brought about by everything from blogs to social networking sites, provide advertisers with audiences that are smaller but much better defined, leading to ads that are more relevant to viewers and more effective for companies' marketing products. Among others, Comcast Spotlight is one such advertiser employing this method in their video on demand menus. These advertisements are targeted to a specific group and can be viewed by anyone wishing to find out more about a particular business or practice, from their home. This causes the viewer to become proactive and actually choose what advertisements they want to view. Niche marketing could also be helped by bringing the issue of colour into advertisements. Different colours play major roles when it comes to marketing strategies, for example, seeing the blue can promote a sense of calmness and gives a sense of security which is why many social networks such as Facebook use blue in their logos. Google AdSense is an example of niche marketing. Google calculates the primary purpose of a website and adjusts ads accordingly; it uses keywords on the page (or even in emails) to find the general ideas of topics disused and places ads that will most likely be clicked on by viewers of the email account or website visitors.

Crowdsourcing

The concept of crowdsourcing has given way to the trend of user-generated advertisements. User-generated ads are created by people, as opposed to an advertising agency or the company themselves, often resulting from brand sponsored advertising competitions. For the 2007 Super Bowl, the Frito-Lays division of PepsiCo held the "Crash the Super Bowl" contest, allowing people to create their own Doritos commercials. Chevrolet held a similar competition for their Tahoe line of SUVs. Due to the success of the Doritos user-generated ads in the 2007 Super Bowl, Frito-Lays relaunched the competition for the 2009 and 2010 Super Bowl. The resulting ads were among the most-watched and most-liked Super Bowl ads. In fact, the winning ad that aired in the 2009 Super Bowl was ranked by the USA Today Super Bowl Ad Meter as the top ad for the year while the winning ads that aired in the 2010 Super Bowl were found by Nielsen's BuzzMetrics to be the "most buzzed-about". Another example of companies using crowdsourcing successfully is the beverage company Jones Soda that encourages consumers to participate in the label design themselves.

This trend has given rise to several online platforms that host user-generated advertising competitions on behalf of a company. Founded in 2007, Zooppa has launched ad competitions for brands such as Google, Nike, Hershey's, General Mills, Microsoft, NBC Universal, Zinio, and Mini Cooper. Crowdsourcing remains controversial, as the long-term impact on the advertising industry is still unclear.

Global Advertising

Advertising has gone through five major stages of development: Domestic, export, international, multi-national, and global. For global advertisers, there are four, potentially competing, business objectives that must be balanced when developing worldwide advertising: building a brand while speaking with one voice, developing economies of scale in the creative process, maximising local effectiveness of ads, and increasing the company's speed of implementation. Born from the evolutionary stages of global marketing are the three primary and fundamentally different approaches to the development of global advertising executions: exporting executions, producing local executions, and importing ideas that travel.

Advertising research is key to determining the success of an ad in any country or region. The ability to identify which elements and moments of an ad contribute to its success is how economies of scale are maximized. Once one knows what works in an ad, that idea or ideas can be imported by any other market. Market research measures, such as Flow of Attention, Flow of Emotion and branding moments provide insight into what is working in an ad in any country or region because the measures are based on the visual, not verbal, elements of the ad.

Foreign Public Messaging

Foreign governments, particularly those that own marketable commercial products or services, often promote their interests and positions through the advertising of those goods because the target audience is not only largely unaware of the forum as a vehicle for foreign messaging but also willing to receive the message while in a mental state of absorbing information from advertisements during television commercial breaks, while reading a periodical, or while passing by billboards in public spaces. A prime example of this messaging technique is advertising campaigns to promote international travel. While advertising foreign destinations and services may stem from the typical goal of increasing revenue by drawing more tourism, some travel campaigns carry the additional or alternative intended purpose of promoting good sentiments or improving existing ones among the target audience towards a given nation or region. It is common for advertising promoting foreign countries to be produced and distributed by the tourism ministries of those countries, so these ads often carry political statements and depictions of the foreign government's desired international public perception. Additionally, a wide range of foreign airlines and travel-related services which advertise separately from the destinations, themselves, are owned by their respective governments; examples include, though are not limited to, the Emirates airline (Dubai), Singapore Airlines (Singapore), Qatar Airways (Qatar), China Airlines (Taiwan/Republic of China), and Air China (People's Republic of China). By depicting their destinations, airlines, and other services in a favorable and pleasant light, countries market themselves to populations abroad in a manner that could mitigate prior public impressions.

Diversification

In the realm of advertising agencies, continued industry diversification has seen observers note that "big global clients don't need big global agencies any more". This is reflected by the growth of non-traditional agencies in various global markets, such as Canadian business TAXI and SMART in Australia and has been referred to as "a revolution in the ad world".

New Technology

Human billboard at the National Multicultural Festival being used to advertise Facebook news feed.

The ability to record shows on digital video recorders (such as TiVo) allow watchers to record the programs for later viewing, enabling them to fast forward through commercials. Additionally, as more seasons of pre-recorded box sets are offered for sale of television programs; fewer people watch the shows on TV. However, the fact that these sets are sold, means the company will receive additional profits from these sets.

To counter this effect, a variety of strategies have been employed. Many advertisers have opted for product placement on TV shows like Survivor. Other strategies include integrating advertising with internet-connected program guidess, advertising on companion devices (like smartphones and tablets) during the show, and creating mobile apps for TV programs. Additionally, some like brands have opted for social television sponsorship.

The emerging technology of drone displays has recently been used for advertising purposes.

Advertising Education

In recent years there have been several media literacy initiatives, and more specifically concerning advertising, that seek to empower citizens in the face of media advertising campaigns.

Advertising education has become popular with bachelor, master and doctorate degrees becoming available in the emphasis. A surge in advertising interest is typically attributed to the strong relationship advertising plays in cultural and technological changes, such as the advance of online social networking. A unique model for teaching advertising is the student-run advertising agency, where advertising students create campaigns for real companies. Organizations such as the American Advertising Federation establish companies with students to create these campaigns.

Purposes

Advertising is at the front of delivering the proper message to customers and prospective customers. The purpose of advertising is to inform the consumers about their product and convince customers that a company's services or products are the best, enhance the image of the company, point out and create a need for products or services, demonstrate new uses for established products, announce new products and programs, reinforce the salespeople's individual messages, draw customers to the business, and to hold existing customers.

Sales Promotions and Brand Loyalty

Sales promotions are another way to advertise. Sales promotions are double purposed because they are used to gather information about what type of customers one draws in and where they are, and to jump start sales. Sales promotions include things like contests and games, sweepstakes, product giveaways, samples coupons, loyalty programs, and discounts. The ultimate goal of sales promotions is to stimulate potential customers to action.

Theory

Hierarchy-of-effects Models

Various competing models of hierarchies of effects attempt to provide a theoretical underpinning to advertising practice.

- The model of Clow and Baack clarifies the objectives of an advertising campaign and for each individual advertisement. The model postulates six steps a buyer moves through when making a purchase:
    - Awareness
    - Knowledge
    - Liking
    - Preference
    - Conviction
    - Purchase

- Means-end theory suggests that an advertisement should contain a message or means that leads the consumer to a desired end-state.
- Leverage points aim to move the consumer from understanding a product's benefits to linking those benefits with personal values.

Marketing Mix

The marketing mix was proposed by professor E. Jerome McCarthy in the 1960s. It consists of four basic elements called the "four Ps". Product is the first P representing the actual product. Price represents the process of determining the value of a product. Place represents the variables of getting the product to the consumer such as distribution channels, market coverage and movement organization. The last P stands for Promotion which is the process of reaching the target market and convincing them to buy the product.

In the 1990s, the concept of four Cs was introduced as a more customer-driven replacement of four P's. There are two theories based on four Cs: Lauterborn's four Cs (consumer, cost, communication, convenience) and Shimizu's four Cs (commodity, cost, communication, channel) in the 7Cs Compass Model (Co-marketing). Communications can include advertising, sales promotion, public relations, publicity, personal selling, corporate identity, internal communication, SNS, and MIS.

Advertising Research

Advertising research is a specialized form of research that works to improve the effectiveness and efficiency of advertising. It entails numerous forms of research which employ different methodologies. Advertising research includes pre-testing (also known as copy testing) and post-testing of ads and campaigns.

Pre-testing includes a wide range of qualitative and quantitative techniques, including: focus groups, in-depth target audience interviews (one-on-one interviews), small-scale quantitative studies and physiological measurement. The goal of these investigations is to better understand how different groups respond to various messages and visual prompts, thereby providing an assessment of how well the advertisement meets its communications goals.

Post-testing employs many of the same techniques as pre-testing, usually with a focus on understanding the change in awareness or attitude attributable to the advertisement. With the emergence of digital advertising technologies, many firms have begun to continuously post-test ads using real-time data. This may take the form of A/B split-testing or multivariate testing.

Continuous ad tracking and the Communicus System are competing examples of post-testing advertising research types.

Semiotics

Meanings between consumers and marketers depict signs and symbols that are encoded in everyday objects. Semiotics is the study of signs and how they are interpreted. Advertising has many hidden signs and meanings within brand names, logos, package designs, print advertisements, and television advertisements. Semiotics aims to study and interpret the message being conveyed in (for example) advertisements. Logos and advertisements can be interpreted at two levels – known as the surface level and the underlying level. The surface level uses signs creatively to create an image or personality for a product. These signs can be images, words, fonts, colors, or slogans. The underlying level is made up of hidden meanings. The combination of images, words, colors, and slogans must be interpreted by the audience or consumer. The "key to advertising analysis" is the signifier and the signified. The signifier is the object and the signified is the mental concept. A product has a signifier and a signified. The signifier is the color, brand name, logo design, and technology. The signified has two meanings known as denotative and connotative. The denotative meaning is the meaning of the product. A television's denotative meaning might be that it is high definition. The connotative meaning is the product's deep and hidden meaning. A connotative meaning of a television would be that it is top-of-the-line.

Apple's commercials used a black silhouette of a person that was the age of Apple's target market. They placed the silhouette in front of a blue screen so that the picture behind the silhouette could be constantly changing. However, the one thing that stays the same in these ads is that there is music in the background and the silhouette is listening to that music on a white iPod through white headphones. Through advertising, the white color on a set of earphones now signifies that the music device is an iPod. The white color signifies almost all of Apple's products.

The semiotics of gender plays a key influence on the way in which signs are interpreted. When considering gender roles in advertising, individuals are influenced by three categories. Certain characteristics of stimuli may enhance or decrease the elaboration of the message (if the product is perceived as feminine or masculine). Second, the characteristics of individuals can affect attention and elaboration of the message (traditional or non-traditional gender role orientation). Lastly, situational factors may be important to influence the elaboration of the message.

There are two types of marketing communication claims-objective and subjective. Objective claims stem from the extent to which the claim associates the brand with a tangible product or service feature. For instance, a camera may have auto-focus features. Subjective claims convey emotional, subjective, impressions of intangible aspects of a product or service. They are non-physical features of a product or service that cannot be directly perceived, as they have no physical reality. For instance the brochure has a beautiful design. Males tend to respond better to objective marketing-communications claims while females tend to respond better to subjective marketing communications claims.

Voiceovers are commonly used in advertising. Most voiceovers are done by men, with figures of up to 94% having been reported. There have been more female voiceovers in recent years, but mainly for food, household products, and feminine-care products.

Promotion

In marketing, promotion refers to any type of marketing communication used to inform or persuade target audiences of the relative merits of a product, service, brand or issue. The aim of promotion is to increase awareness, create interest, generate sales or create brand loyalty. It is one of the basic elements of the market mix, which includes the four Ps, i.e., product, price, place, and promotion.

Promotion is also one of the elements in the promotional mix or promotional plan. These are personal selling, advertising, sales promotion, direct marketing publicity and may also include event marketing, exhibitions and trade shows. A promotional plan specifies how much attention to pay to each of the elements in the promotional mix, and what proportion of the budget should be allocated to each element.

Promotion covers the methods of communication that a marketer uses to provide information about its product. Information can be both verbal and visual.

Purpose

There are three objectives of promotion. These are:

- To present information to consumers and others.
- To increase demand.
- To differentiate a product.

The purpose of a promotion and thus its promotional plan can have a wide range, including: sales increases, new product acceptance, creation of brand equity, positioning, competitive retaliations, or creation of a corporate image.

The term 'promotion' tends to be used internally by the marketing function. To the public or the market, phrases like "special offer" are more common. Examples of a fully integrated, long-term, and large-scale promotion are My Coke Rewards in the USA or Coke Zone in the UK and Pepsi Stuff.

Types

There have been different ways to promote a product in person or with different media. Both person and media can be either physically real or virtual/electronic.

In a Physical Environment

Promotions can be held in physical environments at special events such as concerts, festivals, trade shows, and in the field, such as in grocery or department stores. Interactions in the field allow immediate purchases. The purchase of a product can be incentive with discounts (i.e., coupons), free items, or a contest. This method is used to increase the sales of a given product. Interactions between the brand and the customer are performed by a brand ambassador or promotional model who represents the product in physical environments. Brand ambassadors or promotional models are hired by a marketing company, which in turn is booked by the brand to represent the product or service. Person-to-person interaction, as opposed to media-to-person involvement, establishes connections that add another dimension to promotion. Building a community through promoting goods and services can lead to brand loyalty.

Traditional Media

Examples of traditional media include print media such as newspapers and magazines, electronic media such as radio and television, and outdoor media such as banner or billboard advertisements. Each of these platforms provide ways for brands to reach consumers with advertisements.

Digital Media

Digital media, which includes Internet, social networking and social media sites, is a modern way for brands to interact with consumers as it releases news, information and advertising from the technological limits of print and broadcast infrastructures. Digital media is currently the most effective way for brands to reach their consumers on a daily basis. Over 2.7 billion people are online globally, which is about 40% of the world's population. 67% of all Internet users globally use social media.

Mass communication has led to modern marketing strategies to continue focusing on brand awareness, large distributions and heavy promotions. The fast-paced environment of digital media presents new methods for promotion to utilize new tools now available through technology. With the rise of technological advances, promotions can be done outside of local contexts and across geographic borders to reach a greater number of potential consumers. The goal of a promotion is then to reach the most people possible in a time efficient and a cost efficient manner.

Social media, as a modern marketing tool, offers opportunities to reach larger audiences in an interactive way. These interactions allow for conversation rather than simply educating the customer. Facebook, Snapchat, Instagram, Twitter, Pinterest, Google Plus, Tumblr, as well as alternate audio and media sites like SoundCloud and Mixcloud allow users to interact and promote music online with little to no cost. You can purchase and buy ad space as well as potential customer interactions stores as Likes, Followers, and clicks to your page with the use of third parties. As a participatory media culture, social media platforms or social networking sites are forms of mass communication that, through media technologies, allow large amounts of product and distribution of content to reach the largest audience possible. However, there are downsides to virtual promotions as servers, systems, and websites may crash, fail, or become overloaded with information. You also can stand risk of losing uploaded information and storage and at a use can also be effected by a number of outside variables.

Brands can explore different strategies to keep consumers engaged. One popular tool is branded entertainment, or creating some sort of social game for the user. The benefits of such a platform include submersing the user in the brand's content. Users will be more likely to absorb and not grow tired of advertisements if they are, for example, embedded in the game as opposed to a bothersome pop-up ad.

Personalizing advertisements is another strategy that can work well for brands, as it can increase the likelihood that the brand will be anthropomorphized by the consumer. Personalization increases click-through intentions when data has been collected about the consumer.

Brands must navigate the line between effectively promoting their content to consumers on social media and becoming too invasive in consumers' lives. Vivid Internet ads that include devices such as animation might increase a user's initial attention to the ad. However, this may be seen as a distraction to the user if they are trying to absorb a different part of the site such as reading text. Additionally, when brands make the effort of overtly collecting data about their consumers and then personalizing their ads to them, the consumer's relationship with the advertisements, following this data collection, is frequently positive. However, when data is covertly collected, consumers can quickly feel like the company betrayed their trust. It is important for brands to utilize personalization in their ads, without making the consumer feel vulnerable or that their privacy has been betrayed.

Brand Management

Brand management is a marketing technique which focuses on improving the reputation of a brand or product. The brand is what customers think of when they see or hear the brand name. Many multinational companies' brands are worth billions of dollars.

Essentially, a brand is the image and personality of a product or service that a firm provides.

Good brand management can improve brand loyalty, which subsequently keeps customers coming back. This, in turn, can be beneficial for a company. Put simply; a good brand allows a company to raise prices and increase profits.

In fact, without good brand management, most of the world's biggest companies would not be so successful.

Principles of Brand Management

Define your Brand

It all begins with authenticity, the key purpose, mission, vision, position, character and value. Focus on what you can do best and then communicate your strengths with consistency. There have been several instances where companies acquired other brands, only to sell them off later, because the acquisitions didn't fit into the parent company's brand architecture. Microsoft acquired Razorfish—a major internet and technological innovation company—when it bought a Quantive—a digital marketing service company—for about $6 billion in 2007. But a couple of years later, Microsoft sold off Razorfish for about $530 million.

Simply put, Razorfish wasn't a good fit for Microsoft's brand strategy.

The Brand is your Business Model

Support and challenge your business for maximizing the potential of your brand. Think of personal brands like Richard Branson, Martha Stewart or Barack Obama. These individuals almost built their businesses right atop their personal brand, and everything they offer are an extension of that brand promise.

Consistency

If that wasn't enough, consistency in your message is always the key to differentiate. Own up to your position on all reference points for all that you do. Obama, for instance, focused on only one message during his 2008 presidential campaign: Change. Automobile major BMW has always been branded as the "ultimate driving machine".

Start Inside Out

All those working for your company can tell you what they feel and think of your brand. And that's the story you must place before your customers. Drive the impact beyond mere marketing walls. That's how online apparel store Zappos empowers its employees to bolster customer perception about the brand.

Connect at the Emotional Level

A brand is not just a logo, name, website, public relations exercise, or TV commercials. These are merely tools and not the brand. A brand is a much larger thing, a desirable idea manifested in products or services, places, people, and experience.

Coffee major Starbucks created a third space experience that was exclusive and desirable so that people preferred staying back and pay for the overpriced coffee.

Try selling something which satisfies not only the physical needs of people, but also their emotional needs. They will slowly start to identify with your brand.

Empower Brand Champions

Award those who love your brand and help to drive home a message, so that they can be a part of the brand building process. If your brand advocates stops telling you what you should do and what you shouldn't, it's about time you start evaluating the brand promise.

Go and speak to someone working at an Apple retail outlet, or an iPad owner and you'll see how passionate they are about the company. It's almost a culture and a lifestyle.

Stay Flexible and Relevant

A brand that's well managed should always remain open to adjustments. Remember, branding is not a race but a process. It's not an eventuality. So constantly tweak the message for your target group and refresh your company's image.

A successful brand will never cling to the traditional ways because that delivered results in the past. It has to adapt to the changing market conditions. It will always try to reinvent itself by being flexible. Companies embracing change in a positive way will be able to free themselves to become more creative and savvy.

When the global economy went southwards in 2009, Hyundai Motors introduced an assurance program. It allowed buyers to return their cars if they suffered a job loss, with no outstanding financial obligation or damage to the owner's credit.

Result

At the end of February 2010, only two buyers had returned their cars. But at the same time, Hyundai's sales saw a 14% year-on-year jump. Hyundai was one of the only two companies that was able to increase its revenue in those hard times of truncated business activity, while companies like Honda, saw sales plummeting by over 30%. The Korean automobile major again rebranded its image with another program, by guaranteeing an year's worth of free gasoline at $1.49 per gallon across most models, when gas prices pushed higher during the peak summer travel months. It was less of clever marketing and more of a carefully devised rebranding strategy.

Align your Tactics with Strategy

Convey your brand statement on the most appropriate media platform using specific campaign objectives. Each day, consumers are bombarded with commercial messages. It often becomes an overkill. Many customers actively block commercials on the internet or switch channels on TV. Invest your branding efforts on the correct platform which communicates it to the target audience.

While TV may be the most expensive, it also has a wider reach, and can come up with largely instant results. On the other hand, social media is much cheaper, but has a longer response time. The resources may not give a prompt outcome if that's what you want.

Measure the Effectiveness

Focus on the return on investment (ROI), which is a key indicator to measure the effectiveness of your brand management strategies. It often depends on how well your company can be inspired to carry out these strategies. The effectiveness is also reflected in your brand valuation i.e. how the customers react to your product and price adjustments. Brand readjustments should ultimately lead to better sales and profits. But make sure not to focus solely on increasing sales, when you can achieve better margins by reducing expenses and overheads.

There are several options to test various marketing tactics. Just make sure they complement your brand authenticity and also align with the strategy you have taken.

Keep Enemies Closer

Even if you have one of the most highly desirable and innovative product or service, expect new competitors with a better value proposition to enter the market, some days down the line. A market, regardless of the product or service, is never small enough to discourage new players from entering it and create competition. You'll always find another competitor delivering faster, better, and more importantly, cheaper products or services. Call it innovation economics or hyper-competition, peer challenge could be better for you, believe it or not. It urges you to raise your strategy and give more value.

For instance, look how the big three automobile manufacturers—Ford, General Motors (GM), and Chrysler—was crushed in the past decade by car makers from Japan and Germany. Not only the latter made better cars, they did that more efficiently and commanded a much better brand loyalty. Toyota, in 2008, beat GM, while Honda overtook Chrysler in the US market.

Cultivate your Community

The community is an effective and powerful platform which can engage buyers and also create a loyalty towards the brand. In active communities, members feel an urge to connect to each other, regarding your brand's consumption.

All of us want to be an insider to something. It is usually exciting for us to tell others in our community that we have some exclusive knowledge about something.

In several ways, we take pride in our ego to be part of a professional group or say, a sports team. Guess which car the members of a Jaguar club would consider at the time of purchasing their next vehicle?

A brand community allows companies collaborate with customers across all sections of value creation via crowd sourcing like pricing strategy, product design, availability, and selling metrics.

Brand Strategy Thinking

Design thinking is a "process for creating new choices." It essentially means not to just settle for the available alternatives but to think outside the box, sans being limited. The concept, in effect, applies to the brand strategy creation process that experts often term as brand strategy thinking.

It's always easier to execute tactics, instead of introducing a new strategy because that could imply a possibility of failure. It's always much easier to copy what worked for the competitor than come up with something creative and original.

But the fact is, you can't do that because it violates the very basics of brand management. Branding is about creating the correct experience which involves all stakeholders to devise a better strategy.

Leveraging the ecosystem which includes your partners, employees, customers for helping you articulate the brand strategy so that they can sync together, could be a wonderful idea.

The brand image component of brand management can be maintained by tangible as well as intangible aspects of the product. Tangible aspects of brand management include the core product, price, packaging, augmented product etc. The intangible aspects of brand management include product positioning, customer experience, value added services, customer relationship with the brand. Brand manager is responsible for all these.

Brand Management Process

Brand management process includes the following steps:

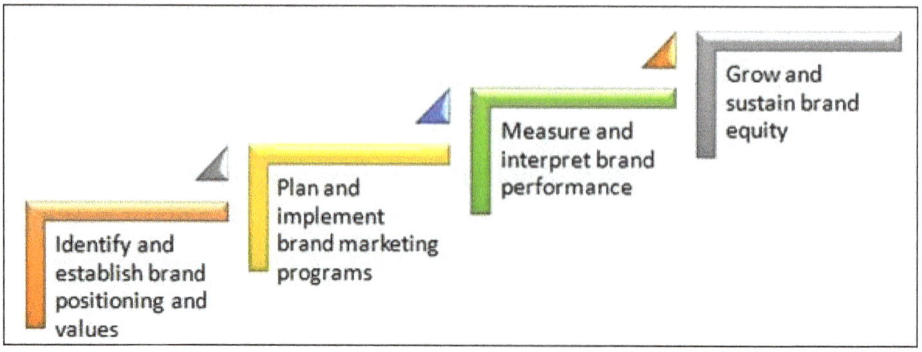

1.Identify Brand Positioning and Value: The first step in the brand management process is to understand the product and service offering in terms of positioning and brand value it offers to the customers. This is the foundation for companies as how they want the customers to perceive their product or service is a part of brand development.

2. Brand Marketing Planning: Brand building is the next step in brand management for a product/ service. This process includes creation of the brand by creating components like pricing, packaging, customer service etc. Also, brand awareness techniques like marketing, branding & advertising also come under this step. Companies use integrated marketing communications (IMC) to promote its products & services.

3. Measuring Brand Performance: It is not simply important to create brand but to also measure its performance vis-à-vis competitors & other market dynamics. This step in brand management identifies parameters like brand recall, brand preference, brand recognition etc.

4. Growth & Sustainability: The final step in the brand management process post evaluation is to improve the brand performance to ensure growth and sustainability. Brand equity is the measure of the quality offered by a product and service.

Importance of Brand Management

Brand management is a concept adopted by companies & marketers to create an emotional connect between customers and their product. Through brand management, an image of the product or brand is created in the mind of the consumer. This becomes the foundation of not only acquiring new customers but also increasing brand loyalty amongst existing users. Also, brand management is important for any business as it helps companies evaluate the performance of the brand and helps them improve and adapt with changing times. Inability to change with customer preferences and needs can lead to the demise of the brand. A good overall brand management can help increase business and have strong advocates for the brand. Brand management is an important marketing strategy which helps companies establish their brand & products.

Brand Management Examples

Some of the leading companies in the world have successfully used brand management to make their brand top in the mind of the consumer. Consider the leading global brands like Nike, Mercedes, Pepsi, Coca Cola, Microsoft etc. All these companies are the best examples of how companies do business using brand management as an integral part of their processes. All these companies produce high quality products & services, and have a strong brand image (core product, brand image). Once the products are ready, these companies use various media channels like TV commercials, social media, online advertising, print ads etc to create brand awareness among customers. The big companies ensure high quality post-purchase customer service and are receptive to critical feedback which helps in improving their brand. Thus, all companies using end-to end brand management processes for effective business are the best examples.

Advantages of Brand Management

There are several benefits of brand management, some of which are highlighted below:

- Brand management helps create an emotional connect between customers and products.

- Effective brand management helps the business grow as consumers become loyal and advocate for the products & services. Customer loyalty further helps boost business.
- Taking critical and important feedback helps companies improve based on consumer insights.
- Brand managements helps companies adapt their strategies with changing times based on the needs and requirements of the customers.
- Tools like brand development index (BDI), help a brand grow and fight competition.

References

- Marketing-definition-meaning, financial-glossary: marketbusinessnews.com, Retrieved 16 June, 2019
- Marketing-management-overview, marketing-management: tutorialspoint.com, Retrieved 15 July, 2019
- Interactive-marketing-definition-types-examples-and-benefits, types-of-marketing: jgdb.com, Retrieved 20 January, 2019
- Marketing-communication: businessjargons.com, Retrieved 18 May, 2019
- Brand-management, financial-glossary: marketbusinessnews.com, Retrieved 18 August, 2019
- 12-basic-principles-of-brand-management: educba.com, Retrieved 29 April, 2019
- Baker, Michael (2003). The Marketing Book (5th ed.). Oxford: Butterworth-Heinemann. pp. 424, 425. ISBN 0585459525. OCLC 52732761

6
Public Relations

A strategic communication procedure that forms favorable relationships between firms and their public is called public relations. Some of the models that fall under its domain are press agentry model, public information model and two-way asymmetric and symmetric model. This chapter delves into the subject of public relations to provide an in-depth understanding of it.

The Public Relations or PR is a practice of maintaining and shaping the image of an individual or an organization to the public in such a way that a favorable point of view is developed for the concerned entity.

In other words, an activity designed to help an organization and its public, such as customers, employees, government, suppliers, etc. who are directly or indirectly associated with the firm, adapt mutually to each other.

The significance of public relations can be traced in marketing. It helps the marketing management to influence the non-customer groups. By doing so, the companies keep this group of customers updated about the new products and formulation the company has introduced into a market through public relations with a hope that some day they will use its product.

The PR also helps in maintaining the cordial relations with the dealers and sales people who are the intermediaries between the organization and the ultimate consumer. Dealer conferences, gifts, in-house publications, display contents, etc. are some of the PR activities performed to gain the dealer support and cooperation. Similar kind of PR activities is carried out for the sales force to win their confidence in the organization.

One of the ultimate purposes of public relations is to influence the purchase decision of the direct consumers and therefore, promotional activities like community relations, media blitz, event management, corporate identity activities and programmes, etc. are carried out to shape the image of the organization.

The PR helps in maintaining relations not only outside the organization but also within the firm, i.e. between the employees and the organization. The employees are the people who work for the organization and sell goods and services on its behalf. So, it is essential for every firm to maintain healthy relationships with its employees through a continuous motivation and employee development programmes. Such as, training on product knowledge, selling, customer knowledge, product handling, etc. that helps in the further grooming of the employee.

Functions of Public Relations

Public relations is different from advertising. Public relations agencies don't buy ads, they don't write stories for reporters, and they don't focus on attractive paid promotions. They rather promote the brand by using editorial content appearing on magazines, newspapers, news channels, websites, blogs, and TV programs.

Using earned or free media for promotion has its own benefits as information on these mediums aren't bought. It has a third party validation and hence isn't viewed with scepticism by the public.

The functions of public relations manager and public relations agencies include:

- Anticipating, analysing, and interpreting the public opinion and attitudes of the public towards the brand and drafting strategies which use free or earned media to influence them.
- Drafting strategies to support brand's every campaign and new move through editorial content.
- Writing and distributing press releases.
- Speechwriting.
- Planning and executing special public outreach and media relations events.
- Writing content for the web (internal and external websites).
- Developing a crisis public relations strategy.
- Handling the social media presence of the brand and responding to public reviews on social media websites.
- Counselling the employees of the organization with regard to policies, course of action, organization's responsibility and their responsibility.
- Dealing with government and legislative agencies on behalf of the organization.
- Dealing with public groups and other organizations with regard to social and other policies of the organization and legislation of the government.
- Handling investor relations.

Public Relations Examples:

PR stunts or strategies range from donating to an affected community to running a brand activation stunt in a mall. Some of the examples of successful public relations campaigns are:

Google's Fight Ebola Campaign

The outbreak of Ebola virus in 2014 was critical as it was spread among many countries and took many lives. Google, to help the people in need and to build up a positive brand image, started a donation campaign where it pledged to give $2 for every $1 donated to the cause through its website.

The public relations strategy attracted the media attention and resulted to be a huge success as Google raised $7.5 million.

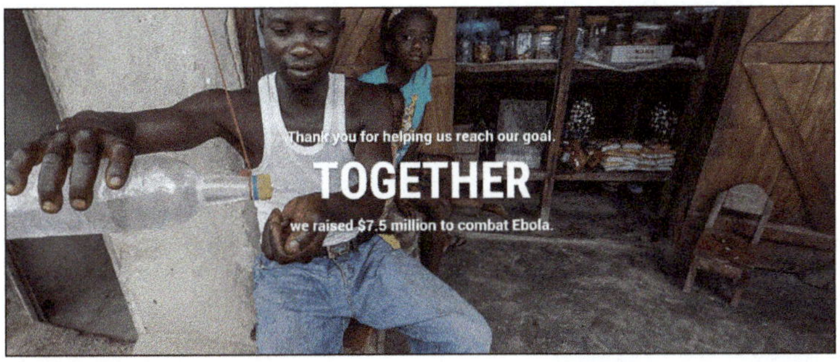

Paramount Pictures the Ring Publicity Stunt

Paramount Pictures, to promote its new horror franchise, The Ring, and to get more user attention, took a step forward and planned a publicity stunt where the protagonist haunted the people in a real-life scenario.

The film's most iconic scene of Samara crawling out of the TV set was recreated in a TV showroom where the protagonist came crawling out of the hidden compartment behind a TV screen and scared people.

Just Eat and a Sick Customer

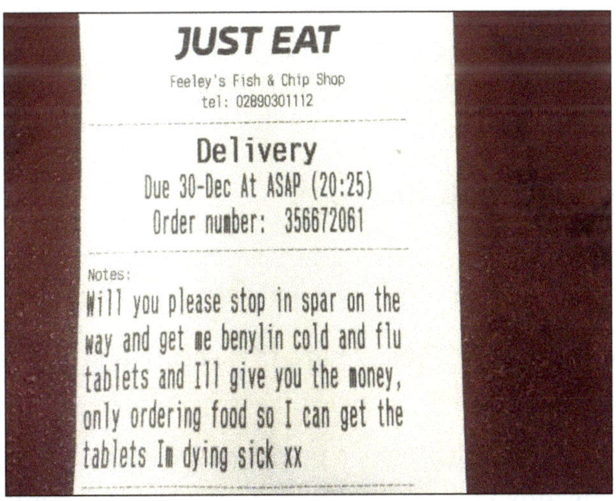

Just Eat is an online food ordering application which lets users add comments to their orders to inform the delivery person about the right address or to leave the order to the neighbour etc.

One unwell customer tried her luck to see if she could get the delivery person to stop en-route and get her some medicines. She wrote:

> "Will you please stop in the Spar on the way and get me some Benylin cold and flu tablets and I'll give you the money. Only ordering food so I can get the tablets."

The delivery person delivered both and this public relations stunt went viral over the media.

Facebook Paris Support Profile Pictures

In response to the tragic shooting in Paris in 2015 where at least 129 people died, Facebook added a France flag filter which the users could apply to their profile pictures to support France. Millions of people applied this filter and appreciated this effort by Facebook.

Advantages Of Public Relations

- Credibility: Public trusts the message coming from a trusted third party more than the advertised content.
- Reach: A good public relations strategy can attract many news outlets, exposing the content to a large audience.
- Cost effectiveness: Public relations is a cost effective technique to reach large audience as compared to paid promotion.

Disadvantages of Public Relations

- No Direct Control: Unlike paid media, there isn't a direct control over the content distributed through the earned media. This is the biggest risk of investing in public relations.
- Hard To Measure Success: It is really hard to measure and evaluate the effectiveness of a PR campaign.
- No Guaranteed Results: Publishing of a press release isn't guaranteed as the brand doesn't pay for it. The media outlet publishes it only if it feels that it'll attract its target audience.

Areas of Public Relations

Public relations is a multifaceted activity involving different audiences as well as different types of organizations, all with different goals and objectives. As a result, there are several specific areas of public relations.

Product Public Relations

Public relations and marketing work together closely when it comes to promoting a new or existing product or service. Public relations plays an important role in new product introductions by creating awareness, differentiating the product from other similar products, and even changing consumer behavior. Public relations can help introduce new products through staging a variety of special events and handling sensitive situations. For example, when the Prince Matchabelli division of Chesebrough-Pond's USA introduced a new men's cologne, there were twenty-one other men's fragrances being introduced that year. To differentiate its new offering, called Hero, Prince Matchabelli created a National Hero Awards Program honoring authentic male heroes and enlisted the participation of Big Brothers/Big Sisters of America to lend credibility to the program. Similarly, when Coleco introduced its Cabbage Patch Kids dolls, public relations helped increase awareness through licensed tie-in products, trade show exhibits, press parties, and even window displays in Cartier jewelry stores.

Public relations is often called on to give existing products and services a boost by creating or renewing visibility. For example, the California Raisins Advisory Board organized a national tour featuring live performances by the California Dancing Raisins to maintain interest in raisins during a summer-long advertising hiatus. The tour generated national and local publicity through media events, advance publicity, trade promotions, and media interviews with performer Ray Charles. Other public relations programs for existing products involve stimulating secondary demand—as when Campbell Soup Co. increased overall demand for soup by publishing a recipe booklet—or identifying new uses for the product. Public relations can interest the media in familiar products and services in a number of ways, including holding seminars for journalists, staging a special media day, and supplying the media with printed materials ranging from "backgrounders" (in-depth news releases) to booklets and brochures. Changes in existing products offer additional public relations opportunities to focus consumers' attention. An effective public relations campaign can help to properly position a product and overcome negative perceptions on the part of the general public.

Employee Relations

Employees are one of the more important audiences a company has, and an ongoing public relations program is necessary to maintain employee good will as well as to uphold the company's image and reputation among its employees. The essence of a good employee relations program is keeping employees informed and providing them with channels of communication to upper levels of management. Bechtel Group, a privately held complex of operating companies, published an annual report for its employees to keep them informed about the company's operations. The company used surveys to determine what information employees considered useful. A range of other communication devices were used, including a monthly tabloid and magazine, a quarterly video magazine, local newsletters, bulletin boards, a call-in telephone service, and "brown bag" lunches where live presentations were made about the company. Suggestion systems are another effective way to improve employee-management communications.

Other public relations programs focusing on employees include training them as company public relations representatives; explaining benefits programs to them; offering them educational, volunteer, and citizenship opportunities; and staging special events such as picnics or open houses for them. Other programs can improve performance and increase employee pride and motivation. Public relations can also play a role in recruiting new employees; handling reorganizations, relocations, and mergers; and resolving labor disputes.

Financial Relations

Financial relations involves communicating not only with a company's stockholders, but also with the wider community of financial analysts and potential investors. An effective investor relations plan can increase the value of a company's stock and make it easier to raise additional capital. In some cases special meetings with financial analysts are necessary to overcome adverse publicity, negative perceptions about a company, or investor indifference. Such meetings may take the form of full-day briefings, formal presentations, or luncheon meetings. A tour of a company's facilities may help generate interest among the financial community. Mailings and ongoing communications can help a company achieve visibility among potential investors and financial analysts.

Annual reports and stockholder meetings are the two most important public relations tools for maintaining good investor relations. Some companies hold regional or quarterly meetings in addition to the usual annual meeting. Other companies reach more stockholders by moving the location of their annual meeting from city to city. Annual reports can be complemented by quarterly reports and dividend check inserts. Companies that wish to provide additional communications with stockholders may send them a newsletter or company magazine. Personal letters to new stockholders and a quick response to inquiries insure an additional measure of good will.

Community Relations

A comprehensive, ongoing community relations program can help virtually any organization achieve visibility as a good community citizen and gain the good will of the community in which it operates. Banks, utilities, radio and television stations, and major retailers are some of the types of organizations most likely to have ongoing programs that might include supporting urban renewal, performing arts programs, social and educational programs, children's programs, community organizations, and construction projects. On a more limited scale, small businesses may achieve community visibility by sponsoring local sports teams or other events. Support may be financial or take the form of employee participation.

Organizations have the opportunity to improve good will and demonstrate a commitment to their communities when they open new offices, expand facilities, and open new factories. One company increased community awareness of its presence by converting a vacant building into a permanent meeting place. Another company built its new headquarters in an abandoned high school that it renovated. One of the more sensitive areas of community relations involves plant closings. A well-planned public relations campaign, combined with appropriate actions, can alleviate the tensions that such closings cause. Some elements of such a campaign might include offering special programs to laid-off workers, informing employees directly about proposed closings, and controlling rumors through candid and direct communications to the community and employees.

Organizations conduct a variety of special programs to improve community relations, including providing employee volunteers to work on community projects, sponsoring educational and literacy programs, staging open houses and conducting plant tours, celebrating anniversaries, and mounting special exhibits. Organizations are recognized as good community citizens when they support programs that improve the quality of life in their community, including crime prevention, employment, environmental programs, clean-up and beautification, recycling, and restoration.

Crisis Communications

Public relations practitioners become heavily involved in crisis communications whenever there is a major accident or natural disaster affecting an organization and its community. Other types of crises involve bankruptcy, product failures, and management wrongdoing. In some cases, crises call for an organization to become involved in helping potential victims; in other cases, the crisis may require rebuilding an organization's image. In any case, experts recommend that business owners prepare a plan in advance to deal with potential crises in an honest and forthright manner. The main objective of such a plan is to provide accurate information quickly in order to reduce uncertainty. After the San Francisco earthquake of 1989, for example, the Bank of America utilized its public relations department to quickly establish communications with customers, the financial community, the media, and offices in 45 countries to assure them the bank was still operating.

Government and Political Relations

Public relations in the political arena covers a wide range of activities, including staging debates, holding seminars for government leaders, influencing proposed legislation, and testifying before a congressional committee. Political candidates engage in public relations, as do government agencies at the federal, state, and local levels.

Trade associations and other types of organizations attempt to block unfavorable legislation and support favorable legislation in a number of ways. The liquor industry in California helped defeat a proposed tax increase by taking charge of the debate early, winning endorsements, recruiting spokespersons, and cultivating grassroots support. A speakers bureau trained some 240 industry volunteers, and key messages were communicated to the public through printed materials and radio and television commercials.

Public Relations in the Public Interest

Organizations attempt to generate good will and position themselves as responsible citizens through a variety of programs conducted in the public interest. Some examples are environmental programs (including water and energy conservation) and antipollution programs. Health and medical programs are sponsored by a wide range of nonprofit organizations, healthcare providers, and other businesses and industries. These range from encouraging other companies to develop AIDS-in-the-workplace policies to the American Cancer Society's Great American Smokeout. Other programs offer political education, leadership and self-improvement, recreational activities, contests, and safety instruction.

Consumer Education

Organizations have undertaken a variety of programs to educate consumers, building good will and helping avoid misunderstandings in the process. Opportunities for educating consumers might include sponsoring television and radio programs, producing manuals and other printed materials, producing materials for classroom use, and releasing the results of surveys. In addition to focusing on specific issues or industries, educational programs may seek to inform consumers about economic matters and business in general.

Other Public Relations Programs

Other types of programs that fall under the umbrella of public relations include corporate identity programs, ranging from name changes and new trademarks to changing a company's overall image. Special events may be held to call attention to an organization and focus the public's good will. These include anniversary celebrations, events related to trade shows, special exhibits, or fairs and festivals. Speakers bureaus and celebrity spokespersons are effective public relations tools for communicating an organization's point of view. Speakers bureaus may be organized by a trade association or an individual company. The face-to-face communication that speakers can deliver is often more effective than messages carried by printed materials, especially when the target audience is small and clearly defined.

Community Relations

Community relations refers to the various methods companies use to establish and maintain a mutually beneficial relationship with the communities in which they operate. The underlying principal of community relations is that when a company accepts its civic responsibility and takes an active interest in the well-being of its community, then it gains a number of long-term benefits in terms of community support, loyalty, and good will. Community involvement builds public image and employee morale, and fosters a sense of teamwork that is essential in long-term success.

A comprehensive, ongoing community relations program can help virtually any organization achieve visibility as a good community citizen. Organizations are recognized as good community citizens when they support programs that improve the quality of life in their community, including crime prevention, employment, environmental programs, clean-up and beautification, recycling, and restoration. Some other examples of ongoing programs might include scholarship programs, urban renewal projects, performing arts programs, social and educational programs, children's activities, community organizations, and construction projects. On a more limited scale, small businesses might achieve community visibility and engender good will by sponsoring local sports teams or other events. Support may be financial or take the form of employee participation.

Good community relations programs offer small businesses a wide variety of benefits. For instance, they give employees a reason to be proud of the company, which increases loyalty and may help to reduce labor and production costs. Furthermore, a company with happy employees and a good reputation in the community is likely to attract highly qualified new employees. A small company also might generate new business through the contacts and leads it generates in its community relations activities. Such contacts might also make it easier for the company to obtain financing for expansion, find promising new locations, or gain favorable treatment in terms of taxes, ordinances, or utilities. Good community relations can also be beneficial in times of crisis, such as a fire or a plant closing, by rallying the community around the affected business.

In today's environment of public suspicion, gaining and maintaining public consent to operate has become a major concern for most businesses. Managers are advised to initiate community outreach programmes in areas consistent with their DNA.

For example, a company which produces or sells sports gear should think about "adopting" a school and contributing to the school's sports department or perhaps donate gear to a neighbourhood football team.

Initiatives such as these can boost a company's image in the eyes of the public who are potential customers. It is for this reason that a company uses these PR tactics. The company develops relationships to help foster its good name while the community receives support from its initiatives.

Communities also appreciate the fact that they can rely on corporations to assist in community development programmes; after all, the community was there before the business and sees it only fair to reap some of the benefits.

The underlying principle of community relations is that when a company accepts its civic responsibility and takes an active interest in the well-being of its community, it gains a number of long-term benefits in terms of community support, loyalty and the fostering of good will. This, in turn, will help to raise awareness of the company's products and services.

A solid, comprehensive community relations programme can help virtually any organisation achieve visibility as a good community citizen.

Crisis Communication

Crisis communication is a sub-specialty of the public relations profession that is designed to protect and defend an individual, company, or organization facing a public challenge to its reputation. The communication scholar Timothy Coombs defines crisis as "the perception of an unpredictable event that threatens important expectancies of stakeholders and can seriously impact an organization's performance and generate negative outcomes" and crisis communication as "the collection, processing, and dissemination of information required to address a crisis situation."

Meaning can be socially constructed; because of this, the way that the stakeholders of an organization view an event (positively, neutrally, or negatively) is a major contributing factor to whether the event will become a crisis. Additionally, it is important to separate a true crisis situation from an incident. The term crisis "should be reserved for serious events that require careful attention from management."

Crisis management has been defined as "a set of factors designed to combat crises and to lessen the actual damages inflicted." Crisis management should not merely be reactionary; it should also consist of preventative measures and preparation in anticipation of potential crises. Effective crisis management has the potential to greatly reduce the amount of damage the organization receives as a result of the crisis, and may even prevent an incident from ever developing into a crisis.

Theories in Crisis Communication Research

In crisis communication literature, several streams of research exist at the same time. Different theories demonstrate certain ways to look at and explain crisis situations.

Image Repair Theory (IRT)

William established image repair theory (IRT) based on apologia studies. IRT assumes that image is an asset that a person or an organization attempts to protect during a crisis. When the person or the organization is attacked, the accused should draft messages to repair its image. Benoit further introduced 5 general and 14 specific response strategies the accused could harness during a crisis. General categories include deny, evading responsibility, reducing offensiveness, corrective action, and mortification.

Situational Crisis Communication Theory (SCCT)

Timothy Coombs started working on situational crisis communication theory (SCCT) in 1995. Originated from attribution theory, SCCT assumes that crises are negative events that stakeholders attempt to attribute responsibility. Coombs believes crisis managers can employ different crisis strategies according to different crisis types. Different from IRT, SCCT is an audience-oriented theory which focuses on stakeholders' perceptions of crisis situations. This idea is in line with Benoit's argument that crisis concerns more about perception than reality.

Social-mediated Crisis Communication (SMCC) Model

As social networks and blogs become popular, people spend more time online during crises. Social-mediated crisis communication (SMCC) model is introduced to investigate crisis management in online context. The model first explains how the source and form of information affect response selections and then proposes crisis response strategies. The model argues that five factors influence an organizations' communication during a crisis: crisis origin, crisis type, infrastructure, message strategy, and message form.

Integrated Crisis Mapping (ICM) Model

Another line of crisis communication research focuses on stakeholders' emotional changes in times of crises. Jin, Pang, and Cameron introduces integrated crisis mapping (ICM) model to understand stakeholders' varied emotion during a crisis. ICM assumes that people keep interpreting their emotions during a crisis.

Covariation-based Approach to Crisis Communication

As an extension of SCCT, Andreas Schwarz suggested to apply Kelley's covariation principle (attribution theory) more consistently in crisis communication to better explain the emergence and perception of causal attributions in crisis situations and deduce certain information strategies from this model and according findings. In this approach the three informational dimensions of consensus, distinctiveness, and consistency are conceptualized for situations of organizational crises (or other types of crisis) to predict the likelihood of stakeholders to make organizational attributions, entity attributions, or circumstance attributions and subsequently influence responsibility perceptions and evaluations of organizational reputation.

Discourse of Renewal

The discourse of renewal theory examines the components an organization can employ when navigating a crisis in order to mitigate significant issues within the organization when entering the post-crisis stage. It is a theory assessed by Gregory Ulmer, Timothy Sellnow, and Matthew Seeger as a framework that "emphasizes learning from the crisis, ethical communication, communication that is prospective in nature, and effective organizational rhetoric".

Categories of Crisis Management

Coombs identifies three phases of crisis management.

- *Pre-crisis*: preparing ahead of time for crisis management in an effort to prevent a future crisis from occurring. This category is also sometimes called the *prodromal* crisis stage.
- *Crisis*: the response to an actual crisis event.
- *Post-crisis*: occurs after the crisis has been resolved; the efforts by the crisis management team to understand why the crisis occurred and to learn from the event.

Inside the management step, Bodeau-Ostermann identifies 6 successive phases: - reaction, where the group behaves on first sight, - extension, because the crisis dilutes itself and touches neighbours, - means (material and human), which constitutes an overview of success/failures of emergency reaction, - focus, stands as a concrete action or event on which the team leaders concentrate to fight crisis, - retraction, is the moment where the group diminishes means involved, in accordance with its aims, - rehabilitation, where, as a last step, result is, for the group, emergence of new values, stronger than the older.

Crisis Response Strategy

Both situational crisis communication theory and image repair theory assume organizations should protect their reputation and image through appropriate responses to the crisis. Therefore, how to draft effective message to defend the crisis becomes the focal point of crisis communication research. Image repair theory provides series of options that organizations usually adopt including denial, evade responsibility, reduce offensiveness, corrective action, and mortification. Specifically, denial strategy contains two sub-strategies, simple denial and shift blame. Evade responsibility strategy includes provocation, defeasibility, accident, good intention. Reduce offensiveness strategy garners bolstering, minimization, differentiation, transcendence, attack accuser, and compensation.

SCCT also offers a handful of strategies: Denial, scapegoat, attack the accuser, excuse, justification, ingratiation, concern, compassion, regret, apology. Coombs argues different strategy should be adopted according different situations.

Crisis Communication Tactics

Pre-crisis

- Researching and collecting information about crisis risks specific to the organization.
- Creating a crisis management plan that includes making decisions ahead of time about who will handle specific aspects of a crisis if and when it occurs.

- Conducting exercises to test the plan at least annually.
- Preparing press release templates for the organization's public relations team in the event of a crisis.
- The chain of command that all employees will follow in the dissemination of information to all publics during a crisis situation.

A rapid response crisis communications team should be organized during the pre-crisis stage and all individuals who will help with the actual crisis communication response should be trained. At this stage the communication professional focuses on detecting and identifying possible risks that could result in a crisis.

In-crisis

Crisis communication tactics during the crisis stage may include the following: The identification of the incident as a crisis by the organization's crisis management team; the collection and processing of pertinent information to the crisis management team for decision making; and also the dissemination of crisis messages to both internal and external publics of the organization.

Post-crisis

- Reviewing and dissecting the successes and failures of the crisis management team in order to make any necessary changes to the organization, its employees, practices, or procedures.
- Providing follow-up crisis messages as necessary.

Timothy Coombs proposes that post-crisis communication should include the following five steps:

- Deliver all information promised to stakeholders as soon as that information is known.
- Keep stakeholders updated on the progression of recovery efforts including any corrective measures being taken and the progress of investigations.
- Analyze the crisis management effort for lessons and integrate those lessons in to the organization's crisis management system.
- Scan the Internet channels for online memorials.
- Consult with victims and their families to determine the organization's role in any anniversary events or memorials.

In general, Timothy Coombs raises some practices regarding to crisis response strategy based on SCCT that crisis managers should consider carefully.

- All victims or potential victims should receive instructing information, including recall information. This is one-half of the base response to a crisis.
- All victims should be provided an expression of sympathy, any information about corrective actions and trauma counseling when needed. This can be called the "care response." This is the second-half of the base response to a crisis.

- For crises with minimal attributions of crisis responsibility and no intensifying factors, instructing information and care response is sufficient.
- For crises with minimal attributions of crisis responsibility and an intensifying factor, add excuse and justification strategies to the instructing information and care response.
- For crises with low attributions of crisis responsibility and no intensifying factors, add excuse and justification strategies to the instructing information and care response.
- For crises with low attributions of crisis responsibility and an intensifying factor, add compensation and apology strategies to the instructing information and care response.
- For crises with strong attributions of crisis responsibility, add compensation and apology strategies to the instructing information and care response.
- The compensation strategy is used anytime victims suffer serious harm.
- The reminder and ingratiation strategies can be used to supplement any response.
- Denial and attack the accuser strategies are best used only for rumor and challenge crises.

Benoit's 5 Major Strategies

Denial

There are two forms of denial: Simple denial which involves denying the involvement or the act, and shifting the blame, which is also known as Scapegoating.

Evasion of Responsibility

Evading responsibility involves the following 4 steps.

- Provocation: Suggesting that the accused only responded after being provoked.
- Defeasibility: Suggesting that lack of control or information is to blame.
- Accidents: Suggesting that it was an accident.
- Good intentions: Suggest that it was done with good intentions in mind, despite the negative outcome.

Reducing

The apologists will attempt to reduce the offensiveness of the acts by:

- Bolstering by describing positive attributes.
- Minimizing to decrease the negative view of the situation.
- Differentiation by comparing the act to other similar acts that ended in worse terms.
- Transcending by discussion in terms of abstract values and group loyalty.

- Attacking the accuser in an attempt to eliminate credibility.
- Offering compensation to victims.

Corrective Action

The apologist will express corrective action when they attempt to correct the situation and prevent it from ever happening again.

Mortification

When the apologist admits wrongful behavior and asks for forgiveness while apologizing.

Media Relations

Media Relations involves working with media for the purpose of informing the public of an organization's mission, policies and practices in a positive, consistent and credible manner. Typically, this means coordinating directly with the people responsible for producing the news and features in the mass media. The goal of media relations is to maximize positive coverage in the mass media without paying for it directly through advertising.

Many people use the terms *public relations* and *media relations* interchangeably; however, doing so is incorrect. Media relations refer to the relationship that a company or organization develops with journalists, while public relations extend that relationship beyond the media to the general public.

It is possible for communication between the media and the organization to be initiated by either side. However dealing with the media presents unique challenges in that the news media cannot be controlled — they have ultimate control over whether stories pitched to them are of interest to their audiences. Because of this fact, ongoing relationships between an organization and the news media are vital. One way to ensure a positive working relationship with media personnel is to become deeply familiar with their "beats" and areas of interests. Media relations and public relations practitioners should read as many magazines, journals, newspapers, and blogs as possible, as they relate to one's practice.

Organizations often compile what is known as a media list, or a list of possible media outlets who may be interested in an organization's information. The media can consist of thousands of magazine publications, newspapers, and TV and radio stations. Therefore, when a "newsworthy" event occurs in an organization, a media list can assist in determining which media outlet may be the most interested in a particular story.

Working with the media on behalf of an organization allows for awareness of the entity to be raised as well as the ability to create an impact with a chosen audience. It allows access to both large and small target audiences and helps in building public support and mobilizing public opinion for an organization. This is all done through a wide range of media and can be used to encourage two-way communication.

Possible reasons an organization may reach out to the media are:

- Launch of a new product/service.
- Initiation of new factories/offices.
- Financial results.
- Organization sponsored events or awards.
- Launch of organization promotional campaigns.
- Recent disasters, strikes or organizational closures.
- Awards/accolades for the company.
- Visits from company dignitaries/celebrities.
- Involvement in local/community activities.
- Community engagement.

Media Relations and Information Subsidy

Information Subsidy consists of information that is provided to the press as supplemental material to help present their reporting. This includes information such as press releases, advertisements and videos of related news events. An advantage of using information subsidies is that they can decrease or eliminate the need for completing additional research on the part of the media. Subsidies can be a good source of information for the media, however, it is important that the media vet the source for accuracy and bias.

By presenting ready-to-publish data, information subsidies can save journalists time and money. A study completed in 1999 estimated that nearly half of the information reported in newspapers came from information subsidies. Yet another survey suggested that most of the information received by journalists is never published. Trust in the source and content of the data are the criteria journalists use when determining whether or not they will use the material provided.

Media Relations and Public Relations Practitioners (PR)

Media and Public Relations Practitioners are very similar in many ways. Both parties aim to share information with the public. This information is intended to benefit the public by educating them on news and other events. Public Relations Practitioners attempt to expand their client's media coverage by staying up to date on news and current events that are relevant to their client. Because PR practitioners are usually focused on a client, some would argue that they are biased or attempt to sway public opinion. The media is constantly looking for a new story. PR practitioners are a good, reliable place for the media to go to for newsworthy events. They often provide newsworthy or public service data, which can save the media the time required to complete their own research and sourcing.

The fact that PR specialists have been providing the news mass media with information for years has not really changed the trust level that the media has for the sources. Trust is a critical component between the media and PR practitioners and it must be present for their to be a successful working relationship. It has been said that part of the problem between journalists and PR

Practitioners is the perception that PR Specialists have not been good at providing journalists with newsworthy material. Journalists should express their thoughts and concerns to these PR Specialists to allow for better communication and improvement of the type and quality of news data. As with any relationship, both parties must be committed to working together to achieve success.

Ethical Pitfalls

The words 'fake news' bombard news outlets today. It is now more important than ever for Public Relations Practitioners to provide honest, truthful, and accurate information to the media. It is equally important that journalists themselves authenticate information that they have been given. There is much pressure for a Public Relations Practitioner to embellish the truth for their client to make news appear better than it really is. PR Practitioners could help the communication process by providing more detail about specific news. For example, if a client calls the recall of a product, the reason for the recall should be thoroughly explained.

One way a PR Practitioner can avoid ethical issues is to be upfront with their clients and the media regarding any potential ethical issues. The pressure for a PR Practitioner can be great because of the need to work with multiple entities in order to produce their information. Having a basis for their personal and professional ethics will go a long way in helping a PR Practitioner. This basis should include considering the interests of themselves, the media, and the entity they are representing. Respect for those involved and social responsibility should also be an inherent part of ethics. Another approach to ethics is based on virtue. This includes learning from others, being prepared to take risks, and practicing complete honesty in their reporting.

Social Media

Many companies use social media campaigns as a form of marketing, but social media also has huge PR potential. Some of a company's greatest PR successes (and disasters) can happen on social media. It's a place where your interactions with a single customer are visible to the whole world. It allows companies to show their lighter side – for example, two fast food chains exchanging friendly Twitter insults. It's also a good place for honest public apologies.

To be a good social media professional you need to be tech-savvy and intuitive and have a great sense of humour.

Here are five key ways that social media is changing PR:

1. Emerging Tech Trends: New apps, tools and technologies are being created each day. Using this innovation, consumers are finding alternative ways to gather and absorb information. In 2018, video was named the most popular form of multimedia content. As PR professionals are realizing the extent to which virtual reality (VR) can deliver value and creativity for clients. VR provides a level of realness and excitement that a press release or a short video simply failed to do in the past. VR results in a deeper emotional connection with stakeholders that is certain to change the game in digital storytelling.

As social sites begin to leverage the limitlessness of VR, there will be no bounds on how professionals will use this tool to support PR and marketing objectives for brands.

2. Two-Way Conversations: Less than 10 years ago, the Public Relations Society of America (PRSA) defined the PR profession as "the strategic communication process that builds mutually beneficial relationships between organizations and their publics." That definition no longer holds true, as public relations, social media and digital marketing have integrated with the wider communications world. Facebook, Instagram, Twitter, YouTube and other social media channels have transformed the communication between companies and the public. The PR process used to be surprisingly one-dimensional, but the future of PR is now a conglomeration, mainly focused on leveraging new innovations to communicate with the public. In the era of instant Twitter and Instagram feedback, companies now have customer service representatives fielding questions in real time via social media.

As the future of PR continues to transform, the line between marketing, customer service and PR will become more and more blurred. People's trust in companies has diminished rapidly over the past decade. In the next five years, there will be a public call for companies to become more transparent – which may lead to 24/7 live video recordings of manufacturing facilities, daily updates from the CEO or even virtual tours of different offices around the world – all communicated directly through social media.

3. Niche-Influencers: Public relations is no longer simply about traditional media. Social communication makes it possible for the average person to create their own platform and cultivate their audience in a way that has never been possible before.The future of PR leverages the macro-influencers (those with fewer than 100,000 followers) and micro-influencers (those with fewer than 10,000 followers). As the pendulum swings towards the small, expect these nimble influencers to continue to make a big impact in the PR world.

4. Dizzying News Cycle: Social and digital media has shortened the life span of news, pushing often-frenzied journalists to turnaround stories in a short time. This has forced PR pros to keep up.

Roughly 6,000 tweets are shared every second on Twitter. While this makes social media a highly effective tool for communicating breaking news coverage, it also means the lifespan of a story is so much shorter than it used to be. Journalists are constantly searching for "the next big thing" and PR pros need to keep up with their turnaround time. In today's turbulent news cycle, journalists and the public turn to Twitter to get the latest news, making the competition to get attention from media even harder. PR professionals will spend less time blanketing news to a wide net of journalists and will instead focus on very targeted media outreach and relationship building. Journalists are often pressed for time in this continuous news cycle, forcing them to prioritize, capture essential stories first and, perhaps, neglect other leads that have some appeal. To ensure this does not happen, be sure to get to the point in pitches and provide the information as quickly as possible, as a reporter would in his or her lead.

5. Access to Journalists: Social media helps public relations professionals get an inside scoop on reporters. By following a journalist on social networking sites, PR pros can gain insight into a reporter's tone of voice, opinions on relevant topics and recent work. Now, this doesn't mean you should drop all other responsibilities and spend 40-plus hours a week sifting through Twitter. In addition to social media being a great resource for finding reporters, it will continue to morph into a platform to connect and pitch journalists. While some media still prefer to be pitched by email, Twitter and LinkedIn are both emerging as platforms where journalists are open to receiving relevant pitches.

Models of Public Relations

The Public Relations or PR helps in shaping the image of the organization with its prospective customers in such a way that a favorable response is created.

When we talk about the models of public relations, the only names that come to the mind is of Grunig and Hunt, who have identified four models of public relations, all of which to some extent are still prevalent in the current market scenario. These models are:

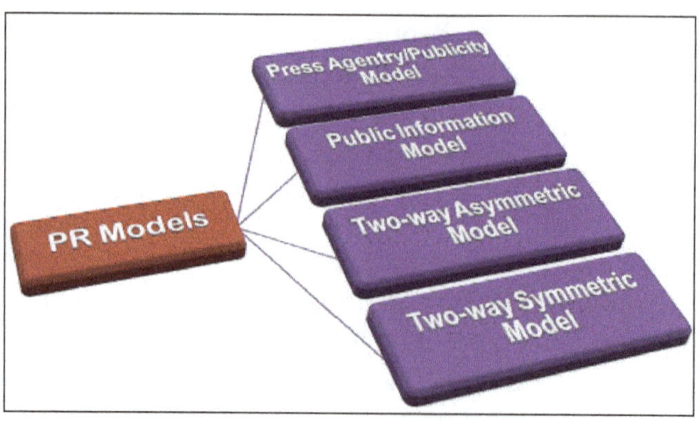

Press Agentry Model

Press agentry model was the earliest PR model. It comes out in the late 19th century Grunig Hunt, 1984. The heyday of this model from 1850 to 1900 and P.T. Barnum was the representative of the historical figure. Press agentry model is one-way communication as the flow of information is only from the sender to the receiver, i.e. source-to-receiver communication. People who send out the message are not much take no account of second party's response, comment, point of view and so on. Press agentry attempts to alter the act of publics whereas do not have the intention to change the behavior of the organization. Public relations whose are under press agentry struggle for publicity in the media in almost any way possible.

Practitioners of press agentry have included so-called fathers of modern PR, Ivy Lee and Edward Bernays. In the early 20th Century, both were Broadway press agents, when Broadway was the capital of the entertainment world, before moving on. Bernays' move into constructed news that accounts for audience perceptions and biases is a sophisticated form of press agentry. His 1915 80-page press packet for the Diaghilev Ballet Russe American tour was an early example, and his work in 1932 publicizing autos for General Motors with testimonials from business and academic leaders was more elaborate.

Press agents did little research aside from monitoring the media in which they sought to place favorable articles about their clients. The prototype practitioner of this model was the American impresario P. T. Barnum. He promoted circuses and other entertainment venues such as the singer Jenny Lind. Publicity continues to be a component of contemporary American PR and is used in sports, entertainment and product publicity, although today's practitioners are less likely to take liberties with the truth. In Press Agentry publicity model, public relations expects enhance the reputation of the organization among the target audience, stakeholders, employees, partners, all other associated with it through manipulation. According to this model, hire public relations expects who create a positive image of their brand in the minds of target audience through arguments and reasoning. They influence their potential customers by simply imposing their ideas, thoughts, creative stories of their brand, USPs of the products and so on. Flow of information takes place only from the public relations expects to the target audiences.

Although J. Grunig and Hunt acknowledged that there had been "public-relations-like" activities throughout history, they claimed that the press agents of the mid-19th century were the first full- name specialists to practice public relations. These press agents practiced the press agentry/ publicity model of public relations for such heroes as Andrew Jackson, Daniel Boone, Buffalo Bill Cody, and Calamity Jane. The most prominent of these practitioners was P.T. Barnum, who skillfully promoted his circus performers using the axiom, "There is a sucker born every minute."

Curiosity and scepticism played a pivotal role in the success of the press agentry model in the 19th Century, as illustrated with Barnum's stunt, and to this day it still does. Butterick points out that we only have to look at the inner editorial pages of the tabloid newspapers, the celebrity magazines or observe when a new movie or CD is launched to see the press agentry model in its purest form. Press agents like Max Clifford are often seen as masters of the industry, carefully manipulating the media coverage of their clients, as Butterick notes; 'even the so-called exclusive pictures of semi-naked celebrities on a beach in a Sunday newspaper can sometimes be the result of a collusion between the star's publicist and photographer'.

Nowadays, press agentry model is still very much in use in the 21st Century. It can easily argue that the ethics involved in this model are highly questionable, and the admission from Grunig & Hunt that the model has an element of propaganda attached to it does nothing to distil the negative connotations attached to PR as propaganda. However, despite these criticisms, it is ultimately that the curiosity and skepticism of which ensures the press agentry model is still alive and well in the modern day. Although the modern day PR practitioner must be more familiar with the truth, the very foundations of the model still exist whether it be to publicize a sporting event, a theatre production, or 'the scariest film of the decade', as in the recent movie release 'Paranormal Activity'. We, the public, will either want to believe what we see, or find out for ourselves if our skepticism can be proven correct which is why this model still works for practitioners seeking to gain the illusive media spotlight and is therefore relevant for the 21st Century.

Press agentry is closely associated with publicity in the entertainment world. Press agentry is the practice of attracting the attention of the press through technique that manufactures news. Methods associated with press agentry include staged events, publicity stunts, faux rallies or gatherings, spinning, and hype. A common practice is the late 1800s and early 1900s, press agentry is not part of mainstream public relations. Rather, it is a practice primarily associated with major entertainment-related events, such as Hollywood premieres and boxing matches. The goal of press agentry is to attract attention rather than gain understanding. Even today, however, the term press agent is sometimes used interchangeably with publicist in traditional Broadway theater and motion picture industries. Today's entertainment industries are populated with publicists rather than press agents. Publicists are individuals skilled in media relations who attempt to get the name of their clients or events in the media by carefully constructing messages that inform, educate, and persuade. Some are astute in branding and positioning strategies to aid the careers and success of their clients.

In contrast, press agents want attention either good or bad in most any form. Press agentry had been called persuasion for short-term advantage through the use of truth bending and even distortion, but it can also be simply the staging of provocative acts to get publicity and draw attention to an individual, event, or cause. Therefore, it is understandable that one of the earliest proponents of press agentry was Phineas Taylor (P.T) Barnum, the famed American showman and promoter who put gun Gen. Tom Thumb on exhibit and launched a mobile circus featuring Jumbo the elephant and freak shows. Barnum was a master of press agentry. For instance, he wrote letters both praising and criticizing his circus show to newspaper under an assumed name.

In the early part of his career, Edward L. Bernays was also a master of press agentry. He persuaded 10 debutantes to hold up Lucky Strike cigarettes manufactured by his client, the American Tobacco Company, as "torches of freedom" while participating in New York's Easter parade. In 1929, Bernays staged a global news event by organizing the "Light's Golden Jubilee," a worldwide calebration commemorating the 50th anniversary of the electric light bulb for his client, General Electric. Bernays managed to secure several prominent individuals for that event, including carmaker Henry Ford, electricity scientist Thomas Edison, and President Herbert Hoover.

Henry Rogers, one of the founders of Rogers and Cowan, the largest and most successful West Coast entertainment publicity firm, became well known when he promoted an unknown contract player for Columbia Pictures named Rita Hayworth. He contacted Look magazine with a telegram from the Fashion Couturiers Association of America, a fictitious group, claiming that Hayworth was the best-dressed off-screen actress. Look magazine took the bait and put Hayworth on the cover and published 10 pages of her photographs.

Characteristic of Press Agentry

Press agentry is ink. A sales-driven approach does whatever it takes to get exposure for clients in the media without resorting to paid advertising. Press agentry is not above truth-bending or lying to reach its pragmatic objective. It will make up facts if it needs to do so. It is persuasion for short-term advantage. Press agentry is a long-standing part of PR, and it won't go away. Press agentry has transformed over the decades into "ink with ethics," that is getting exposure while maintaining respect for facts, but if all else fails, getting exposure is more important than facts.

Press agentry relies on spin. It is interpreting facts to fit one's view and to get media coverage. Christopher Buckley's hilarious novel, "Thank You for Smoking" lampoons this type of practitioner brilliantly, and post-presidential debate commentary from Democrats and Republicans is a quadrennial example of spinning. Press agentry includes any technique that manufactures news which are publicity stunts, faux surveys, fake committees, constructed events and other tactics practitioners continue to use.

Propaganda classified as one of the characteristic of press agentry model. The term of propaganda in press agentry model, refer to PR practitioner exaggerate and more hype than facts in order to get publicity for their client. They will not care the public feedback and just want the public behave as they want. This model involves a 'propaganda' function and academics such as Butterick, Theaker, and Johnston & Zawawi agree that accuracy and credibility are somewhat compromised as the goal of the model is to influence the audience by manufacturing news, be that by way of stunts or 'explicit' publicity seeking. Butterick states that practitioners who use this model become 'press agents', utilising a range of PR tools from press releases to publicity stunts which in turn ensures that an audience takes a specific course of action.

Public Information Model

Public Information Model basically is to inform the public without carry any emphasizing promotion and publicity. This model does not seek to direct persuade or change the attitude of the public but is to disseminate any relevant information to them. Therefore, it is thus predicated that if the public has sufficient information that is relevant and truthful about the organization, then the public will believe and behave to what the organization desired. In Public Information Model, Public Relations practitioners often being refer as the "journalist in residence", whose job is to report objectively information about their organizations to the public.

In addition, Public Information Models explained the importance of maintain and enhancing the image of the company or organizations by disseminating information to the target public. It has been characterized as a one way communication techniques used by Public Relations practitioners. Although both Press Agentry and Public Information Model has been characterized as one way communications, the Public Information model differs because the purpose is to giving out clear and factual information to the public. In fact, this model is a one way communication where the process start off with information flows from sender (PR practitioners of the organizations) to the receiver (target audience or public). This technique included press release, features story, video release or any communication related to the information of the company that is directed among the public.

In this model, a good Public Relations practitioner is able to disseminate the information by putting in their organizations ideas or approaches and uses it to influences their target public. Therefore in this model, Public Relations practitioner has to constructs their writing in creative and informative way. This creative can be applied into the newsletter of the company, magazine, brochures with any related information about the organizations like the products, testimonials, organization's successful background, top management people and etc.

People are exposed to different kind of media messages in their daily life. Mass media are very important particular on Public Relations Practitioner for delivering their messages to the target audience. Grunig and Hunt explains that media relations is very important among Public Relations when it comes to Press Agentry and Public Information Model. Therefore, Public Relations practitioner as the third-party information endorser for the media is responsible to giving out the information that is credible and valuable to the public.

Today, the Public Information Model can be found in mostly in government agencies, NGOs, education and health institutions or in some other businesses. In fact, the concept of this model is to give out the information to the public usually through the media by hoping someone will pay attention to the information. The example can be seen in one of the Malaysian Government's policies, 1 Malaysia Concept. Agenda setting theory explains the powerful influence in the media that able to create public awareness on important issues. The media cannot tell what the people to think but has the ability to inform the people what to think about. In order word, Public Relations practitioners able to raise the importance of an issue through the repetition of news in the media. Malaysia is a multicultural society of which the population is made up by different types of ethnic groups includes Malays, Chinese, Indian and the Native. In fact, Malaysians are very sensitive to the issue that particular related to ethnicity and races. Thus, national unity has become the top agenda to the public and thus it has become a Public Relations discourse in Malaysia. In that case, PR practitioner has utilised the mainstream media to disseminate the messages and information that is associates to unity to the Malaysian citizen. Everyday Malaysian citizen and also foreigner have been bombarded by with the messages of 1 Malaysian Concept by the mainstream media. The 1 Malaysia logo and slogan is ubiquitous due to mass advertising and commercials in mainstream media. Therefore, by observing at the very general perspective, the Public Information Model has been practiced in 1 Malaysia concept is to create the awareness on the importance of unity in the society.

The Public Information Model has also been applied in the public service announcements that related to health, safety and environment. One of the examples is the Tak Nak!, an anti-smoking campaign conducted by Malaysia Ministry of Health. The purpose of this is campaign to create awareness of the dangerous and harmful effect of smoking to the public. The campaign usually associates smoking to deadly diseases such as lung cancer and heart attack. The Tak Nak! Campaign is considered as a Public Information Model because it basically provides the information about the chemical substances that can be found in the cigarettes and how it is harmful to the individuals or the people around them. In fact, Public Information Model also been practiced in some campaign like HIV prevention, Crime Awareness, or any social issues that basically aimed to educate the public. In brief, these campaigns are characterised as a one way communication, in which the PR practitioner only involves in creating awareness and telling the information to the public.

Similarly, Public Information Model also being used for crisis management. The outbreak of Severe

Acute Respiratory Syndrome (SARS) in Southern China in November 2002 has been recognised as one of the global threats in 21th century. SARS had eventually caused hundreds of death and also bring a worldwide impact on economic and the travel industry. However, Public Information Model has been practiced by the Singapore Government and media to overcome the crisis. Information regarding the SARS outbreak was widely distributed by the media and government. The information such as the SARS knowledge, symptoms, prevention and safety precaution has been distributed to the public. The Singapore Ministry of Health has established the channels that provide sufficient and comprehensive information to the public. All types of media were used, including a public television channel, radio, newspaper and internet to ensure constant information update and keep the public informed of the risks for infection and preventive measures. In fact, Singapore was taken out of the official list of SARS-infected countries by the World Health Organization (WHO) in 2003 due to the quick responses of Singapore Government and their media in controlling the crisis. Therefore, the above example has highlighted the importance of the Public Information Model for PR practitioners when handling the crisis management.

Meanwhile, the higher education institutions have also been spotted on practicing the Public Information Model. We often can see the university and college create the publicity materials such as press release, banner, brochure, flyer or even static web content. In fact, the process usually involved is disseminating the details and information about the history, achievement, facilities, event, faculty and courses.

In recent years, private sector has started to realised the importance of providing and explaining the company policies to their stakeholder. Public Information Model plays an important role when comes to new innovation that needs to explains to the public. The diffusion of innovation theory explains the adoption of the idea, practice, culture or object that is perceived to be new in the society. The theory explains that media as well as interpersonal communication play the important role in providing the information to influence others opinion.

Two-way Asymmetric Model

This model is developed by Edward. L. Bernays. As the name suggests, this model supports the two-way communication between the sender and the receiver, but however the communication is not balanced. This is because the PR experts position the image of the organization and a brand in the minds of the customer through manipulation and forces them to behave in a manner as expected by them. Thus, the objective of this method is to understand the psychology of the customers and manipulate it accordingly so as to get the favorable reactions.

Two-way Symmetric Model

The two-way symmetrical model of public relations as described in Grunig's Excellence Theory is focused primarily in making sure that decisions made by an organization are mutually beneficial between itself and its audiences. The goal of Grunig's symmetrical communication model is one that embraces negotiation between the organization and its publics, and one that also fosters mutual understanding. During this aspect of Grunig's research, his idea for symmetrical communication "also was stimulated by Carter's and Chaffee and McLeod's conceptualization of coorientation." The roots for this model "represented a movement away from theories of attitudes held by one person and research on how to develop messages to change the orientations (attitudes) of person." This model is drastically different in comparison to the stereotypical view of the PR practitioner as a manipulative figure who uses smoke and mirrors to control audiences. The symmetrical model "proposed that individuals, organizations, and publics should use communication to adjust their ideas and behavior to those of others rather than try to control how others think and behave."

The symmetrical model of communication is a democratic framework for the PR practitioner to follow, and one that can both be effective or detrimental, depending on the situation. The overall goal of creating mutual understanding between parties also is much more palatable for audiences, because in human nature, no one desires to be controlled. If a person is controlled or feels inferior to another person or organization, they will not develop trust, and they are likely to withdraw completely from a relationship. The same goes for the organizational-public relationship as well. If we create a sense of open communication and build trust through the two-way symmetrical model, we are more likely to be in a positive position when a time of crisis does occur because of strong relationships that have created a strong reputation. The use of two-way symmetrical communication by a PR practitioner who functions at the strategic management level also allows our audiences to have a voice at the executive table. This model creates a level playing field for negotiation and mutual understanding to take place between the organization and its publics. The two-way model provides an organization with the tools and path needed to create a strong company reputation built upon solid, long-lasting relationships, because both the organization and its audiences are provided with a voice in processes and developing issues or problems. The two-way symmetrical model for communication maintains both the organization's best interests and its audiences' best interests at the forefront in the most fair and balanced way possible. Through the use of this model, both the organization and its audiences can collaborate together to both grow and strengthen an overall organization, leading it to greater success.

Public Relations for Small Businesses

Like other types of organizations, small businesses can benefit from public relations in terms of their relationships with customers, employees, investors, suppliers, or other interested members of the community. Since small business owners are the most visible representatives of their own companies, they frequently handle many of the public relations functions in person. If the activity is principally associated with public appearances and participation in public events, the owner's natural abilities will be to the fore. But if a campaign needs to be launched, and funds are available, professional help may well be needed.

Effective PR professionals will be, above all, knowledgeable about press relations. For on-going and routine assistance, the small business is well served by engaging the services of an experienced freelance writer with an extensive journalism background now specializing in helping companies "tell their story." Such individuals, very often one-person operations, have wide contacts and know not only how to prepare but also how to get materials placed with the right media. If a large campaign looms ahead, such consultants are also the ideal contact for selecting the right firm for a major campaign.

While communication is the essence of public relations, an effective public relations campaign is based on action as well as words. Whether it is practiced formally or informally, public relations is an essential function for the survival of any organization. Small business owners cannot afford to neglect public relations. But lavish parties and gifts are not necessary–it is possible to vastly improve a small business's image within its community while also controlling public relations expenditures. Sponsoring a local softball team, speaking at a chamber of commerce meeting, and volunteering at a neighborhood clean-up are among the wide variety of public relations activities readily available to small businesses.

References

- Public-relations: businessjargons.com, Retrieved 14 May, 2019
- What-is-public-relations-pr-functions-types-examples: feedough.com, Retrieved 18 March, 2019
- Public-relations, encyclopedia: inc.com, Retrieved 16 June, 2019
- How-important-is-community-relations-to-a-company: prmrinc.net, Retrieved 14 February, 2019
- Five-ways-social-media-is-changing-PR: cision.com, Retrieved 16 May, 2019
- Models-of-public-relations: businessjargons.com, Retrieved 28 January, 2019
- Introduction-of-press-agentry-model-media-essay: ukessays.com, Retrieved 19 February, 2019
- The-two-way-symmetrical-model-of-communication: excellencetheory.wordpress.com, Retrieved 09 August, 2019

Permissions

All chapters in this book are published with permission under the Creative Commons Attribution Share Alike License or equivalent. Every chapter published in this book has been scrutinized by our experts. Their significance has been extensively debated. The topics covered herein carry significant information for a comprehensive understanding. They may even be implemented as practical applications or may be referred to as a beginning point for further studies.

We would like to thank the editorial team for lending their expertise to make the book truly unique. They have played a crucial role in the development of this book. Without their invaluable contributions this book wouldn't have been possible. They have made vital efforts to compile up to date information on the varied aspects of this subject to make this book a valuable addition to the collection of many professionals and students.

This book was conceptualized with the vision of imparting up-to-date and integrated information in this field. To ensure the same, a matchless editorial board was set up. Every individual on the board went through rigorous rounds of assessment to prove their worth. After which they invested a large part of their time researching and compiling the most relevant data for our readers.

The editorial board has been involved in producing this book since its inception. They have spent rigorous hours researching and exploring the diverse topics which have resulted in the successful publishing of this book. They have passed on their knowledge of decades through this book. To expedite this challenging task, the publisher supported the team at every step. A small team of assistant editors was also appointed to further simplify the editing procedure and attain best results for the readers.

Apart from the editorial board, the designing team has also invested a significant amount of their time in understanding the subject and creating the most relevant covers. They scrutinized every image to scout for the most suitable representation of the subject and create an appropriate cover for the book.

The publishing team has been an ardent support to the editorial, designing and production team. Their endless efforts to recruit the best for this project, has resulted in the accomplishment of this book. They are a veteran in the field of academics and their pool of knowledge is as vast as their experience in printing. Their expertise and guidance has proved useful at every step. Their uncompromising quality standards have made this book an exceptional effort. Their encouragement from time to time has been an inspiration for everyone.

The publisher and the editorial board hope that this book will prove to be a valuable piece of knowledge for students, practitioners and scholars across the globe.

Index

CPSIA information can be obtained
at www.ICGtesting.com
Printed in the USA
LVHW060904030122
707669LV00002B/347

9 781647 260743